GOOGLE APPS
MADE EASY

Learn To Work In The Cloud

By James Bernstein

Copyright © 2019 by James Bernstein. All rights reserved.

All rights reserved. This book or any portion thereof may not be reproduced or used in any manner whatsoever without the express written permission of the publisher except for the use of brief quotations in a book review.

Printed in the United States of America

Bernstein, James
Google Apps Made Easy
Book 7 in the Computers Made Easy series

For more information on reproducing sections of this book or sales of this book, go to www.onlinecomputertips.com

Contents

Introduction 8

Chapter 1 - Introducing Google Apps 9
What are Google Apps? 9
Signing up for a Google Account 9
Changing Your Account Settings 12
Finding Your Google Apps 18
Personalizing Your Google Account Photo 21
Installing Google Apps on Your Smartphone and Tablet 22
Google Apps Covered in This Book 24

Chapter 2 – Google Drive 25
Introducing Google Drive 25
Google One Plans and Features 25
Using Google Drive 27
    Creating Folders and Uploading Files 28
    Managing Files and Folders 31
Google Drive Desktop Client 43
Sharing Files and Folders 51
Google Drive Smartphone \ Tablet App 62

Chapter 3 – Google Docs 66
Docs Interface 66
Menu Items 73
    File Menu 73
    Edit Menu 80
    View Menu 83
    Insert Menu 85
    Format Menu 92

    Tools Menu 96

    Add-ons Menu 101

    Help Menu 102

  Creating a Document 103

    Right Click Options 109

  Formatting a Document 122

    Editing Text 122

    Word Art 128

    Line Spacing 130

    Numbered and Bulleted Lists 131

    Page Setup 134

  Printing and Publishing a Document 136

  Publishing a Document 140

  Sharing a Document 144

Chapter 4 – Google Sheets 151

  Sheets Interface 151

  Sheets Specific Menu Items 152

    File Menu 153

    Edit Menu 156

    Insert Menu 161

    Format Menu 167

    Data Menu 173

    Tools Menu 190

  Creating a Spreadsheet 193

  Formatting a Spreadsheet 199

  Performing Calculations and Using Formulas 205

  Creating a Chart 211

  Printing a Spreadsheet 220

Chapter 5 – Google Slides 224
Slides Interface 224
Slides Specific Menu Items 226
- *File Menu* 226
- *View Menu* 227
- *Insert Menu* 233
- *Format Menu* 240
- *Slide Menu* 243
- *Arrange Menu* 249
- *Tools Menu* 251

Creating a Presentation 254
Formatting a Presentation 261
Adding Animations and Transitions 278
- *Transitions* 278
- *Animations* 281

Printing a Presentation 284

Chapter 6 – Google Forms 290
Creating a Form 292
Customizing a Form 303
Sending Out a Form 307
Viewing Responses 309
Forms Options 312

Chapter 7 – Google Keep 316
Keep Interface 316
Taking Notes 318
Setting Reminders 330
Searching for Notes 335
Settings 337

Sharing Notes 340

Google Keep Chrome Extension 342

Chapter 8 – Google Photos 345

Photos Interface 345

Adding Photos 348

Desktop Uploader\Backup and Sync 352

Creating Albums 357

Photo Assistant 361

Photo Books 362

Sharing 368

Settings 372

Mobile Devices 375

Chapter 9 – Gmail 379

Gmail Interface 379

Categories 391

Sending and Receiving Emails 392

Sending Email 392

Receiving Email 402

Printing Emails 408

Managing Your Email 411

Managing Spam 421

Account Settings 422

Calendar Interface 430

Adding Events 433

Reminders 441

Tasks 444

Adding Additional Calendars 446

Settings 452

Chapter 11 – Contacts 455

Contacts Interface 455

Creating a Contact 461

Labels 463

Importing and Exporting Contacts 466

Importing Contacts 466

Exporting Contacts 467

Printing Contacts 468

Other Contacts 470

Introduction

The focus of this book is to explain what Google Apps are and how to use the specific apps that suit your needs. The goal is not to make you a Google Apps expert, but rather to get to the point where you are proficient with the applications and can work on becoming an expert. Not everyone will have a need for all of the apps that Google provides, but the goal is to inform you about the available apps so you can choose which ones will work for you.

Google has been providing apps for many years now and keeps adding more and more as time goes on. They even have their G Suite that you can subscribe to if you want to take your app usage to the next level at the workplace, but for most home users and even small business owners, the free apps should do the job just fine.

As I mentioned, you will most likely not have a need to use all of the apps that will be covered in this book, but I wanted to focus on the most commonly used and popular apps available. There are also other apps that Google offers, but to cover everything they have available would make the book longer than anyone would care to read! Plus, for my examples, I will be using a Windows 10 based computer, so some of the options or features might differ on your tablet or other mobile device. I will also be using Google's Chrome web browser to optimize my user experience and minimize browser-related issues.

You will find that many of these apps are integrated with other apps and other Google services. This is done so you can seamlessly go from one app to another without having to wonder where your data is or figure out how to tie everything together manually. Many of the apps have similar features as well, so once you learn how to use one efficiently, there's a good chance that knowledge will transfer over to other apps. So, on that note, let's start working in the cloud!

Chapter 1 - Introducing Google Apps

What are Google Apps?
Google Apps is a term used to describe the group of web based applications provided by Google that you can use for a variety of things such as email, creating documents, calendars, note taking, file storage and sharing, and so on. Most of these apps are free to use, and once you have a Google account, you automatically have access to start using these apps.

Since they are web based and platform independent, you can run them on almost any device from your Windows PC, MacBook, Android smartphone, iPhone, iPad, and many other devices. One thing you will need is an Internet connection, since most of the things you will do with these apps are "cloud based" and done online.

One of the best things about these apps being run in the cloud and having the ability to also store your files in the cloud is that it makes it easier to share your files and your work with others, which make collaboration much easier. There's no need to email attachments back and forth and copy files to flash drives because everything is stored online, and it's just a matter of allowing others access to your data so they can participate in the work process.

Another great thing about working online is that all of your data will be consistent between your devices. So, if you make a change in a Google Docs document on your PC and then open that file on your iPad, the changes will be automatically synchronized. Speaking of synchronization, there are also options to synchronize local copies of files with the copies in the cloud so that you are always working with the most up to date data.

Signing up for a Google Account
The first thing you need to do before being able to use all of these apps is to sign up for a Google account. Since all of these apps will be tied to *you* specifically, it's necessary to have a way to log in so you have all of the information that belongs to you each time you use an app.

To create a Google account simply to go **www.google.com** and click on the Sign In button. If you don't already have an account, then you will be prompted to create one (as seen in figure 1.1).

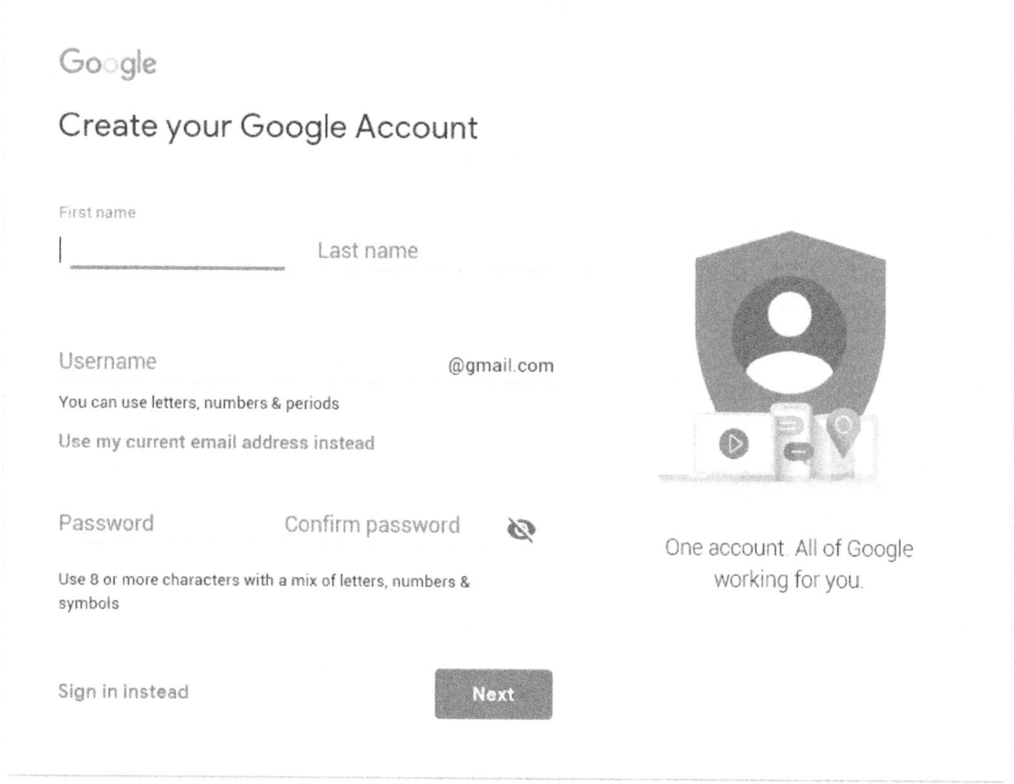

Chapter 1 – Introducing Google Apps

Figure 1.1

Simply enter your first and last name and choose a username, which will also be used for your Gmail email account ending in @gmail.com. If the username has already been taken, then you will be prompted to enter a new one. Notice that there is an option that says *Use my current email address instead*. This can be done if you do not want a Gmail email address, but still want to create a Google account with your current email address. (I would suggest creating a Gmail email address just to make things easier when using Google Apps.)

Then you will need to come up with a password that has 8 or more characters and uses letters, numbers, and symbols (such as ! or # for example) and click on *Next*.

After that, you will need to enter your phone number so Google can verify it is really you. It will send you a six digit number via text message that you will have to enter in the next step. Doing this will also tie your phone number to your Google account, which comes in handy for things like password recovery if you forget your password. If you don't have a password you can have Google call you with the code instead of texting it.

Chapter 1 – Introducing Google Apps

Next, you enter a recovery email address (which can also be used for password recovery), as well as your birth date information. The birth date information is used because some Google services have age requirements. The gender information it asks for is optional and is not shown to other Google users. You can also edit your Google account later if you wish to change or add anything.

You may be asked to add your phone number to your account to use for Google services. This is optional, but if you click on the *More options* link you can specify exactly what you want or don't want your phone number to be used for (figure 1.2).

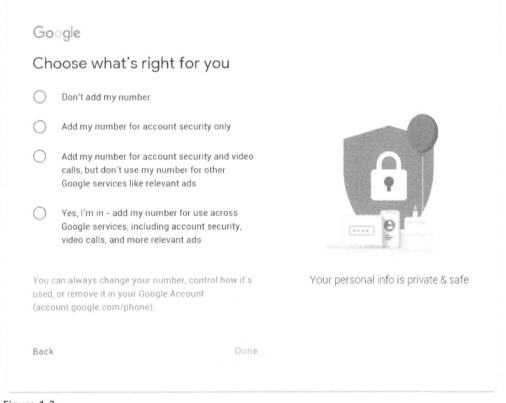

Figure 1.2

If you *don't* want your number to be used at all, simply click on *Skip,* and you will be brought to the *Privacy and Terms* agreement, which you can read if you like. To continue, you will need to click on the *I agree* button. Finally, after clicking on *I agree,* your account will be created and you will be logged in automatically. If you are on the Google home page, then you will see your first initial up in the right hand corner. You can go into your settings and edit your profile and add a picture if you like.

If you have an Android-based smartphone or tablet, then you most likely have a Google account since it is required to have one to download apps on Android devices.

Changing Your Account Settings

Before you get too involved in using your new Google Apps, you might want to take a look at your Google settings to make sure all of the security and privacy settings are set the way you like. To get to your settings, click on the circle with your initials in it on the top right of the screen on the Google homepage (www.google.com), and then click on the *Google Account* button.

As you can see in figure 1.3, there are a lot of things you can do from here, and I will briefly go over some of the more important settings you should look at.

Chapter 1 – Introducing Google Apps

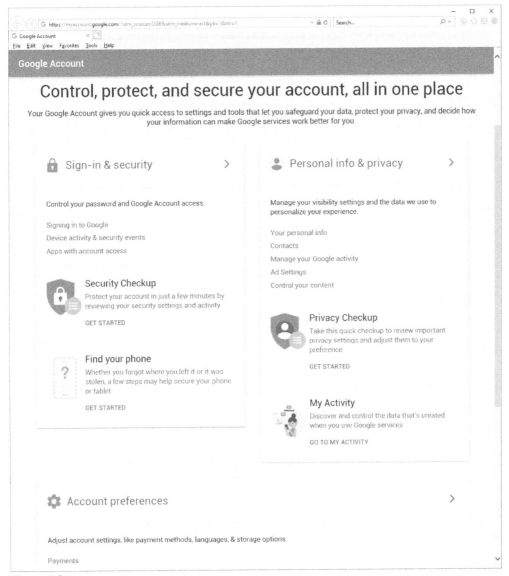

Figure 1.3

Clicking on one of the right arrows (>) in any section will bring you to a screen that has all of the settings that you can manage (figure 1.4).

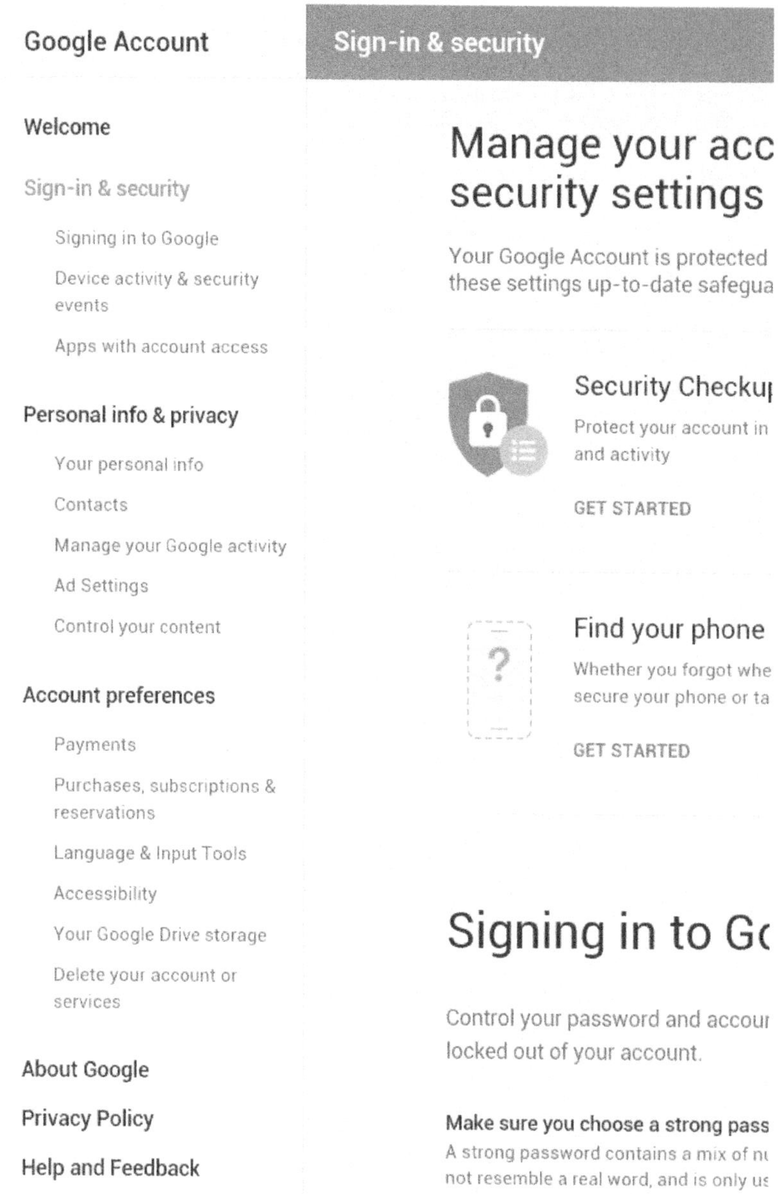

Chapter 1 – Introducing Google Apps

Figure 1.4

Sign-in & security

- **Security Checkup** – Running the Security Checkup will look at your account activity to show you things like what devices you are signed into, what location you are signed in to, and how your recovery methods are looking (figure 1.5). You can click the down arrow next to each one for more details.

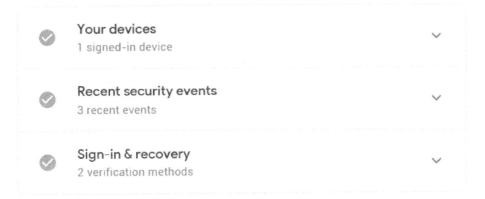

Figure 1.5

- **Signing in to Google** – Here is where you can configure password and account access as well as change your password or set up 2-step verification, which will require you to enter a password and also a verification code each time you sign in.

- **Delete activity & security events** — This area also shows recent security events and devices that you have recently used to log in with, so if you see a device that is not yours, you will know that someone figured out your password and you can change it.

- **Apps with account access** – Many apps require access to your account to get information that they use within that app. Here you can manage the apps that you want to allow access to your account. For the most part, this will be third party apps and not your Google Apps, which should already have access to your account. There is also an option here to sync passwords that you save for various sites.

Personal info & privacy

- **Your personal info** – This shows things like your name, email address, phone number, birthday, gender, and so on. From here you can decide on whether or not you want this information shared, and also make changes if needed.

- **Contacts** – Here you will find the names, email addresses, and phone numbers of the people you interact with using your Google Apps. You can also open the Google Contacts app from here as well.

- **Manage your Google activity** – When you use certain Google services, apps, or devices (such as an Android smartphone), Google will save data pertaining to your activities such as where you were, what apps you used, web activity, and so on. As an Android user myself, I would get monthly reports showing a map of everywhere I have been and when. Fortunately, you can turn off this kind of tracking by clicking on the *go to activity controls* link in this section. The Google Dashboard in this section will show you a summary of all the things Google is tracking (figure 1.6).

Chapter 1 – Introducing Google Apps

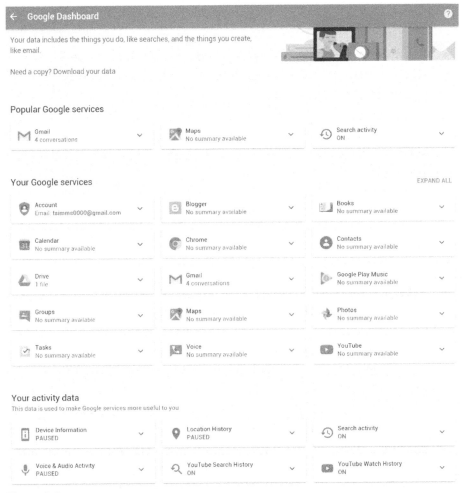

Figure 1.6

- **Ad Settings** – As I'm sure you know, online advertising is a way of life these days, and Google and other companies like to tailor their ads to things you are interested in. In this section, you can fine tune what types of advertisements are shown to you.

- **Control your content** – Your content includes things like bookmarks, Google Drive files, Google Photos, activity, purchases, and so on. So, if you want to download a copy to your local computer, you can do so from here and select exactly what content you want to download or even archive. The Inactive Account Manager setting will let you decide what happens to your account if you stop using it or even pass away. (Grim, I know!)

Chapter 1 – Introducing Google Apps

Account Preferences

- **Payments** – Google will let you pay for goods and services using your Google account (called Google Pay), but you will need to add a payment method before doing so.

- **Purchases, subscriptions & reservations** – If you *do* buy any goods or services using your Google account, then you can view and manage them from here.

- **Language & Input Tools** – Here you can set the default language Google uses with your apps, as well as things like keyboard layout and spell checking.

- **Accessibility** – If you need assistance with seeing your screen, you can enable things like the screen reader and high contrast colors.

- **Your Google Drive storage** – Your Google account comes with 15GB of free cloud storage, which I will have an entire chapter on, but from here you can see how it's being used.

- **Delete your account or services** – From here, you can delete Google specific products from your account or delete your account and its data altogether if you don't want to be a Google user anymore.

Finding Your Google Apps
Now that you are signed up with your new Google account (assuming you didn't already have one), you might be wondering how to find the apps that you plan on using, or even the ones you want to try out before deciding if they are right for you or not.

There are several ways to go about finding and opening your Google Apps, but if you are on the Google homepage, then all you need to do is click on the icon that consists of nine small boxes to bring up many of the Google Apps (figure 1.7).

Chapter 1 – Introducing Google Apps

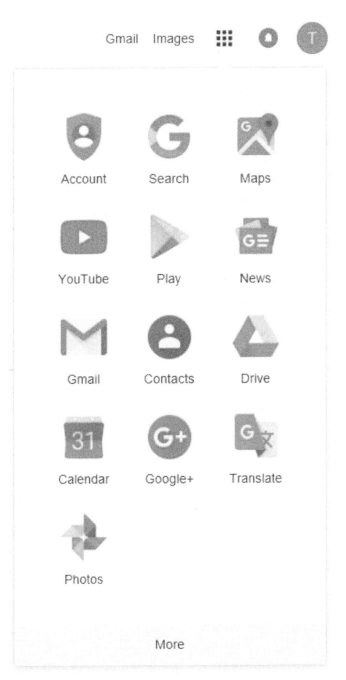

Figure 1.7

If you don't see what you are looking for, then try clicking on *More* to bring up additional apps (figure 1.8)

Chapter 1 – Introducing Google Apps

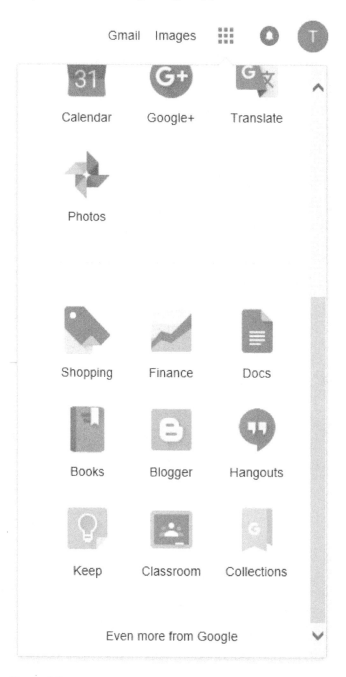

Figure 1.8

If you *still* can't find what you're looking for, you can simply do a Google search for that app and then open it from the search results. Once you figure out what apps you will be using, it might be a good idea to make bookmarks for each one and then make a bookmark folder to put them in so they are all in one place.

Chapter 1 – Introducing Google Apps

Personalizing Your Google Account Photo

If you plan on collaborating with other people and sharing things like your documents and calendar, then you might want to spruce up your account with a personalized photo. By default, Google will just use your initial as your profile picture, but if you click on Change (figure 1.9), you can add a photo of yourself or anything else you want to use to represent yourself.

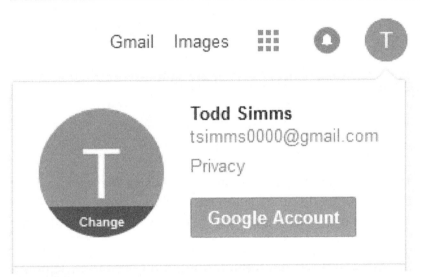

Figure 1.9

Once you click on *change*, you will then have the options to upload a photo, choose a photo from your existing Google photos (if you have any), or take one with your webcam. Then you can crop your photo (as well as rotate it) if you like. When everything looks good, simply click on *Set as profile photo* and you are done. Then, when you go back to your Google page, it will show your picture rather than your initials (as shown in figure 1.10).

Figure 1.10

When you share items with other people or send them emails from your Gmail account to theirs, your new picture will be displayed alongside your name (as shown in figure 1.11) for them to see.

Shared with me

Name	Shared by
Today	
📄 Getting started	👤 Todd Simms

Figure 1.11

Installing Google Apps on Your Smartphone and Tablet

Since Google Apps are meant to be used from any location and any device, it only makes sense that you should be able to install these apps on your smartphone or tablet so you can use them on the go.

If you have an Android based smartphone or tablet, then using these apps will be easier than if you have an iPhone or an iPad (since Google owns Android and makes sure that everything will work properly between their apps and their devices).

 Your Android device most likely already has some Google Apps installed (such as Photos, Gmail, or Docs) depending on which model you have.

If you go to the Google Play Store and just type in Google in the search box, it will bring up most of their apps and also show you which ones you have installed on your device (figure 1.12).

Chapter 1 – Introducing Google Apps

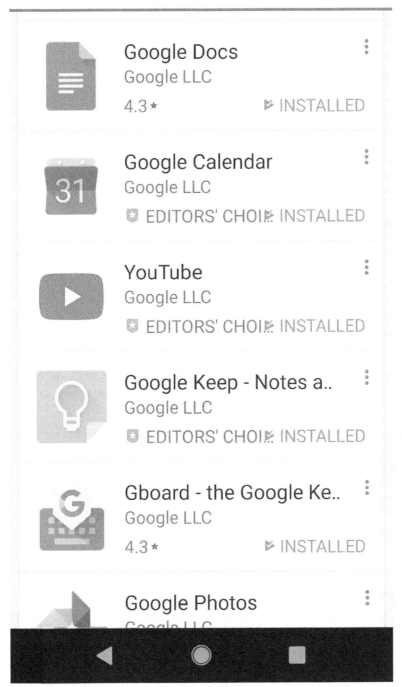

Figure 1.12

If you don't have one of the apps that you would like to use, simply install the app just like you would any other app. If you have an iPhone or iPad, you can still install all or most of the Google Apps you would like to use on your device.

Chapter 1 – Introducing Google Apps

Google Apps Covered in This Book

There are many Google Apps you can use, and most of them are free, but you most likely won't have a need for many of them. Here is a list of the Google Apps I will be covering in this book, and a quick description of what each one does:

- **Docs** – This is Google's word processor program, similar to Microsoft Word. You can use it to create things like letters, resumes, lists, and so on.

- **Sheets** – This is Google's spreadsheet program, similar to Microsoft Excel. It has a similar look and feel to Excel as well.

- **Slides** – This is Google's presentation program, similar to Microsoft PowerPoint. It can be used to create slideshows and custom presentations that you can show during meetings and so on.

- **Forms** – This app is used to create custom forms such as applications and surveys that users can fill out and then send back to you.

- **Keep** – Keep is used to do things such as take notes, create lists, and also make audio reminders so you don't forget the things you need to do.

- **Drive** – Google gives its members free online storage space that is kept "in the cloud" (meaning it can be accessed from just about anywhere). You can also use it to share files with other people.

- **Gmail** – Gmail is Google's email program, and is one of the most widely used email services with millions of users.

- **Calendar** – Calendar can be used to do things such as schedule meetings and set reminders for appointments and other events.

- **Contacts** – If you have an Android smartphone, then all of your contacts are automatically added to your Google contacts. These will also be used with other apps, such as Gmail, so you will always have your contacts available to you.

Now that you have an idea of what Google Apps are and what they can do for you, let's start going into some details about each one.

Chapter 2 – Google Drive

Introducing Google Drive

Since many of the Google Apps I will be going over in this book rely on storing documents "in the cloud", I wanted to begin with Google Drive, since this is the place you will most likely be using to store the files that you use with your other Google Apps. As you read through this book, you will start to see how everything ties together and how the apps are linked with each other.

Everyone has heard of Google, and they seem to be getting their hands more and more into other areas of technology, so it only seems appropriate that they would be involved in the cloud storage business. (And they have been involved in the cloud storage business for some time now.)

The cloud storage service provided by Google used to be just called Google Drive, but recently they have changed the name to rebrand their cloud storage solution to Google One. Now they offer family plans and even things like special hotel pricing as a way to entice you into signing up. In other words, the new Google One name includes more than just online storage, but you can also combine things like Google Photos and Gmail to simplify your Google services. Even though the new name is Google One, they still call the storage portion of the plan Google Drive, so that is what I will be focusing on for this chapter.

Google One Plans and Features

Google One has quite a few plans to choose from, but for the most part, the plan you choose really only gives you extra storage capacity more than additional features over more expensive plans. That will most likely change in the future, so be sure to check it out before choosing your plan. With Google One\Google Drive, you can do things such as save your Gmail attachments right to your Google Drive, edit your photos with Google Photos, and work directly on your work files using Google Docs, Sheets, and Slides.

As for the Google One pricing options, here is a breakdown of the plans as of the writing of this book:

15GB Plan (Google Drive)
- Free

Chapter 2 – Google Drive

- 15GB of storage space

100GB Plan
- $1.99/month
- 100GB of storage space
- Access to Google experts
- Optional family member access
- Extra member benefits

200GB Plan
- $2.99/month
- 200GB of storage space
- Access to Google experts
- Optional family member access
- Extra member benefits

2TB Plan
- $9.99/month
- 2TB of storage space
- Access to Google experts
- Optional family member access
- Extra member benefits

10TB Plan
- $99.99/month
- 10TB of storage space
- Access to Google experts
- Optional family member access
- Extra member benefits

20TB Plan
- $199.99/month
- 20TB of storage space
- Access to Google experts
- Optional family member access
- Extra member benefits

Chapter 1 – Introducing Google Apps

30TB Plan
- $299.99/month
- 30TB of storage space
- Access to Google experts
- Optional family member access
- Extra member benefits

Using Google Drive

If you already have a Google account or Gmail address, then you already have access to Google Drive. If not, then all you need to do is head over to Google and create an account like I discussed in Chapter 1. You can also use that address to access your account once you create one.

If you take a look at figure 2.1, you can see what my Google Drive storage space looks like. There is the main storage area labeled *My Drive,* and then you can have subfolders underneath that like I do. Think of My Drive as your C drive in Windows, and you can then create subfolders under that and then subfolders within subfolders.

Chapter 2 – Google Drive

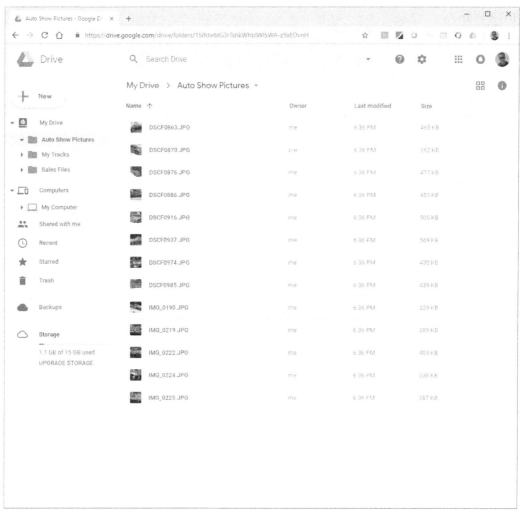

Figure 2.1

Also notice how there's a column for the owner of the files, as well as the date and\or time it was last modified, and the amount of space the files takes up on your drive. If it's a new file, it will just show the time, and older files will show the date. You can also sort by each one of these columns by clicking on the column header. In my example they are sorted by name, indicated by the up arrow next to the column heading that says *Name*.

Creating Folders and Uploading Files
It's very easy to create a new folder in Google Drive. All you need to do is click right on the location where you want to create your folder (such as My Drive), choose *New Folder*, and give it a name. Then you can go into that folder and upload some files. To do so, simply right click on a blank area and choose *Upload*

Chapter 2 – Google Drive

files, or you can actually drag and drop the files from your computer right into your web browser. When you upload files, you will see a status box for the upload, and when everything is complete, you will see a screen similar to figure 2.2.

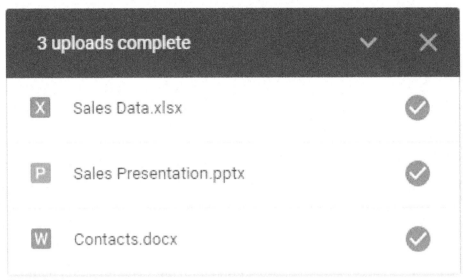

Figure 2.2

Then, when you are back at that folder, you will see your newly added files (like shown in figure 2.3).

Chapter 2 – Google Drive

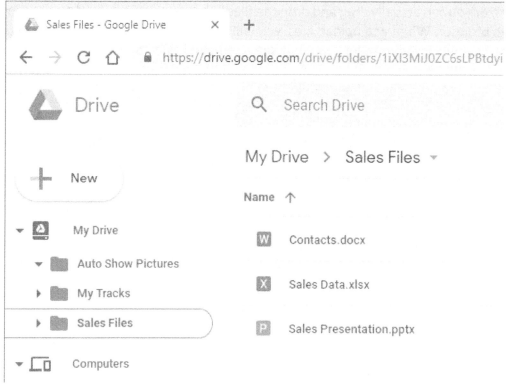

Figure 2.3

You can upload as many files as you have room for. You can also upload folders using the same methods that you can use for uploading files.

If you upload the same file to your drive, then you will have the option to overwrite the current file or keep the file you are uploading as a separate file, and will get a notification as shown in figure 2.4. Also note the version number, which means I have uploaded this file three times.

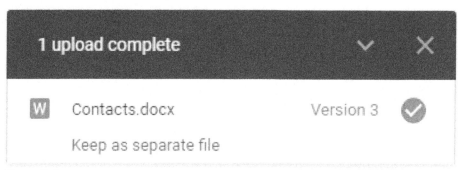

Figure 2.4

Chapter 2 – Google Drive

You might have noticed while you were right clicking that there are options for things like Google Docs and Google Sheets (figure 2.5). This is because Google wants you to use its Google Docs service, which is similar to Microsoft's Office 365, and allows you to use things like a word processor and spreadsheet app online rather than having to install one on your computer. (I will be getting into these apps later in the book.)

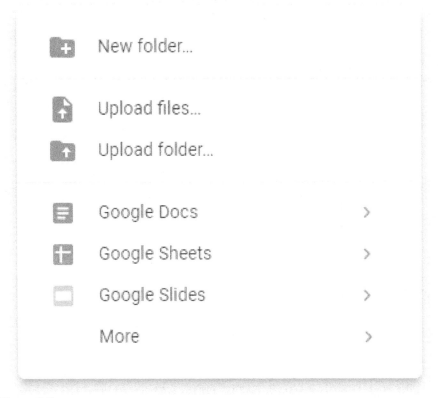

Figure 2.5

Managing Files and Folders
Once you get your folders created and files uploaded, you will need to know how to manage them so you know where things are and so your storage doesn't turn into a mess of files that are unmanageable.

Going back to figure 2.3, let's say we need to move the file called *Contacts.docx* to a new folder for a user called Mary. The first thing to do is right click on a blank spot within the Sales Files folder and choose *New folder*. Then let's call it *Mary's Files* and click on *Create*.

Chapter 2 – Google Drive

Now, as you can see in figure 2.6, we have a folder called *Mary's Files*, and we just need to move the Contacts.docx file into that folder. There are a couple of ways we can this.

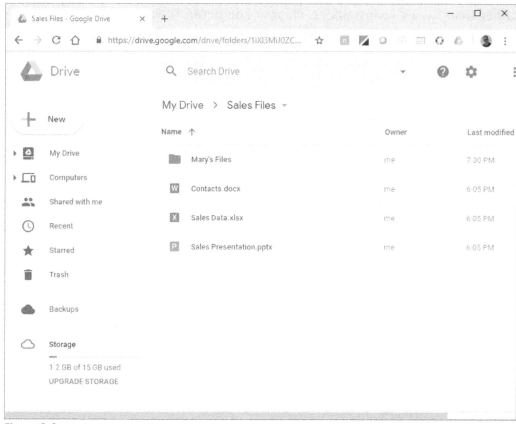

Figure 2.6

One way is to right click the Contacts.docx file, choose *Move to*, and then choose the *Mary's Files* folder (figure 2.7), which will get it moved into that folder.

Chapter 2 – Google Drive

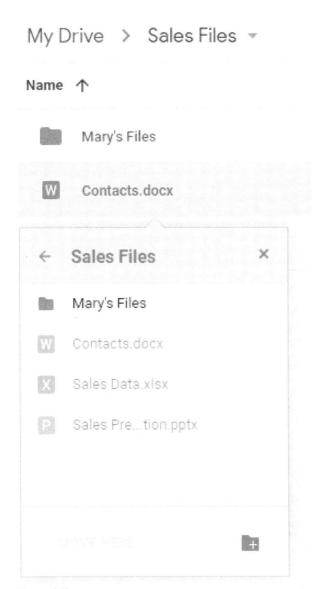

Figure 2.7

An easier way to do this is to just click on the *Contacts.docx* file and drag it into the *Mary's Files* folder. Either way, you will get a message similar to figure 2.8 telling you what happened.

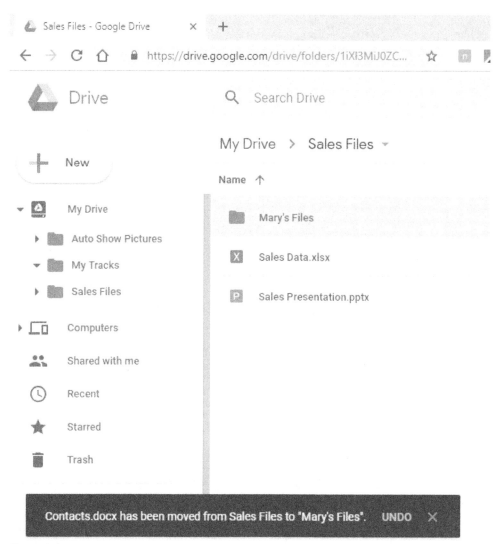

Figure 2.8

If you were then to go into the *Mary's Files* folder, you would find that the *Contacts.docx* file is now located in that folder.

Now I want to talk about the right click options that you have for files. When you right click a file, you will get a menu similar to figure 2.9, with many options to choose from.

Chapter 2 – Google Drive

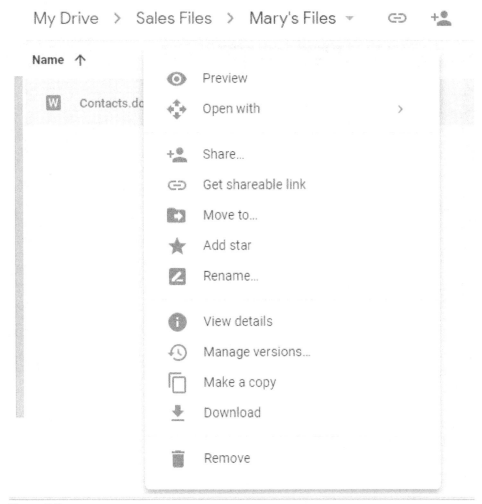

Figure 2.9

Here is what each of the right click options will do to your file:

- **Preview** – This option will allow you to preview your file right from your browser (assuming it's a supported file type). If you look at figure 2.9, I have opened the *Contacts.docx* file as a preview and can see the names and numbers in the file.

  Google Drive will also suggest other methods of opening your file based on the type of file it is. Back in figure 2.10, you can see that it suggested opening the file using Word 2016, and if you click the dropdown arrow next to that, there will be other options such as WordPad and Google Docs, which you can try if the preview function doesn't work.

35

Chapter 2 – Google Drive

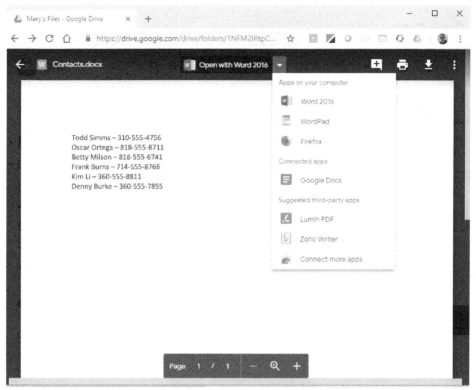

Figure 2.10

- **Open with** – This will give you choices of programs to open the file with (similar to the ones in figure 2.10).

- **Share** – This allows you to share your file with other people via a link or an email invite.

- **Get sharable link** – The same thing applies about sharing for this option, but what this does is create a link to your shared file that people can click on to have access to your file.

- **Move to** – I already discussed moving a file, but once again this will allow you to move a file from one folder to another.

- **Add star** – If you want a particular file to stand out, then you can add a star to it (figure 2.11), which will remind you that there is something special about it. There is also a Starred section in the main OneDrive area where you can view all of your starred files in one place.

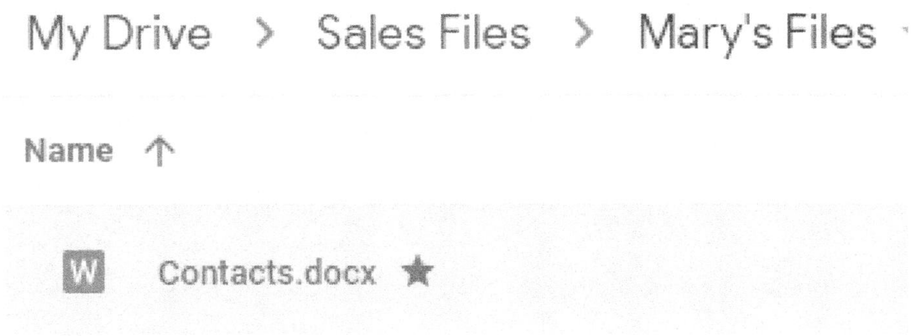

My Drive > Sales Files > Mary's Files

Name ↑

W   Contacts.docx ★

Figure 2.11

- **Rename** — This is pretty self-explanatory, but one thing you need to keep in mind is that if you change the file extension (in this case it's .docx) then you might not be able to open the file anymore since Windows (and Mac\Linux) use file extensions to tell the operating system what program it should open the file with.

- **View details** — Here you can view the details and activity of a certain file. As you can see in figure 2.12, there is a Details section and an Activity section, and each one shows different information about the file, such as its size, location, owner, as well as edit and move activity (etc.).

Chapter 2 – Google Drive

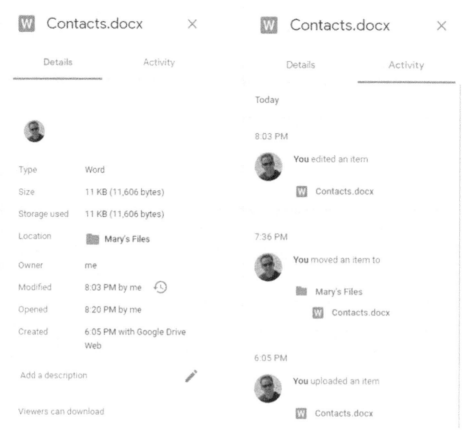

Figure 2.12

- **Manage versions** – If you have multiple versions of a file that you have either changed and saved, or uploaded a new copy and overwritten the existing copy, then you will have some options as to what you can do with those various versions (figure 2.13). Google will keep your older versions for thirty days (or 100 versions) before removing them, so if you need to go back to an older version, you will be able to do so. Then you can click on the three dots menu to either download the file, delete the file, or have Google keep the file forever.

Chapter 2 – Google Drive

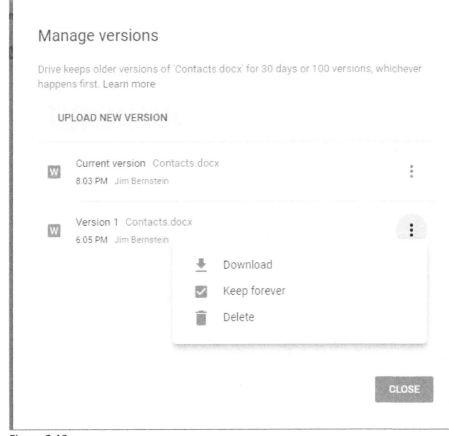

Figure 2.13

- **Make a copy** – This option will simply create a copy of the file and place it in the same folder with the same name, except it will say *"Copy of"* in front of it.

- **Download** – If you want to have a copy of this file on your local computer, then choose this option and select the folder on your hard drive where you want to download the file to.

- **Remove** – This option will remove the file from your Google Drive and place it the Trash, where you can go and restore the file if needed. To do so, just right click the file in the Trash and choose *Restore*. Or you can choose *Delete forever* to permanently remove it.

These same options are available from the toolbar that appears when you click on a file (figure 2.14). The three vertical dots will give you additional options.

Chapter 2 – Google Drive

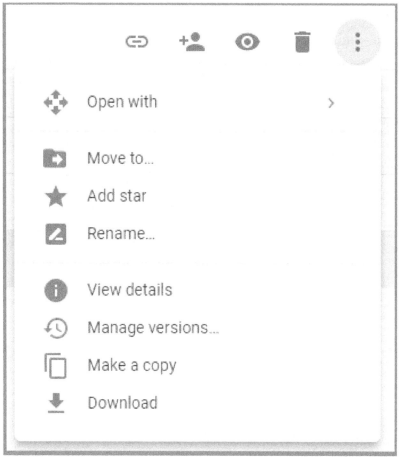

Figure 2.14

When you right click on a folder instead of a file, you get most of the same options, but there are a couple that are different (as highlighted in figure 2.15).

Chapter 2 – Google Drive

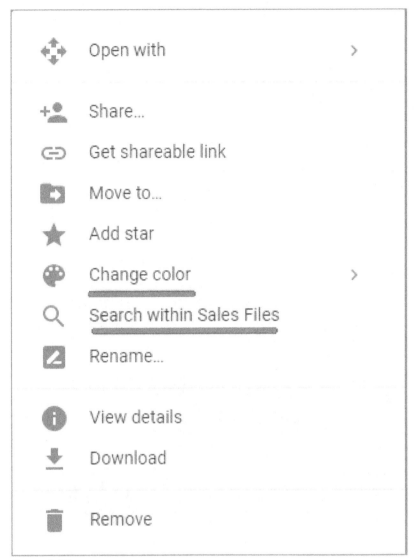

Figure 2.15

The *Change color* choice will change the color of the folder from the default grey to whatever color you like.

The *Search within* choice will let you search for files within the folder you right clicked on. You can search by name and also by file type.

One last thing I want to mention in this section is the view button. You can view your files in both list view and in grid view. Clicking on the button that looks like figure 2.16 will change the view of your files from just the file name to a thumbnail type view, which works well for pictures (figure 2.17). You can switch back and forth between these views in your folders.

Chapter 2 – Google Drive

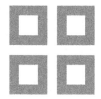

Figure 2.16

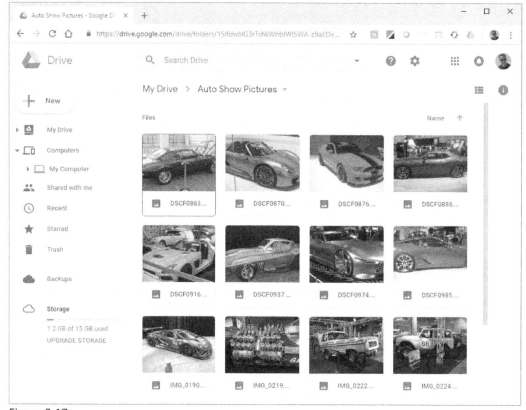

Figure 2.17

The View button is your friend, and it will make it a lot easier to manage your files because you can change the view based on the type of files you are looking at, so be sure to give it a try.

Chapter 2 – Google Drive

Google Drive Desktop Client
Google has a desktop client that comes in handy for managing your files so you can do this right from your computer rather than having to do it from the Google Drive site.

To install the client, simply do a Google search for the client, or you can go to **https://www.google.com/drive/download/** and click on the version you want. If you are using the free Google Drive and are using this at home and want the easy-to-install version, then download the one that says Personal (figure 2.18).

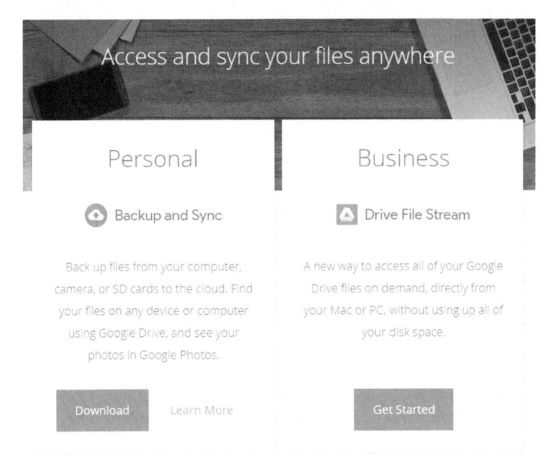

Figure 2.18

Next, you should see a screen similar to figure 2.19, and you will click on *Get Started*.

Chapter 2 – Google Drive

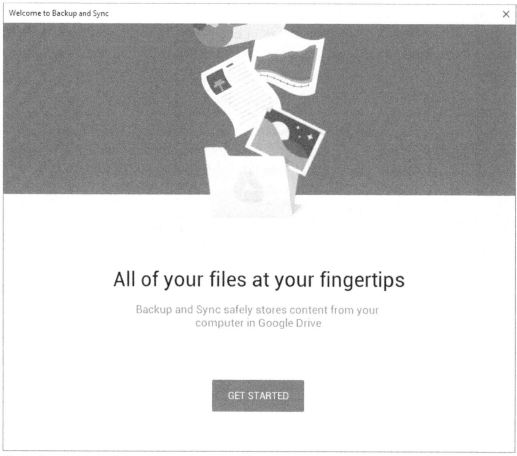

Figure 2.19

Then you will sign in with your Gmail account and password. Finally, it will want you to choose folders from your local computer to synchronize with your One Drive. You can keep the defaults for what files are to be backed up, or you can click on *CHOOSE FOLDER* to choose your own files to be backed up. In my case, I will clear all the boxes in figure 2.20 and choose just one folder called *WA* to be synchronized. You will see how this comes into play later on in the chapter.

Chapter 2 – Google Drive

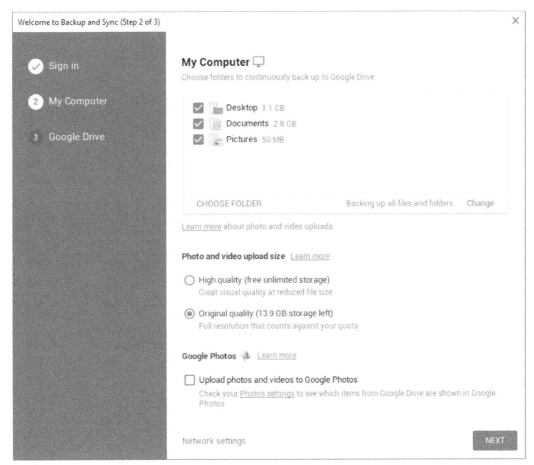

Figure 2.20

Also, notice the options for photo and video upload size. You can choose either *high quality* or *original quality*. If you choose high quality, you will get unlimited storage for your files, but if you want to keep them at their original size, you are stuck with the amount of storage you have, because choosing original size will take up more room on your Google Drive.

Clicking on *Change* will tell the client if it should backup all the files and folders in the location you select, or if you want it to only backup photos and videos from that folder. If you look at figure 2.21, you can also see there's an option under *Advanced settings* to ignore files with certain extensions. So, let's say you don't want any Microsoft Excel files synced to your drive. Since Excel uses .xlsx for its file extension, you would put xlsx in the box and click on *ADD*.

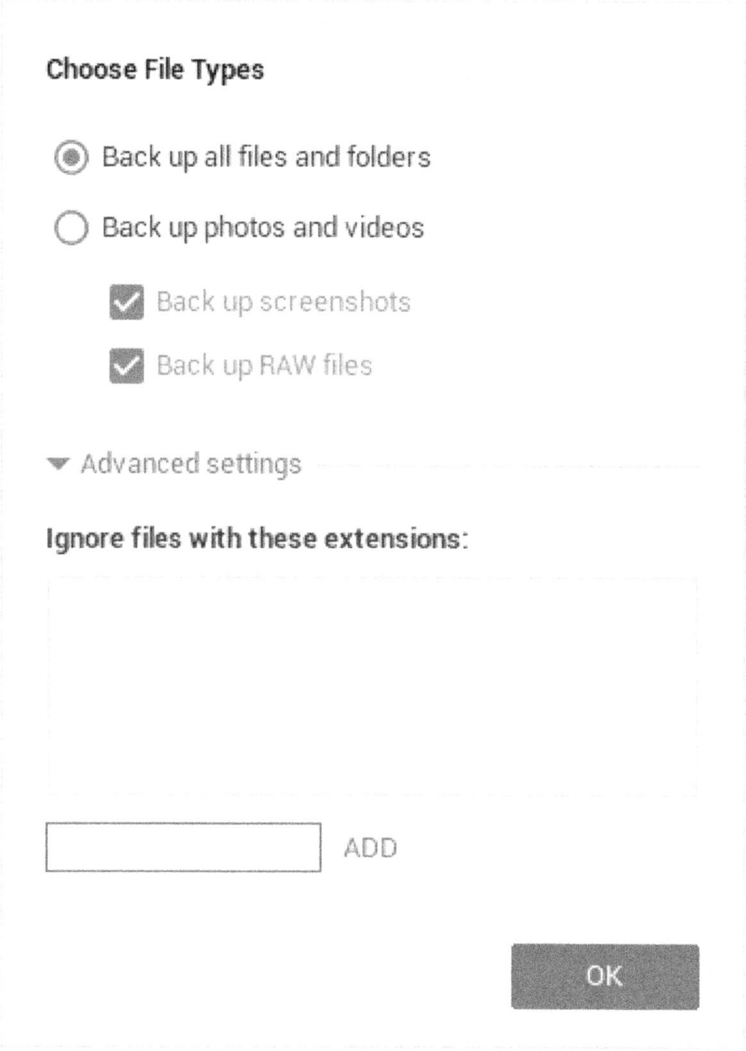

Figure 2.21

Next, it will ask you to sync your My Drive contents with your local computer. The default location on your computer where it will put these files is **C:\Users***username***\Google Drive,** where *username* is the name that you log into your computer with.

Finally, there is the checkbox that says *Sync My Drive to this computer* (figure 2.22). If you are planning on using the client, then you will most likely want to leave this checked, otherwise you won't have any of your Google Drive files on your computer.

Chapter 2 – Google Drive

The other option for *Sync everything in My Drive* or *Sync only these folders* will tell the client to either sync the entire contents of your Google Drive, or only the folders you specify.

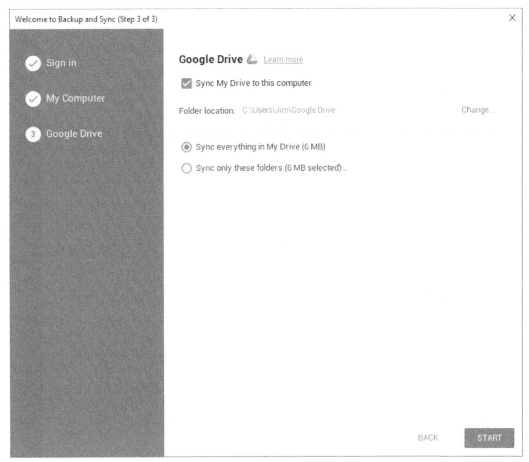

Figure 2.22

When everything looks good, you can click on Start get things synchronizing between your computer and your Google Drive. You will see the status of the copy at the lower right hand side of your screen (figure 2.23), and if you close it, you can right click the Google cloud icon in the system tray to bring it back up.

 Syncing your files with your Google Drive is not a replacement for regular backups, but it is better than doing nothing in case you are not the type who likes to make sure your files are safe!

Chapter 2 – Google Drive

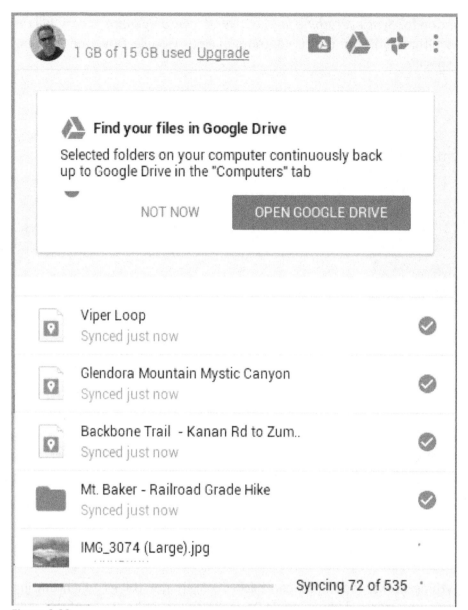

Figure 2.23

Now if you go to Windows Explorer, you should have a shortcut for your Google Drive on the left side of the windows (figure 2.24). If not, then you can browse to **C:\Users*username*\Google Drive** to see your local files. You can also make a shortcut to this folder on your desktop (etc.) if you know how.

Chapter 2 – Google Drive

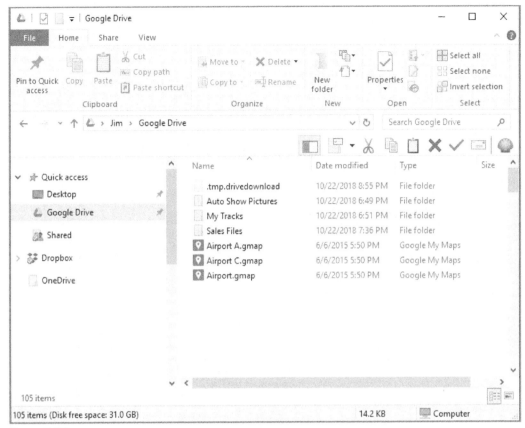

Figure 2.24

Now that you have the Google client installed, you can right click on any folder on your computer and choose *Google Drive > Sync this folder* (figure 2.25) to have the client add that folder to your online storage space.

Chapter 2 – Google Drive

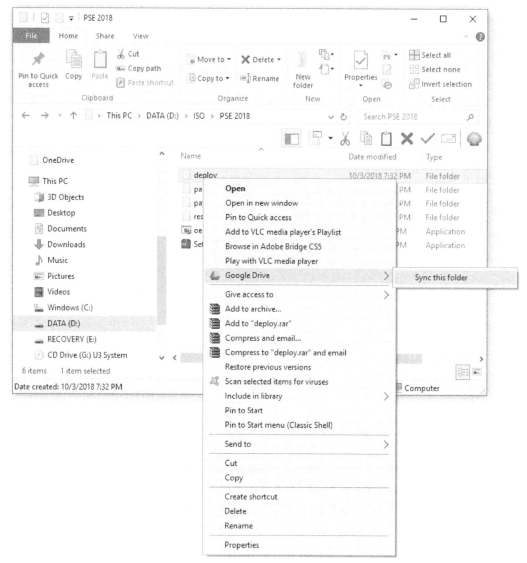

Figure 2.25

Going back to your Google Drive folder on the Google website, you will see a section labeled *Computers*, and underneath that will be your computer that you added during the client installation, as well as any folders you told it to sync at the same time. Notice in figure 2.26 I have the *deploy* folder listed since I just added it in the previous step, as well as the *WA* folder I discussed earlier when I was picking my folders to synchronize.

Chapter 2 – Google Drive

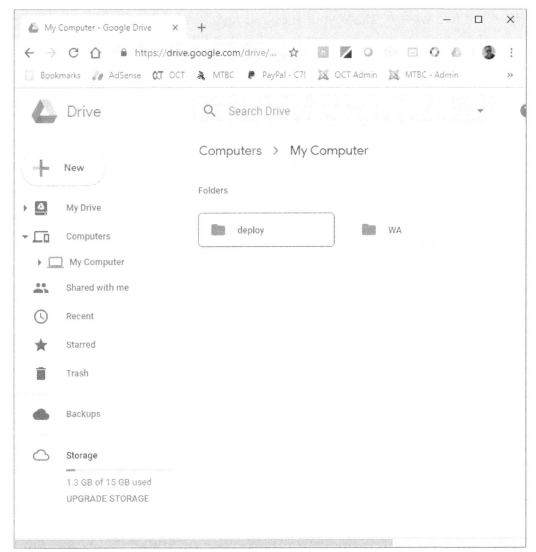

Figure 2.26

If you don't like the default name of *My Computer*, then you can right click on it and choose *Rename* and change it to whatever you like. I think I will rename mine *Jim's Computer*.

Sharing Files and Folders
Just like the other cloud storage services I have discussed so far, Google Drive also offers file and folder sharing capabilities so you can share and collaborate with other people.

Chapter 2 – Google Drive

There are two ways to share your files and folders with Google Drive. You can share them directly and have others use them as if they were their own, or you can create a link that they can download the file from.

When I right click on a file and choose Share, I enter the email address of the person or people I want to share the file with, and then decide if they can edit, comment, or only view the file (figure 2.27).

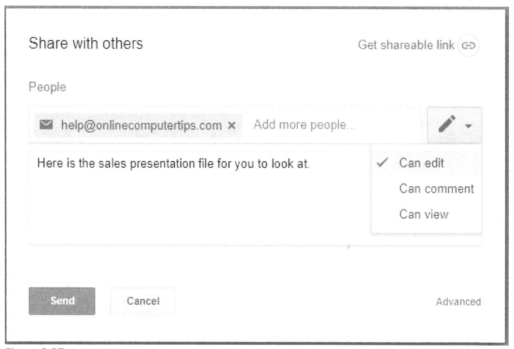

Figure 2.27

As you can see in figure 2.28, this person doesn't have a Google account, so my only option is to send an invitation or send a link (which I will discuss next). If I choose the *Send an Invitation* option, then they will need to create a Google account within fourteen days to be able to access the file.

Chapter 2 – Google Drive

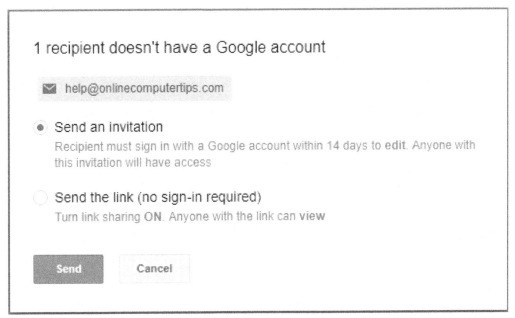

Figure 2.28

Going back to figure 2.27, there is an Advanced option that you can click on to see additional choices you can make to add restrictions to the file before sharing it (figure 2.29).

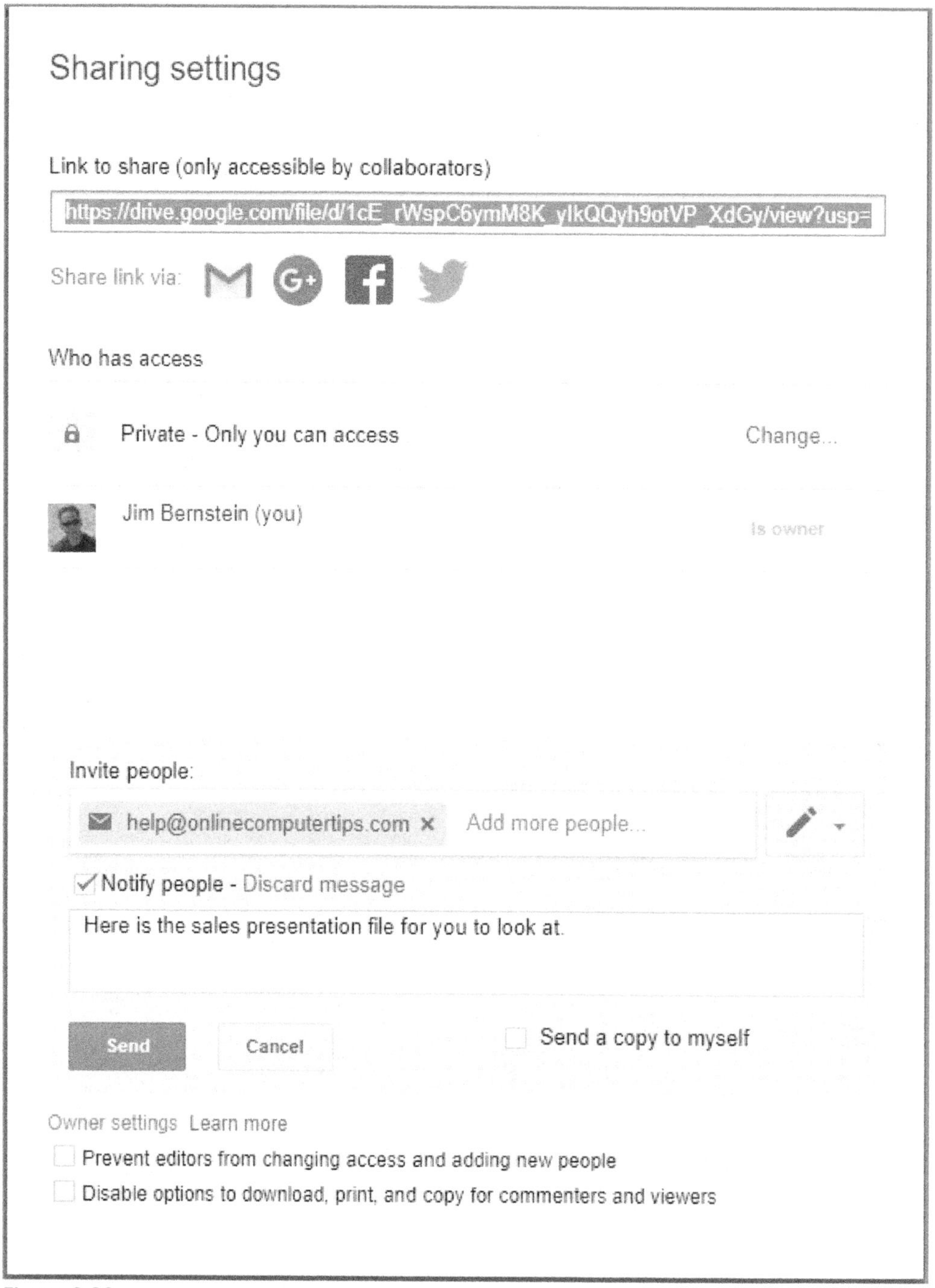

Chapter 2 – Google Drive

Figure 2.29

I am going to send the invitation even though this user doesn't have a Google account. When the end user gets the email, they will see the file name that they have access to as well as the personalized message I added to the invitation (figure 2.30). Notice the message saying they can access the item without logging in and

Chapter 2 – Google Drive

to only forward it to people you trust. When they click on the link, it will open the file in their browser if it's supported. Otherwise, it will give you the option to download the file to your computer or try a different online app to open the file.

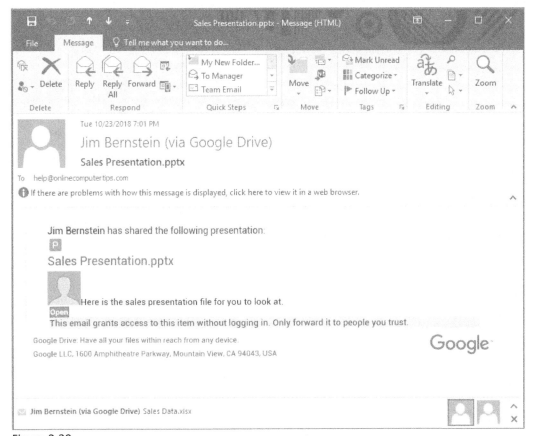

Figure 2.30

When you share a folder, you get different permission options that you can assign with it compared to sharing files (figure 2.31).

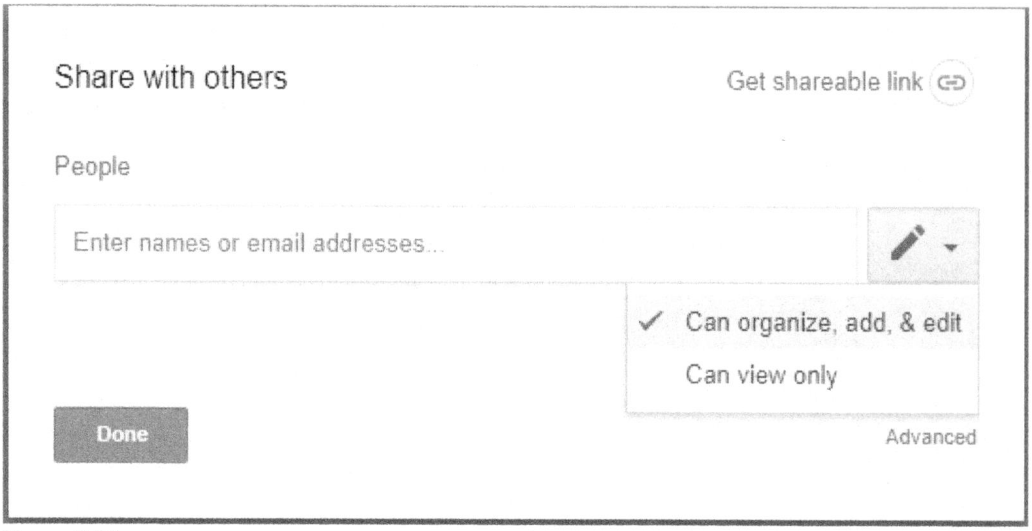

Chapter 2 – Google Drive

Share with others	Get shareable link

People

Enter names or email addresses...

✓ Can organize, add, & edit
Can view only

Done   Advanced

Figure 2.31

The Advanced options are a little bit different as well (figure 2.32).

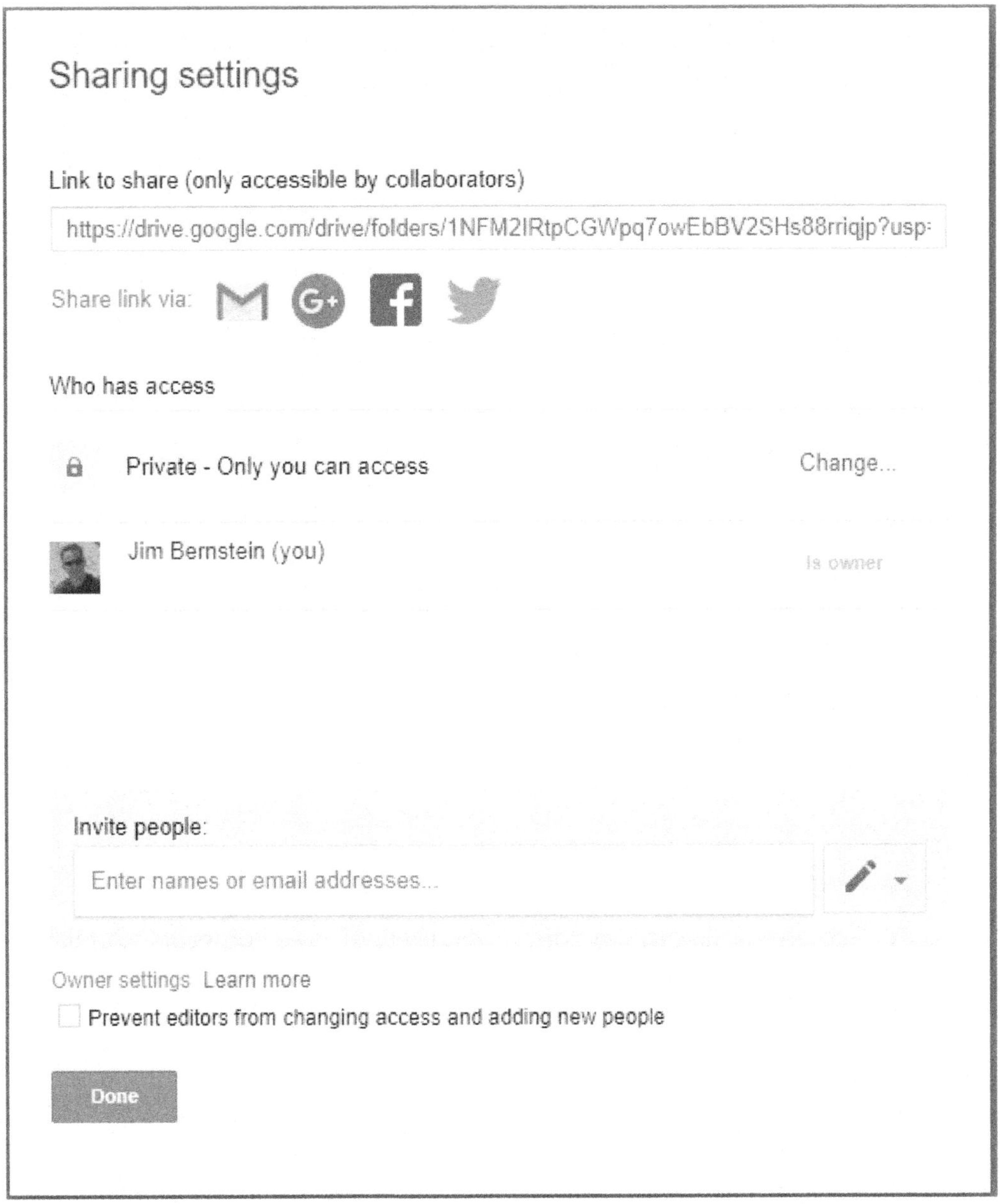

Chapter 2 – Google Drive

Sharing settings

Link to share (only accessible by collaborators)

https://drive.google.com/drive/folders/1NFM2IRtpCGWpq7owEbBV2SHs88rriqjp?usp=

Share link via:

Who has access

🔒 Private - Only you can access   Change...

Jim Bernstein (you)   Is owner

Invite people:

Enter names or email addresses...

Owner settings Learn more
☐ Prevent editors from changing access and adding new people

Done

Figure 2.32

Here is what the email will look like when you share a folder with someone (figure 2.33).

Chapter 2 – Google Drive

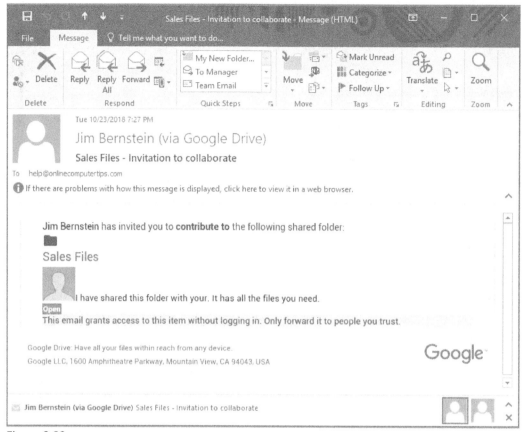

Figure 2.33

When they click on the link called *Sales Files*, they will see something similar to figure 2.34 in their web browser.

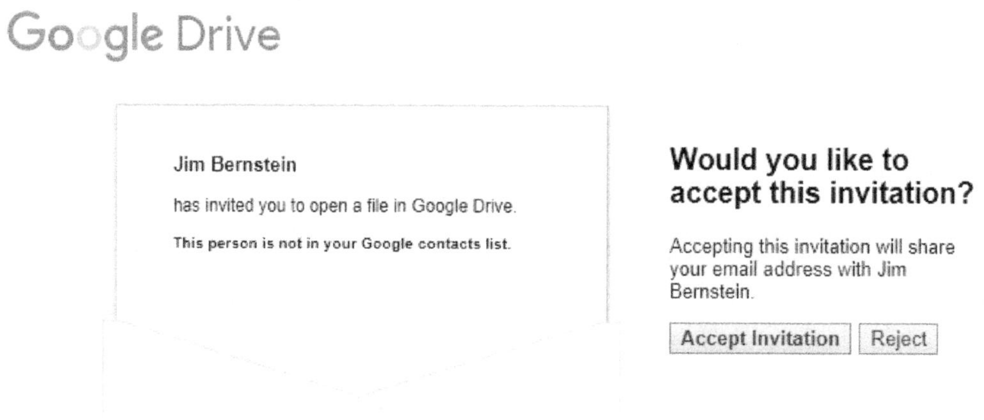

Figure 2.34

Chapter 2 – Google Drive

When they click on the *Accept Invitation* button, they will be brought to a One Drive page with only that folder displayed, and they will not be able to see any of your other files or folders.

Sharing links is a little different, and comes in handy if you just want to share a single file with someone rather than emailing it to them. Most email systems have limits on file attachment size, so if you have a large file in your Google Drive, then sending a link is a great way for the other person to get access to that file without you having to send them a huge email.

I added another file to the Sales Files folder called *Sales Brochure.pub,* which is a Microsoft Publisher file. I will now send a link to the same email address I was sending the other links to. All I need to do is right click on the *Sales Brochure.pub* file, choose *Get shareable link,* and then a box will pop up with the link and an option to turn link sharing on or off (figure 2.35). It will be on by default.

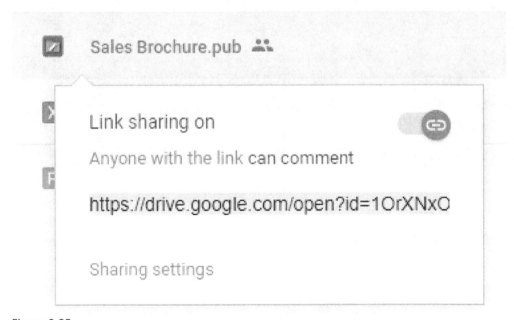

Figure 2.35

Then I can just copy the link and send it in an email and the person on the other end can then click on it and open or download the file. If they can't preview it in their browser, they will get the message to download the file or try another online app (figure 2.36).

Chapter 2 – Google Drive

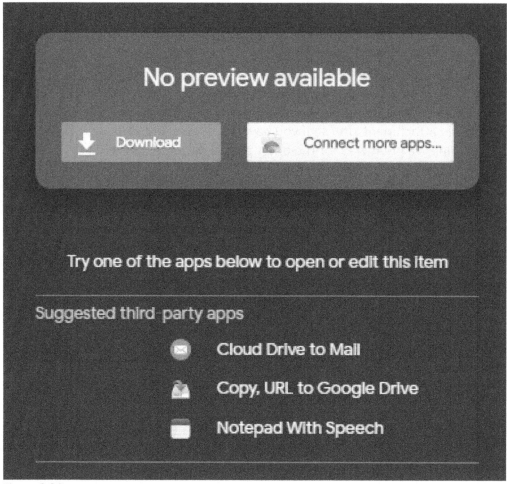

Figure 2.36

If you click on Sharing settings (as seen in figure 2.35), you will get more options that you can apply to your shared link (as shown in figure 2.37).

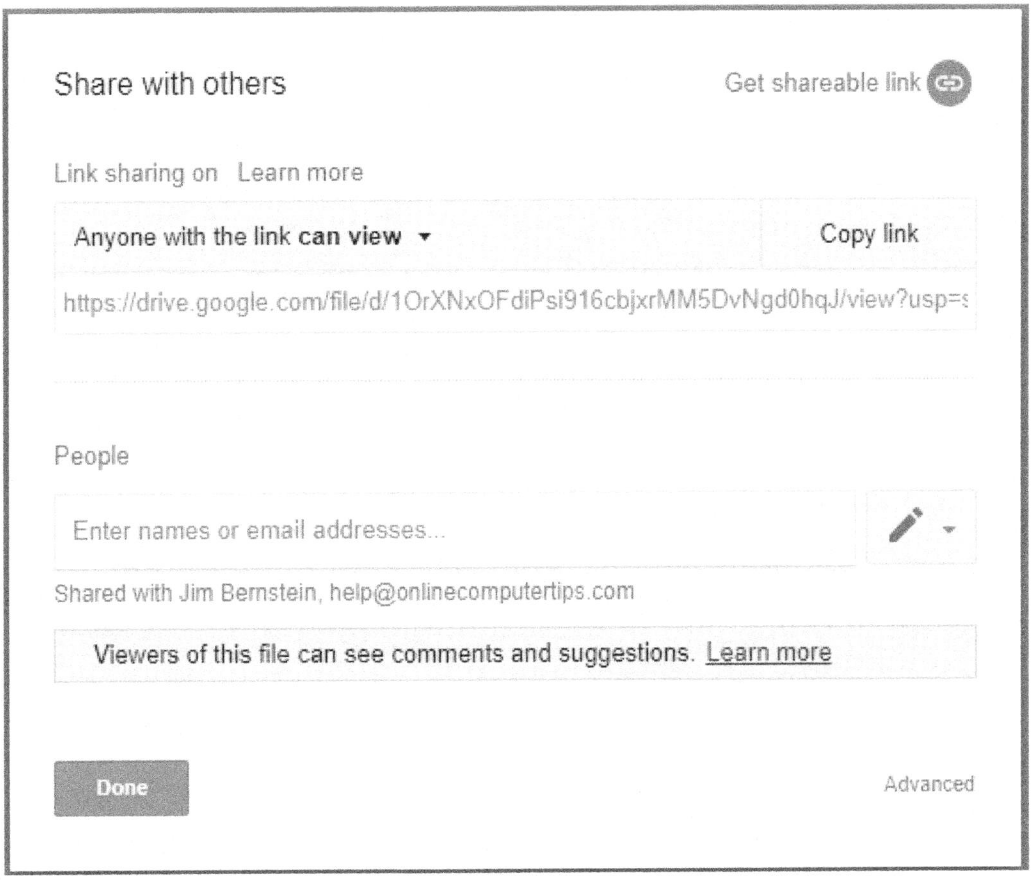

Chapter 2 – Google Drive

```
Share with others                         Get shareable link 🔗

Link sharing on  Learn more

  Anyone with the link can view ▼                      Copy link

  https://drive.google.com/file/d/1OrXNxOFdiPsi916cbjxrMM5DvNgd0hqJ/view?usp=s


People

  Enter names or email addresses...                       ✏️ ▼

Shared with Jim Bernstein, help@onlinecomputertips.com

  Viewers of this file can see comments and suggestions. Learn more


  Done                                                    Advanced
```

Figure 2.37

And clicking on *Advanced* will bring you to the same advanced settings as we saw back in figure 2.29.

These link creating steps are pretty much the same for sharing folders, so give it a try on your own to see if it makes sense to you.

One more thing I want to mention about sharing is the *Shared with me* section that you can find on the left sidebar under *Computers*. This will show you any files and folders that have been shared with you by other Google users. It will show you the names, who shared it, and the share date (figure 2.38). You can also share these shared files with other people if you like.

Chapter 2 – Google Drive

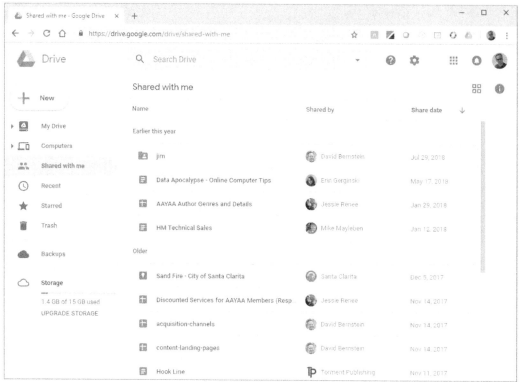

Figure 2.38

Google Drive Smartphone \ Tablet App

It's possible to access your Google Drive files and folders from your smartphone or tablet, but you will need to install the app to do so. To install the Google Drive app on your phone or tablet, you will need to go to the Google Play Store or Apple App Store and search for Google Drive, then download and install it. If you install the Google 1 (not Google *one*) app, it will want you to use a pay-for account, so that's up to you if you want the extra storage space and features.

When you first run the app, it might ask you which Google account you want to use if you have more than one. If you only have one, then you don't need to worry about it. Then you will see that the interface looks pretty much the same as what you see when using your web browser (figure 2.39).

Chapter 2 – Google Drive

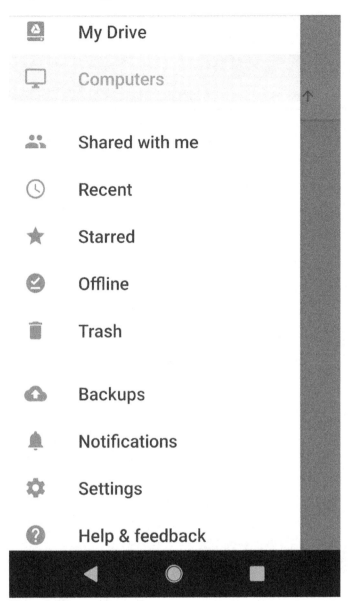

Figure 2.39

Just like with the OneDrive website, you can do the same things with your files and folders such as open, download, share, copy, and so on (as seen in figure 2.40). All you need to do is find the file or folder you want to work with and tap on the three vertical dots next to it to bring up your options.

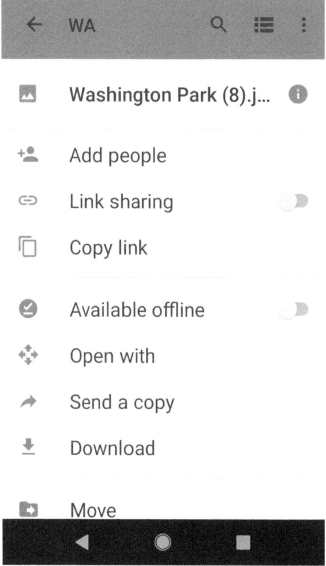
Figure 2.40

There is an option called *Offline* that allows you to mark files as offline so you can view them if you don't have an Internet connection. Any changes made to the file while it's offline will be synced back to your OneDrive folder once your device is connected to the Internet again.

Finally, I want to discuss the Backup settings that come with your Google cloud storage account. If you are using a mobile device, then you have the option to backup device specific settings like apps, contacts, and passwords to your Google Drive. To enable this feature, just go to the OneDrive app and then to Backups, and enable the backup feature (figure 2.41).

Chapter 2 – Google Drive

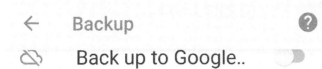

Easily restore your data or switch phones at any time. Learn more

Backup includes:
 - Apps and apps data
 - Call history
 - Contacts
 - Device settings (including Wi-Fi passwords and permissions)
 - SMS

Your backups are uploaded to Google and encrypted using your Google Account password. For some data, your device's screen lock PIN, pattern, or password is also used for encryption.

Figure 2.41

 When backing up to your Google Drive, just remember that your information is only as secure as Google says it is. The term "cloud" only means a server at a different location from yours, and who knows what country it's really located in!

Chapter 3 – Google Docs

I wanted to go over Google Docs before the other office productivity apps because it's the one that is probably used by the most people. Google Docs is Google's word processor application (similar to the popular Microsoft Word program). Once we start diving into how Docs works, you will see that it has many of the same functionality of Word (if in fact you are a current Word user).

Docs Interface

To access Google Docs all you need to do is go to the Google Docs website (https://docs.google.com/), or do a search for Google Docs and get to it that way. If you are already logged into your Google account, then it will take you to the Docs interface (as shown in figure 3.1). If you are not logged in, then you will be prompted to enter your Gmail address and password.

Since I have logged into Docs before, it shows me my recent documents on the bottom of the screen as well as an option to start a new blank document or a document from one of the built in templates. There are many templates to choose from, from resumes to letters to brochures and so on.

Templates are a great way to help to see what kind of things you can do in Google Docs. Try opening one up and playing around with it to see if you can figure out how it was put together.

Chapter 3 – Google Docs

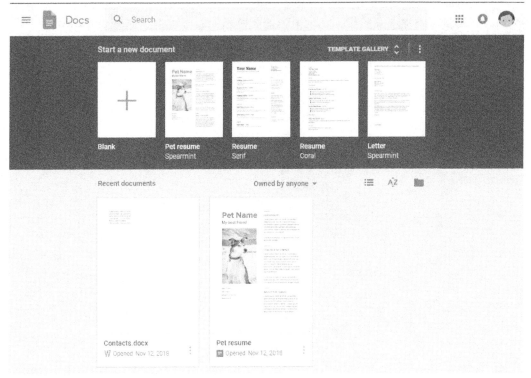

Figure 3.1

In order to start using Docs, we will either need to open a recent document, create a new blank document, or create a document from one of the templates. For my example I will use a template called *Lesson Plan* from the template gallery (figure 3.2). Once I click on that template it will open up in Docs and be ready for us to start editing.

Chapter 3 – Google Docs

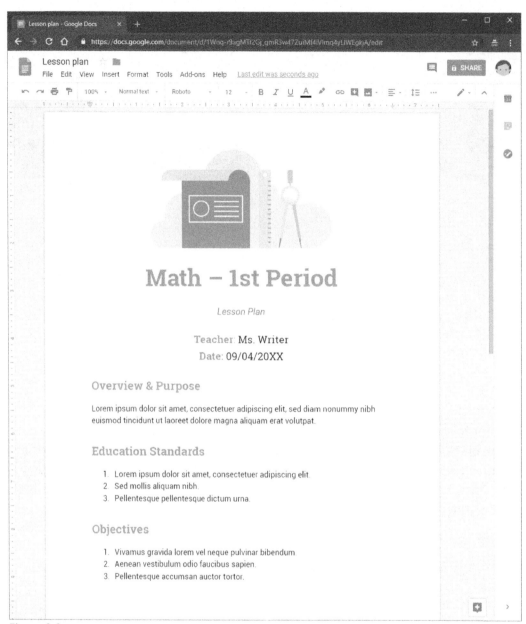

Figure 3.2

Now you can see the toolbars and menu items that you can use when working on your documents. The options are not quite as extensive as the ones with Word, but there are plenty of tools to help you get the job done.

Many of the tool icons are obvious, such as the ones for changing the font type, size, and color. Plus there are buttons to do things like center and justify the text or insert images and hyperlinks. Plus, if you need to know what a button does, simply hold your mouse over the button and the tooltip will appear, telling you what that button does and also give you the keyboard shortcut for that function. For example, in figure 3.3 you can see that the button allows you to insert a link in your document, and you can also press *Ctrl+K* on your keyboard to do the same thing.

Figure 3.3

You will also notice next to the name of the document that there is an option to mark it with a star, which will mark it as starred in your Google Drive, and also allow you to access this particular document faster in the future.

Next to the star is a folder icon, which will allow you to move your document to a different folder within your Google Drive to help you keep things more organized. This is one of the reasons you should set up your Google Drive before getting too into the other Google apps, so things will make a little more sense.

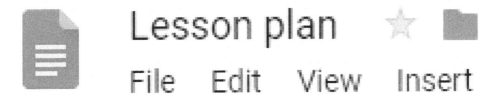

Figure 3.4

At the upper right of the screen, you will see a message looking icon (figure 3.5), and this is where you can view or add any comments about this particular document. If it's shared with others, you can see their comments here as well. Speaking of shared, clicking on the *share* button will allow you to share the document with other people or groups, just like I discussed in the chapter on Google Drive. The icon to the right can be used to view your account settings or sign out of your account if needed.

Chapter 3 – Google Docs

Figure 3.5

On the right hand side of the screen, there will also be some icons that are used for quick access to your calendar, Google Keep, and your Tasks. If you use these apps, this can come in handy, otherwise you can just ignore them.

Figure 3.6

Another thing I want to mention on the right side of the screen is the Editing Mode dropdown selection (figure 3.7).

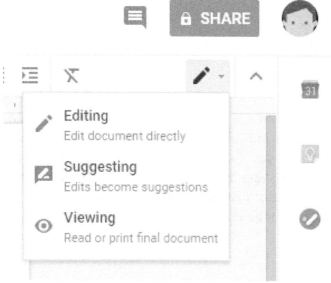

Figure 3.7

Chapter 3 – Google Docs

There are three different modes to choose from:

- **Editing** – *Editing* mode is what you will be using most of the time. This mode allows you to edit your document, meaning you can add text and images, change formatting, and so on.

- **Suggesting** – If you are sharing your document with others for collaboration purposes, the *Suggesting* mode can be used to make changes that are marked as suggested changes, and anyone with edit permissions on the document can accept or reject your suggestions. It's similar to the Track Changes feature in Microsoft Word. As you can see in figure 3.8, Todd Simms added the words *of this course,* which is marked with brackets above and below the text and also changed the text to red. Now there is an option to accept or reject the changes with the checkmark or the X.

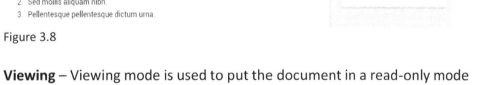

Figure 3.8

- **Viewing** – Viewing mode is used to put the document in a read-only mode where no changes can be made.

Clicking on an object or highlighting some text will bring up an insert comment button (figure 3.9).

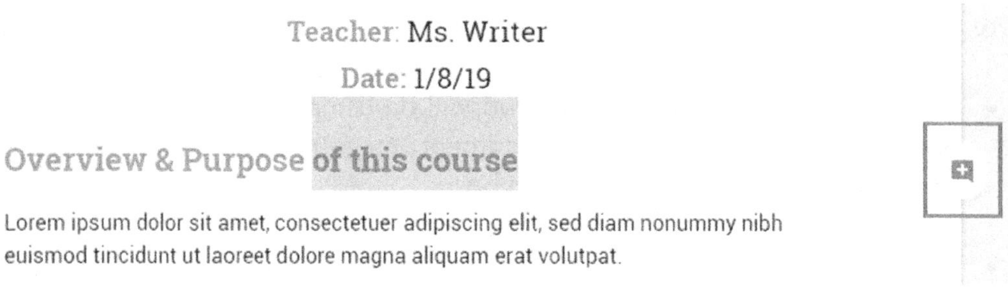

Figure 3.9

Clicking on that button will allow you to type in a comment for the particular item you selected, whether it be text or an image etc.

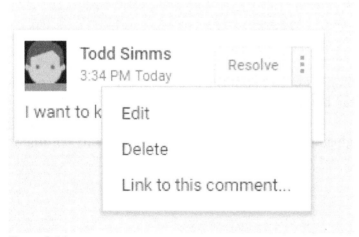

Figure 3.10

After you type in your comment, it will be shown to the right hand side of the page, and you will have some things you or others can do with that comment.

Figure 3.11

Clicking on *Resolve* will mark the comment as resolved and hide the discussion. Clicking on *Edit* or *Delete* are obvious, but when you click on *Link to this comment* you will be provided with a link that you can copy and paste into an email to send

Chapter 3 – Google Docs

off to someone else so they can look over your comment. In order for that person to see your comment, they will need to have permission to access the document, otherwise they can request permission from the page the link brings them to.

Menu Items

Now I would like to go over the tools and functions that you can use from the menu items within Docs. Many of these are obvious, so I will go into more detail about the ones that might not be too obvious. Keep in mind that many of the items you will find under the various menus will be the same as what is available in the toolbars.

File Menu

The File menu is where you will find many of your administrative functions, such as opening a current document or creating a new one.

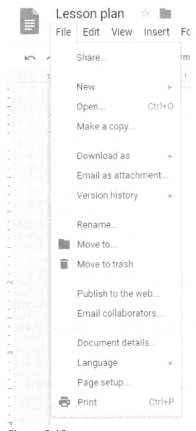

Figure 3.12

Chapter 3 – Google Docs

I will now briefly go over all of the items within the File menu:

- **Share** – I mentioned sharing your document earlier in the chapter, but if you decide to share your work with other people, you can use this option to send out invitations so that they can then view and\or edit your documents. All you need to do is type in their email address and choose if they can edit, comment, or view your document, and click on *Send*.

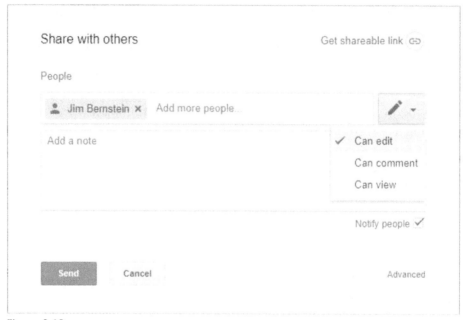

Figure 3.13

- **New** – The *New* option brings you back to where we were at the beginning of the chapter, where you can either choose to create a new blank document or create a new document from one of the included templates.

- **Open** – The Open option will let you open previously saved documents from your Google Drive, as well as documents that have been shared with you by others. If you want to upload a new document to work on you can do that from here as well.

- **Make a copy** – This option will make a copy of the existing document in the location of your choosing. You can name the copy anything you wish, otherwise it will be named **Copy of *document name***. There will also be checkbox options to share the copy with the same people as the original was shared with, and also an option to copy comments and suggestions.

- **Download as** – If you want to download a copy of the document to your local computer or other device, then you can do so using this option. You have several choices as to what type of document you want to save it as, such as a Word document, PDF, text file, and so on.

- **Email as attachment** – If you want to send your actual document to someone rather than inviting them to view it from your account, you can use the *Email as attachment option* (figure 3.14).

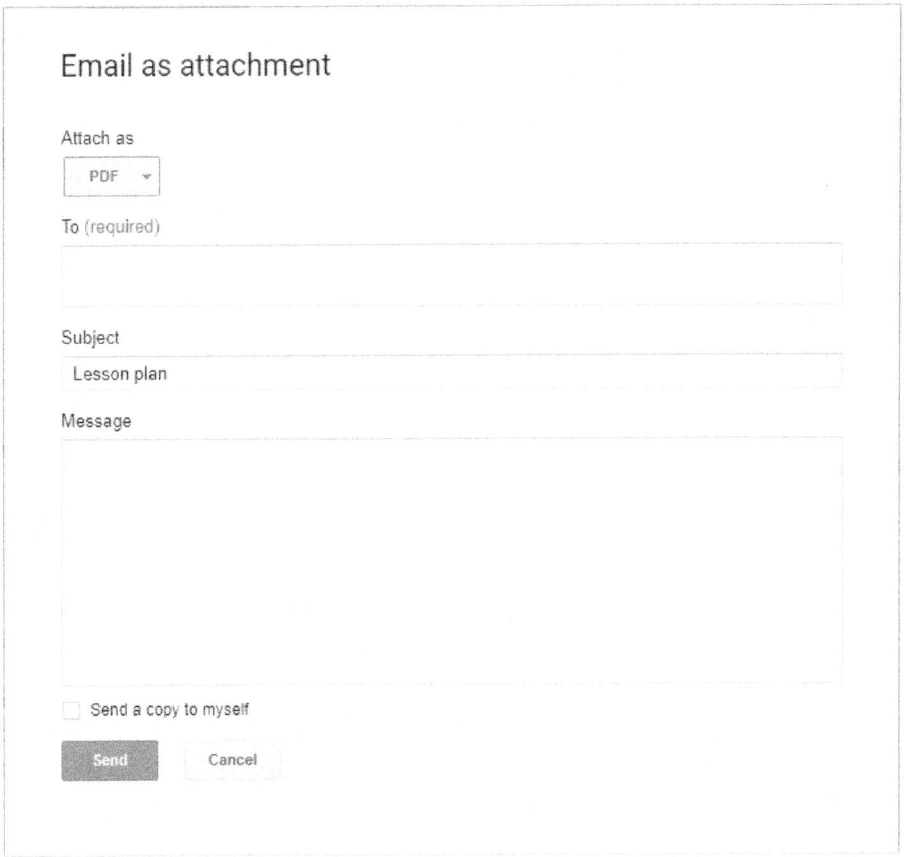

Figure 3.14

Here you can choose what type of file you can have your attachment sent as by clicking on the down arrow under *Attach as*. Or you can use the *Paste the item itself into the email* option if you want the document to be displayed in the body of the email.

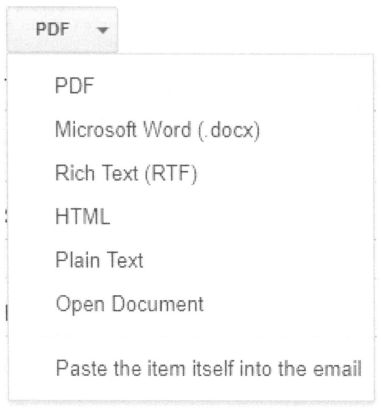

Figure 3.15

- **Version History** – As Google Docs saves your changes, it will keep various versions of the file in case you want to revert back to a different version, and maybe recover some changes as shown in figure 3.16. Clicking on the three vertical dots next to a version will allow you to copy that version, or give that version a specific name (figure 3.17). You also have the option to have Docs only show named versions so your version history only shows the versions you want to see.

Chapter 3 – Google Docs

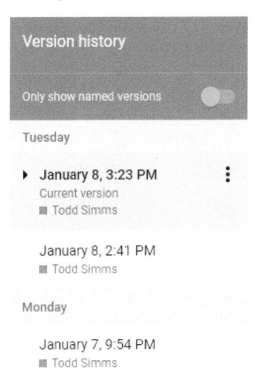

Figure 3.16

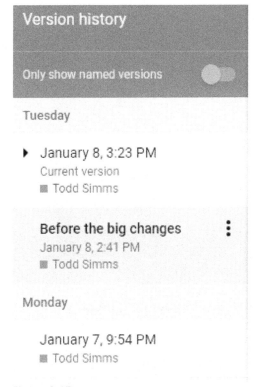

Figure 3.17

- **Rename** – The *Rename* option simply renames your document to a name of your choosing. As you can see in figure 3.18, when I clicked on *Rename*, it highlighted *Lesson plan,* allowing me to change it to something else if desired.

Figure 3.18

- **Move to** – Using this option does the same thing as clicking the folder icon next to the star, and will allow you to move the file to a different location on your Google Drive or move it to your local computer.

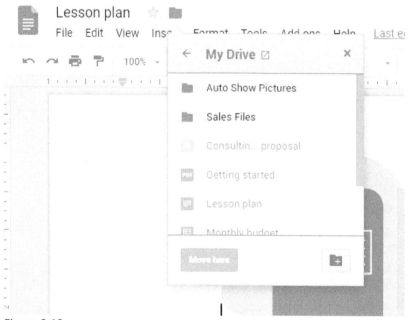

Figure 3.19

- **Move to trash** – If you want to delete your document, you can use this option. (You can recover it from your trash if you change your mind later.)

- **Publish to the web** – If you would like to share your document as a read only webpage version of the file, then this is where *Publish to the web* can come in handy. When you use this option, Docs will create a link when you click on *Publish* that you can copy and then send to other people so they can view your document within their web browser.

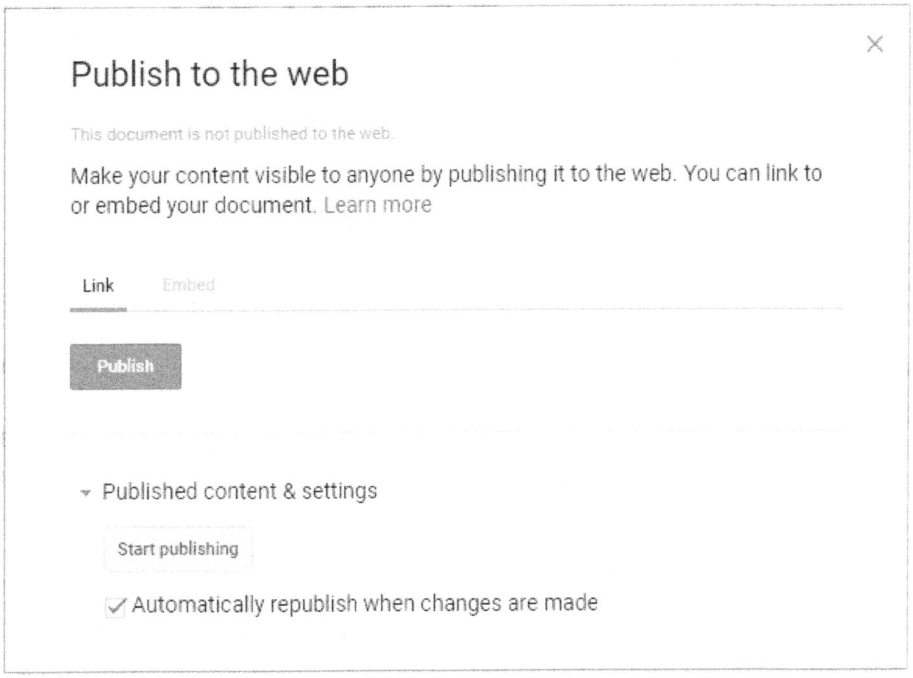

Figure 3.20

If you check the box at the bottom that says *Automatically republish when changes are made*, then when you make changes, the people with access to your shared link can refresh their browser and see your updated document. After you publish your document the *Start publishing* button will change to *Stop publishing* if you don't want your document to be available to people with the link anymore.

- **Email collaborators** – If you want to send a message to everyone who is a collaborator on this document, then use the *Email collaborators* option. Docs will automatically add everyone to the email who has access to the document, but you can uncheck any names that you don't want the email sent to.

- **Document details** – Choosing this option will give you basic information about the document you are working on such as its location, owner, modified date, and created date.

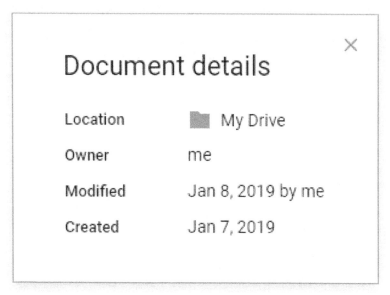

Figure 3.21

- **Language** – This is where you would change your typing language from its default.

- **Page setup** – *Page setup* allows you to change things such as the page orientation, margin sizes, paper size, and page color. You can also make your changes and then have Docs use them as the default for all new documents you create.

- **Print** – When it's time for you print your document, you will do so from the *Print* option. Docs has its own print interface, but if you are used to the print interface that your computer normally uses for locally installed programs, you can click on the link that says *Print using system dialog*.

Edit Menu
There are not as many options on the Edit menu as there are on the File menu, but I still want to take a little time and go over them. Take a note of the shortcut key option to the right of each menu item. These can be used rather than clicking on the menu and then sub-menu item to do the same task.

Chapter 3 – Google Docs

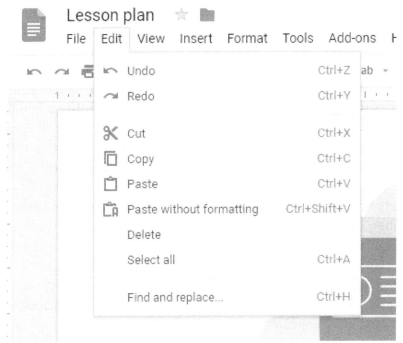

Figure 3.22

Here is what each of the items in the Edit menu does:

- **Undo** – If you make a change and want to revert back to the way it was before the change, you can use the *Undo* option. (This won't work if you have closed the document and then reopened it before using the Undo option.)

- **Redo** – If you undo a change and then decide you want it back after all, then you can use the *Redo* option. (This won't work if you have closed the document and then reopened it before using the Redo option.)

- **Cut** – When you want to remove some text or an image from a page or section and then place it in another page or section, you can highlight it and then choose *Cut*. Then you can paste it in where you would like it to be.

- **Copy** – When you want to make a copy of some text or an image and place it elsewhere, you will use Copy. This leaves the original text or image in place.

- **Paste** – After you cut or copy text or an image, you will use the *Paste* option to place that text or image within your document. Just be sure that your cursor is where you want the text or image to be before choosing Paste.

- **Paste without formatting** – Normally when you paste something into your document, Docs will keep the format of the text the same as the original text you cut or copied when you pasted it into your document. If you choose *Paste without formatting,* then it will paste the text in as the default text style that your version of Docs uses for new documents.

- **Delete** – *Delete* will simply remove any text or images you have selected. (Just remember you can use the *Undo* option to bring them back if needed.)

- **Select all** – If you want to highlight everything in your document all at once, simply choose the *Select all* option to do so. Then you can cut, copy, delete, or change the text and images you have highlighted.

- **Find and replace** – Many times you will want to replace a word with a different word within your document. For example, let's say you wanted to replace *John* with *Jon*. Rather than search for each instance of *John*, you can use the *Find and replace* option to have Docs do it for you. You can do this one instance at a time, or have Docs replace all of the text in one shot. If you look at figure 3.23, you will see that there are two instances of the name *John* in my document.

Figure 3.23

Find and replace can come in handy to make punctuation and capitalization changes as well. So, if you wanted to change : to ; or change Mcdonald to McDonald, you can use the find and replace option to do so.

View Menu
Docs allows you to customize your view so you can see only what you want to see on the screen, allowing for less clutter or viewing of more of the toolbars and so on.

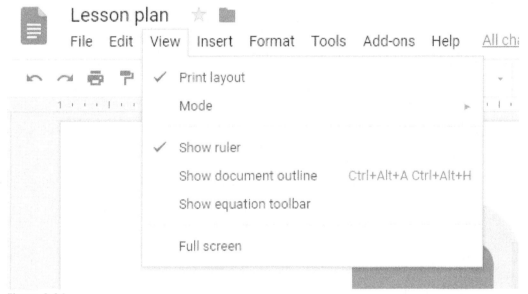

Figure 3.24

There are only a few options on this menu, and I will now go over what each one does:

- **Print layout** – The *Print layout* allows you to see your headers, footers, and margins between pages as if you have printed out the document.

- **Mode** – This will give you the same options I discussed earlier in the chapter when I went over the Editing, Suggesting, and Viewing modes.

Chapter 3 – Google Docs

- **Show ruler** – By default, Docs will show a ruler on the left hand side of the page, allowing you to measure things like images and other items to see what size they will take on the page. You can turn the ruler off if you don't need it, or don't want to see it.

- **Show document outline** – If your document is in an outlined format, you can use the *Show document outline* option to have it show each section. Then you can click on that section header to take you to that part of the document.

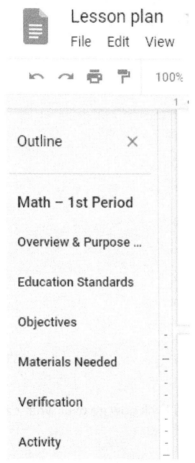
Figure 3.25

- **Show equation toolbar** – If for some rare reason you need to place a mathematical equation into your document, you can use the Equation Toolbar to do so, and selecting *Show equation toolbar* will make it available for use.

- **Full screen** – Choosing the *Full screen* option will hide the controls (toolbars), giving you more space to work. To bring the toolbars back simply press the Esc key on your keyboard.

Insert Menu

There are many items that you can insert into your document, and the Insert menu is where you will go for most of these types of tasks.

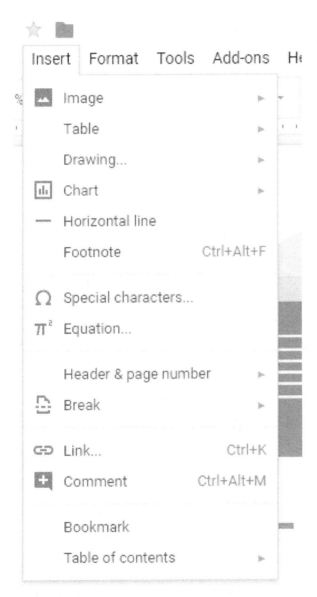

Figure 3.26

Chapter 3 – Google Docs

Now I would like to go over the items in the Insert menu:

- **Image** – Docs allows you to insert images\pictures into your document, and then you can place them where you want and resized them and so on. As you can see in figure 3.27, there are various locations you can insert an image from, such as your computer, Google Drive, a website location, and even your camera if you are working on your phone or tablet, etc.

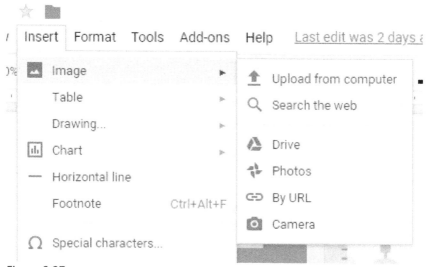

Figure 3.27

- **Table** – There may come a time where you want to make a listing of items in a table format. This is easy to do with Docs, and all you need to do is go to the Table option from the Insert menu, choose the size of the table you want, and then fill it in as desired.

Quantity	Size	Color	Availability
74	Large	Brown	4/19
62	Medium	Yellow	3/19
28	Small	Red	7/19

Figure 3.28

- **Drawing** – The *Drawing* option will bring up a drawing board where you can do things like add shapes, text, and even freehand draw if you like. Once you save your drawing it will be inserted into your document.

86

Chapter 3 – Google Docs

Figure 3.29

- **Chart** – Charts can be inserted into your document as well, and there are a couple of ways to do this. If you want to start from scratch, you can insert a new chart which can be a bar (figure 3.30), column, line, or pie chart. Or you can link to a Sheets spreadsheet (next chapter) and pull the information from there to create your chart.

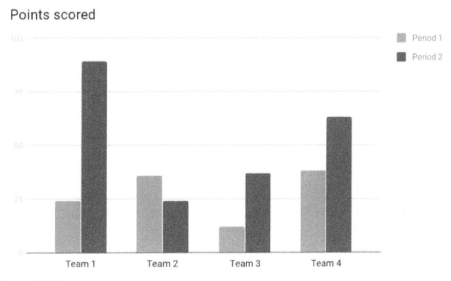

Figure 3.30

If you create a new one from within your document, you will have an option when you click on the chart to open the link to the source of the charts data (figure 3.31). Clicking this will bring you to a Sheets file that will be created for you with some demonstration data that you can edit to fit your needs. After you make your changes in Sheets, simply go back to the chart in Docs and click on the Update button (figure 3.32) to have your data updated in your Docs chart.

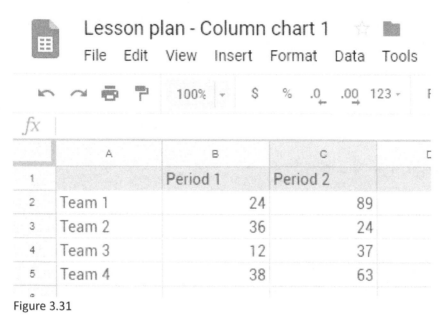

Figure 3.31

Figure 3.32

- **Horizontal line** – This option will simply insert a horizontal line across the page wherever you have the mouse cursor.

- **Footnote** – *Footnotes* are used to add information to the bottom part of the page outside of the margin. As you insert footnotes, they will be numbered, starting with the number 1.

- **Special characters** – Special characters are exactly what they sound like, characters that are different from your standard letters, numbers, and symbols (such as copy write symbols or emoji's and so on). If you look at the top right of figure 3.33, you will see that there are various categories to choose from, and you can even draw your own symbol and have Docs see if there is a match for it.

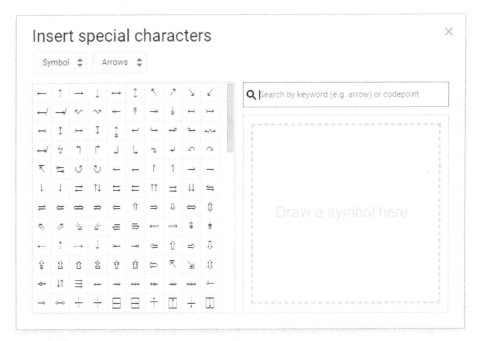

Figure 3.33

- **Equation** – This will bring up the Equation Toolbar like I discussed in the previous section.

- **Header & page number** – Headers and page numbers are commonly used in things like books or other documents that you might want to be numbered or to have a page title or header showing. You can also add footers from this option.

- **Break** – The *Break* option allows you to insert a page break to create a new page after the point where your mouse cursor is positioned. If you have created any columns in your document, you can also insert a column break as well.

- **Link** – With everything being online these days, it's very common to see links to websites within documents. With the *Link* option, all you need to do is enter the website address you want to link to, and then the text that you want displayed in the document. Keep in mind that it's common to have the display text be the same as the link address.

If your document has headings, then you can create a link that will take you back to a particular heading when clicked on.

- **Comment** – I mentioned comments earlier in the chapter, but once again they can be used to add a comment off to the side of the page that relates to a specific part of your document. Then other people that you are sharing the document with will be able to see that comment as well.

- **Bookmark** – *Bookmarks* are used to link within a document to a specific section or page. To create a bookmark, go to the location where you want to place that bookmark, and then choose *Insert > Bookmark* and give it a name (figure 3.34).

Figure 3.34

Next, you will go to the section of your document that you want to link to that bookmark and highlight it. Then go to *Insert > Link* and expand the Bookmarks section to find the bookmark you have created (figure 3.35). Finally, choose the bookmark that you created from the previous step and click *Apply*.

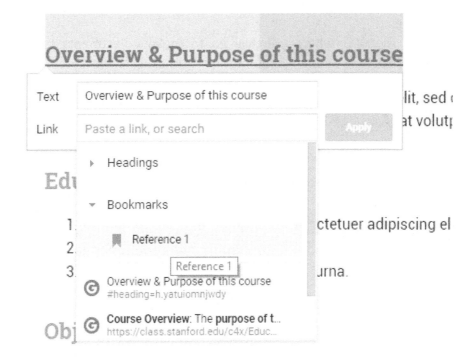

Figure 3.35

- **Table of contents** – If you are writing a book or manual (etc.), you will probably need a table of contents at the beginning if you want your readers to easily be able to find what they are looking for. If you are using headers in your document, then Docs can create a table of contents automatically for you and even add the proper page numbers after each section (I will go over heading text in the next section).

Overview & Purpose of this course	1
Education Standards	1
Objectives	1
Materials Needed	1
Verification	2
Activity	2

Figure 3.36

If you happen to make some changes you your document and the page numbers change, then all you need to do is right click on your table of contents and choose *Update table of contents.*

Chapter 3 – Google Docs

Format Menu

The Format menu is where you will go to make adjustments to how your document looks, such as changing fonts and formatting shapes, etc.

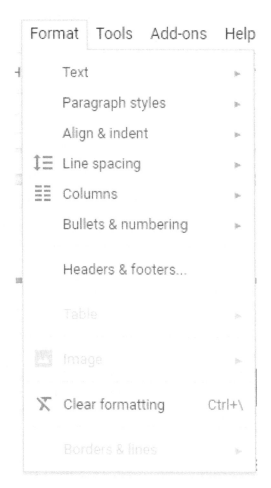

Figure 3.37

Since I will have a section on formatting your document later in this chapter, I will briefly go over the options from this menu.

- **Text** – This menu option allows you to change how your text looks in regards to things like bold, underline, text size, and capitalization.

Chapter 3 – Google Docs

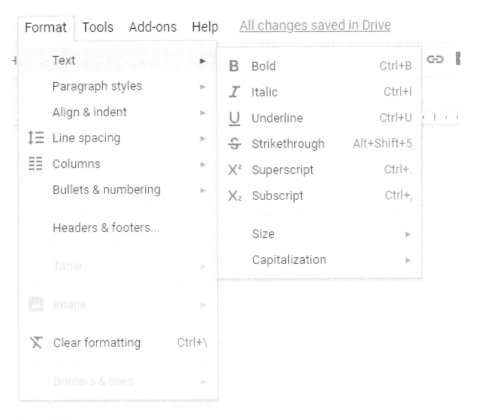

Figure 3.38

- **Paragraph styles** – *Paragraph styles* allow you to format an entire paragraph with various types of styles. For example, you can add a border with various types of line styles and shading. This is also where you can change text from normal text to a heading style text like I mentioned was required to create a table of contents.

- **Align & indent** – Many times you will need to set text alignment of a paragraph or entire document to be aligned to the left or right, centered or justified. Or you might need to indent a paragraph to make it stand out from the rest. If that's the case, then this is where you would do it from.

- **Line spacing** – *Line spacing* is just what it sounds like, the amount of space between the lines of text in your document. The default line spacing is 1.15, and you can also choose other spacing such as single, double, or even customize your own setting.

- **Columns** – Columns can be used to separate your text for things like lists and so on. In earlier versions of Google Docs, you would have to create tables with columns to get this done, but now you can do this from the Format menu if you want another option. You can go into the *More options* section to customize your columns and do things such as add lines between them.

Figure 3.39

- **Bullets & numbering** – Bullets & numbering is used when you have created lists and want the items in the list to be separated with numbers and sub numbers, or a character like a bullet.

    - Category 1
        - Sub category 1
    - Category 2
        - Sub category 2
    - Category 3
        - Sub category 3

    1. Category 1
        a. Sub category 1
    2. Category 2
        a. Sub category 2
    3. Category 3
        a. Sub category 3

Figure 3.40

Once you create a bulleted or numbered list, then you can customize it by going to Format > Bullets & numbering > List options. (You will need to have the list highlighted to use this option.)

- **Headers & footers** – Headers are used to display information like chapter titles at the top of the page, while footers are used to display things like page numbers at the bottom of the page. This option will allow you to specify how many inches the header and footer is from the top and bottom of the page.

- **Table** – In order to use the *Table* option, you will need to have a table in your document, and also have the mouse cursor somewhere within that table. This option lets you do things such as insert and delete rows and columns, as well as merge and unmerge cells. The *Table properties* choice is used to configure things like borders, colors, alignment, and so on (figure 3.41).

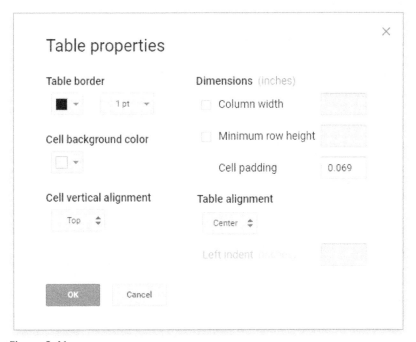

Figure 3.41

- **Image** – When you have images\pictures in your document, you can use the Image settings to do things such as crop the image or replace it with a different one. The *Image options* feature lets you do things like recolor the image and also adjust things like transparency, brightness, and contrast.

- **Clear formatting** – Most documents will have some kind of formatting, whether it be colored or underlined text (etc.), and many times you want to switch that text back to the default unformatted text. To do so, simply highlight the text and choose the *Clear formatting* feature to remove any formatting that was previously applied.

- **Borders & lines** – If you have any items that have a border around them or use a line above or below them, then you can use this option to change things such as the border weight (thickness) and dash type if any.

Tools Menu

The Tools menu is most likely not going to be used as often as some of the other menus, but does have some helpful tools.

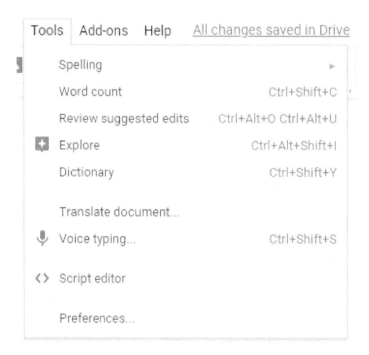

Figure 3.42

Even though you won't be using this menu as much as the others it's still a good idea to know what you can do from the items within it.

- **Spelling** – By default, Docs will underline spelling mistakes in red, but if you want to turn off that feature, then you can do so from here. You can also run a manual spell check if you want Docs to search over your entire document for errors. There is even a Personal dictionary option where you can add words that are not in the Docs dictionary so it won't mark them as misspelled.

- **Word count** – Word count will not only tell you how many words you have in your document, but also how many pages, characters, and characters excluding spaces your document has.

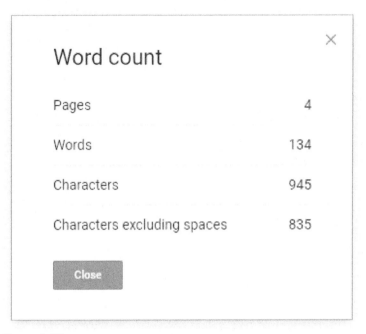

Figure 3.43

- **Review suggested edits** – As I mentioned earlier in the chapter, you can use Suggesting mode to suggest changes to a document that can then be viewed by others and either accepted or rejected. To see the suggested edits in your document, you would use this feature. You can also accept all or reject all from this setting and preview what the document would look like if you either accepted all of the edits, or rejected all of the edits.

- **Explore** – The *Explore* feature is pretty neat because it will go through your document and pick out topics that you can then look up online to get more information on. It will also work for images that it finds. Plus, you can enter in your own search terms if you want to look for something specific.

Chapter 3 – Google Docs

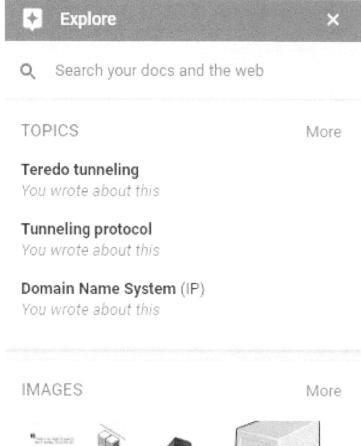

Figure 3.44

- **Dictionary** – The *Dictionary* option is another cool feature that you can use to get definitions of words in your document or others that you want to search for. Simply highlight the word you want to look up in your document and choose the Dictionary option, and it will go out on the Internet and then display its meaning.

Figure 3.45

- **Translate Document** – This is a really neat feature as well because Docs can take your entire document and translate it to a language of your choosing. It will open the translated document in a new tab\page so you will still have access to the original.

- **Voice typing** – *Voice typing* works in a similar fashion to how you would use the voice to text feature on your smartphone. If you have a device that is capable of recording your voice, you can have Docs translate your voice to words in your document. You can even choose a different language if you speak more than one. For PC users, you can use this feature if you have a microphone attached to your computer.

Figure 3.46

- **Script editor** – Unless you are a JavaScript developer and want to write code for Google Apps, you will never use this feature.

- **Preferences** – This is where you can change the way Docs works when it comes to settings such as automatic capitalization, link detection, and substitution of characters. As you can see in figure 3.47, you can have Docs automatically substitute something you type with a properly formatted version, such as replacing the copyright symbol © when you type in (c).

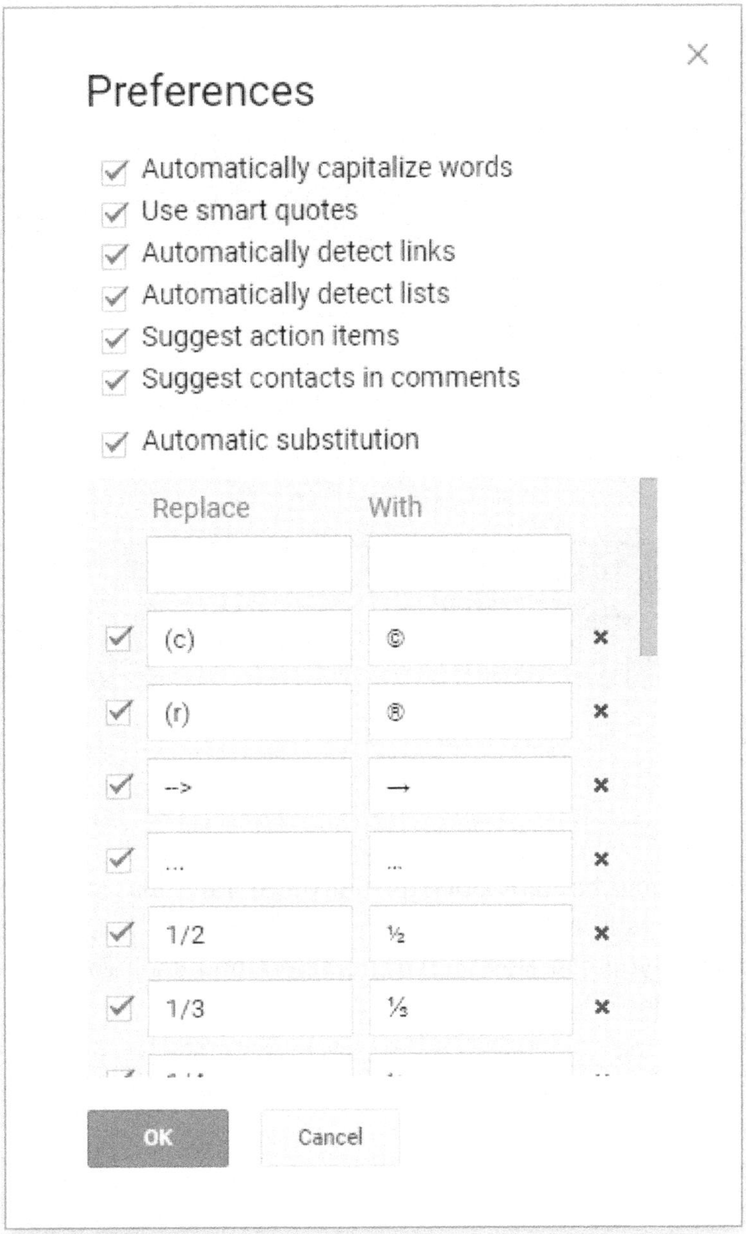

Figure 3.47

Add-ons Menu
Out of the box, Docs will not come with any add-ons, but there are many available that you can download and use with Docs to do things such as create labels, use additional fonts, or have access to clipart libraries. The top left of the Add-ons box (figure 3.48) will have a dropdown where you can select various categories such as business tools, education, productivity, and so on.

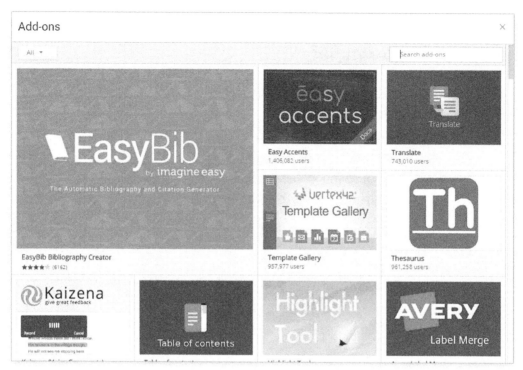

Figure 3.48

Help Menu
This menu option should be fairly obvious, but there are a few other things you can do from here as well. Besides clicking on the Docs Help item to bring up a listing of help topics, you can also search the help menu itself to hopefully find exactly what you are looking for.

Chapter 3 – Google Docs

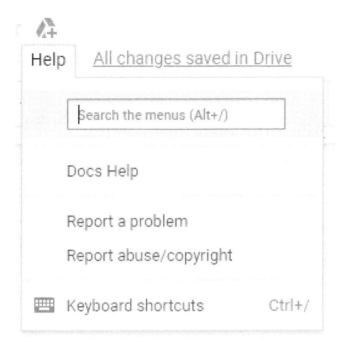

Figure 3.49

The *Report a problem* feature can be used to report any glitches you find in the software to Google so they can fix problems to make Docs work better. (I can't tell you for sure if anyone actually looks at it though!)

The *Report abuse\copyright* feature can be used to report a document to google that has illegal or plagiarized information in it. When you report the document, you can pick what category it falls under, such as spam, hate speech, illegal activity, copyright infringement, and so on.

Finally, the Keyboard shortcuts section will show you the available keyboard shortcuts that you can use within Docs. A keyboard shortcut is when you press a certain key combination that accomplishes the same task as one of the menu items does. For example, you can press Ctrl-b on your keyboard to make text bold rather than having to find it in the Format menu or on the toolbar.

Creating a Document
Now that you know what all the menu items do, it's time to create a new document and see how the process works. If you are used to using another word processing program like Microsoft Word, then you will find the process very familiar.

Chapter 3 – Google Docs

When you first open Docs, it will give you options to create a new blank document, or start with one of the available templates from the Template Gallery. For my example I want to start with a blank document, so all I need to do is click on *Blank* under *Start a new document*.

The first thing you will want to do is give your document a name (unless you don't plan on keeping it, then you can just leave the default Untitled document name as is). To change the name, simply click on Untitled document, and it will become highlighted. Then you can then change it to whatever you like. I will change mine to *Notes*.

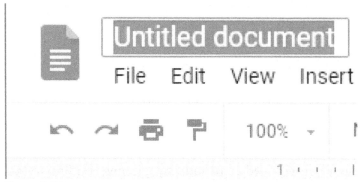
Figure 3.50

Now you can click within the blank page to get a cursor to start typing your text. Docs will automatically place the new text you type at the upper topmost section of the page, so if you want to start a few lines down, you can press the Enter key on your keyboard as many times as you need. (I am assuming you know how to type in text in a document, otherwise you might need to get some practice before even using Docs.) I am actually going to use the text from this chapter for my examples, so if it looks familiar, you will know why!

Chapter 3 – Google Docs

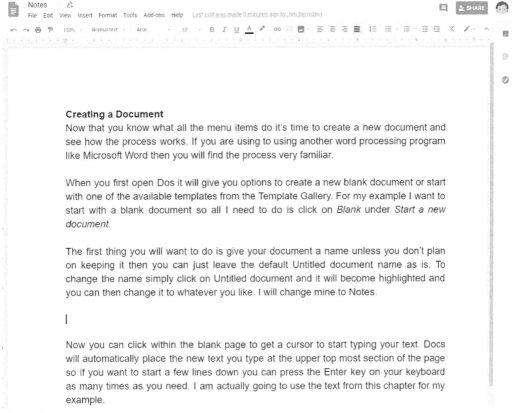

Figure 3.51

Now that I have some text in my document, I want to add an image between the third and last paragraph. To do so, I will put my cursor in between the paragraphs (as you can see in figure 3.51).

There are several ways to accomplish this task. I can copy and paste the image from this document over to my Notes document, but for this example I will insert an image from my local computer by browsing to its location from the Insert > Image menu (figure 3.52).

Chapter 3 – Google Docs

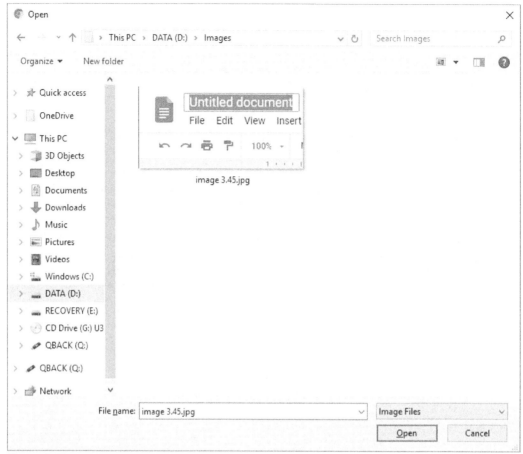

Figure 3.52

If I had the image on my Google Drive, I could have chosen that option and then browsed to it on my drive and inserted into my document from there.

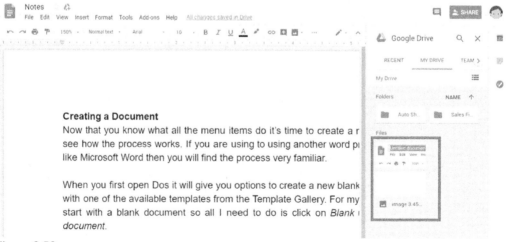

Figure 3.53

Regardless of my method, now I have my image within my document exactly where I wanted it.

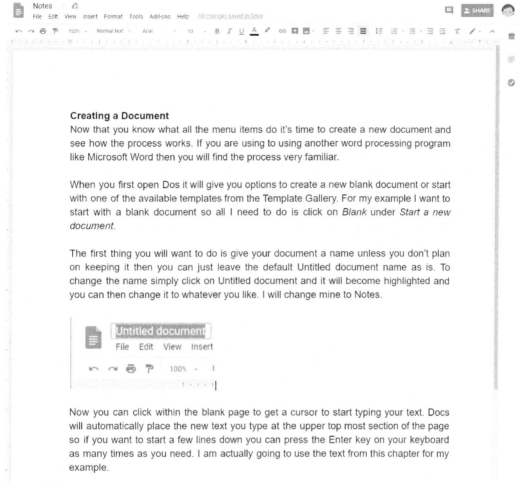

Figure 3.54

When you click on the image within your document, you will see that you have a couple of options as to how to position it (as shown in figure 3.55).

Chapter 3 – Google Docs

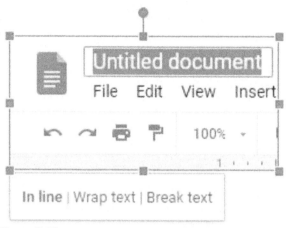

Figure 3.55

In line will be the default, which simply separates the text to be above and below the image like shown in figure 3.54. *Wrap text* will wrap the text around the image as shown in figure 3.56.

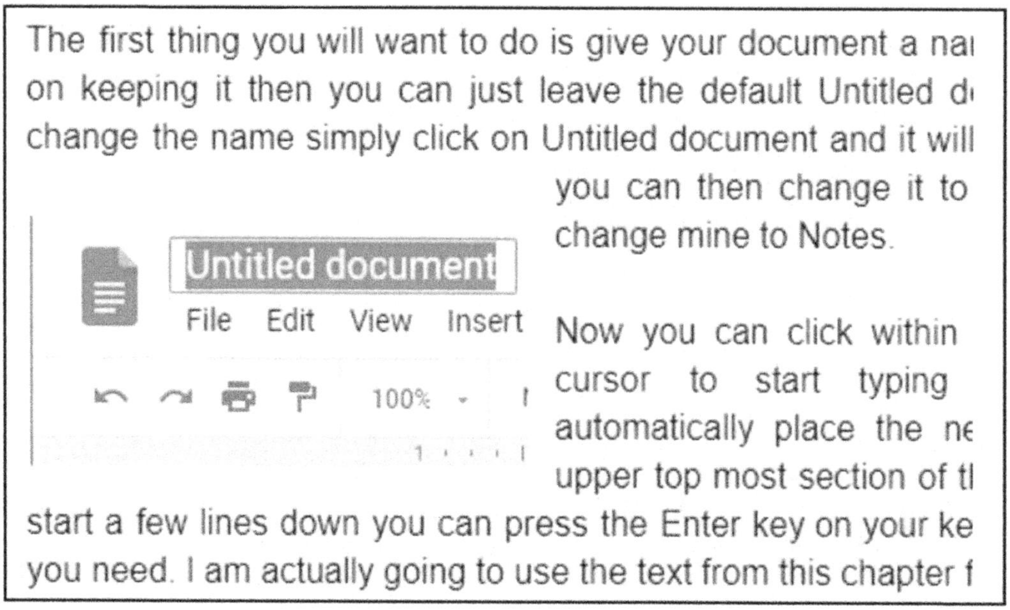

Figure 3.56

Break text is similar to the In line option, except you can decide how far you want the text to be away from the top and bottom of your image (such as ½ inch, ¼ inch, and so on).

To resize the image in your document, simply click on one of the small boxes in the corner of the image when it's highlighted (as shown in figure 3.55 above).

When using a corner box, it will stretch the image and keep its proportions the same and just make it larger. If you use one of the top or side boxes to resize your image, it will get stretched out like in figure 3.57.

Figure 3.57

If you would like to copy the image and use it again in the same document or in a different document, all you need to is right click on it, choose *Copy,* and then right click where you want the copied image to go and choose *Paste*.

The same copy and paste procedure works for copying text from one area to another, or to another document, but you have a couple of different choices as to how you want to paste your text. You can either choose *Paste,* which will paste the text using the same formatting as the current text, or you can choose *Paste without formatting,* which will remove all the formatting such as bold and colors when pasting the text into your document.

Right Click Options
Speaking of right clicking on text and images, I would now like to take a moment to go over some of the right click menu items. Figure 3.58 shows the options when right clicking on some highlighted text.

Chapter 3 – Google Docs

```
Now you can click within the blank page to get a
    Cut                                      Ctrl+X      at the
    Copy                                     Ctrl+C      an pr
    Paste                                    Ctrl+V      ing to
    Paste without formatting            Ctrl+Shift+V
    Delete

    Explore 'Now you can click w...'    Ctrl+Alt+Shift+I
    Define 'Now you can click w...'     Ctrl+Shift+Y

    Comment                              Ctrl+Alt+M
    Suggest edits

    Save to Keep

    Link...                                  Ctrl+K

    Select all matching text
    Update 'Normal text' to match
    Clear formatting                         Ctrl+\
```

Figure 3.58

The first group of options are either obvious, or items that I have already gone over, and the *Explore* and *Define* items have been gone over already in this chapter, but basically they will either do web, image, and drive searches for that text if you choose Explore, and looked up in a dictionary if you use Define. When using *Define*, try to stick to just one word or a term to get the best results.

Here is what the other options do. There may be a little repetition from earlier in the chapter, but that never hurts! Plus, some of this information falls into the *formatting a document* section that is coming up next.

- **Comment** – This will let you make a comment about that text that will be visible to the other collaborators on the document.

- **Suggest Edits** – This will put the document into Suggesting Mode, where you can then add suggested changes to the text you have highlighted.

Chapter 3 – Google Docs

- **Save to Keep** – Google Keep is a note taking app that I will be discussing in Chapter 7, but using this option allows you to send the highlighted text to your Keep notebook. Keep can be accessed from within Docs, allowing you to see all of your notes.

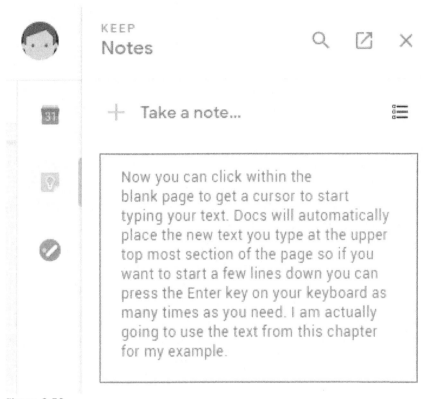

Figure 3.59

- **Link** – You can make a word or many words in your document into a link that can be clicked on to take you to a place such as a website by using the *Link* option. Once you choose *Link*, you will be prompted to enter the link address, and can also change the link text if you desire.

Now you can click within the blank page to get a cursor to start typing your text. Docs will automatically place the new text you type at the upper top most section of the page so if you want to start a few lines down you can press the Enter key on your keyboard as many times as you need. I am actually going to use the text from this chapter for my example.
Text
Now you can click within the blank page to
Link
www.onlinecomputertips.com
Apply
Online Computer Tips: Home
https://www.onlinecomputertips.com/
Hardware - Online Computer Tips
https://www.onlinecomputertips.com...
Find more

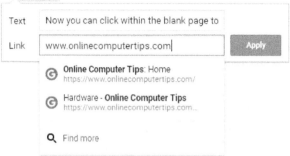

Figure 3.60

Once you make the link, the text will appear as a link with underlined text, and clicking on the text will take you to the address that you entered in the Link box when creating the link. Normally you wouldn't make a link out of an entire paragraph, but I just did so for my example.

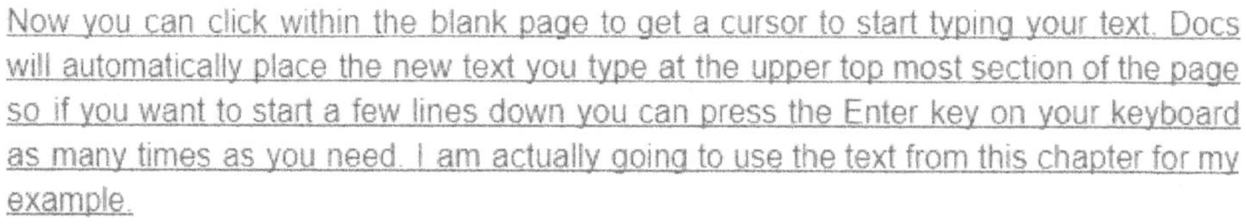

Now you can click within the blank page to get a cursor to start typing your text. Docs will automatically place the new text you type at the upper top most section of the page so if you want to start a few lines down you can press the Enter key on your keyboard as many times as you need. I am actually going to use the text from this chapter for my example.

Figure 3.61

- **Select all matching text** – This is an interesting feature because it will allow you to highlight some text that is formatted a specific way and then find all of the other text that matches that same formatting. In figure 3.62, you can see the word **blank** was highlighted, and when the *Select all matching text* option was chosen, Docs highlighted all of the other text that was bolded like the word **blank** was.

Creating a Document

Now that you know what all the menu items do it's time to create a new document and see how the process works. If you are using to using another word processing program like **Microsoft Word** then you will find the process very familiar.

When you first open Docs it will give you options to create a new blank document or start with one of the available templates from the **Template Gallery**. For my example I want to start with a blank document so all I need to do is click on Blank under Start a new document.

The first thing you will want to do is give your document a name unless you don't plan on keeping it then you can just leave the default Untitled document name as is. To change the name simply click on Untitled document and it will become highlighted and

you can then change it to whatever you like. I will change mine to Notes.

Now you can click within the **blank** page to get a cursor to start typing your text. Docs will automatically place the new text you type at the upper top most section of the page so if you want to start a few lines down you can press the Enter key on your keyboard as many times as you need. I am actually going to use the text from this chapter for my example.

Figure 3.62

- **Update normal text to match** – This can be used to have Docs update the format of all of the text in your document to match the highlighted text. For example, let's say you highlighted a word that was bold and the color red, and chose *Update normal text to match*. Docs would then update the rest of your text in your document to be bold and red as well.

- **Clear formatting** – If you have formatted text that you want to reset to unformatted text, then you can use the *Clear formatting* option.

Chapter 3 – Google Docs

Next, I would like to discuss what you can do when right clicking on an *image* rather than text.

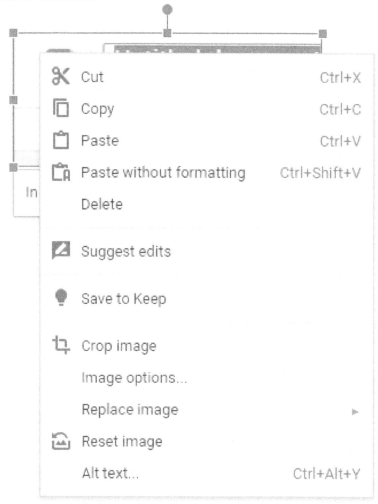

Figure 3.63

Many of the options are the same as they are for text, so I will only go over the ones that are specific to images.

- **Crop image** – Crop image allows you to crop the image to cut out certain parts of that image. Let's say I had a picture of my dog in the snow like shown in figure 3.64, and wanted to crop it so it showed just my dog.

Dog in the snow during January.
Figure 3.64

What I would do is right click on the picture and choose *Crop*. Then you will see some black "handles" on all sides of the image that you can use to drag in to crop the actual image.

Dog in the snow during January.
Figure 3.65

When you get it the way you want, just press Enter on your keyboard and you will have your cropped image (as shown in figure 3.67).

Dog in the snow during January.
Figure 3.66

Dog in the snow during January.

Figure 3.67

Then you can click on the cropped image and resize it so it looks exactly the way you want.

 If you are concerned with image quality for printing purposes, keep in mind that when you increase the image size by dragging it to make it larger, generally the image quality will decrease.

Dog in the snow during January.

Figure 3.68

- **Image options** – Docs allows you to touch up your pictures from within the document itself if you think they need a little adjustment. You can choose from some built-in color profiles from the *Recolor* section, or add a little transparency to your image as well. There are also settings to adjust the brightness and contrast of your image.

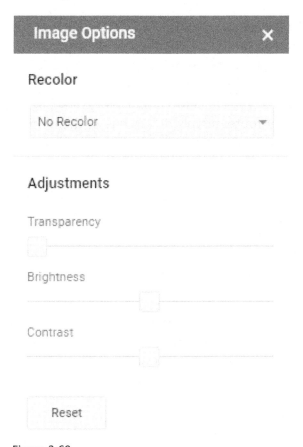

Figure 3.69

- **Replace image** – This option allows you to swap out your image with another one from your computer, Google Drive, camera, and so on.

- **Reset image** – You will only see the Reset image option if you have made changes to that image that can be reset (such as cropping it). When you use this option, the image will be returned to its former state.

- **Alt text** – Alt text is used by screen readers who might have trouble seeing your image so they can get an idea of what it is. You can put in a short title and description here.

Inserting Headers, Footers, and Page Numbers
I mentioned headers, footers, and page numbers earlier in this chapter, but wanted to take a minute to go over how to use them in Docs. All of these can be put into your document from the *Insert* menu within Docs.

If you choose *Headers*, it will allow you to enter header information at the top of the page, while *Footers* will do the same thing at the bottom of the page. Once you type in your text for your header or footer, you can click on *Options* to determine how far you want the header or footer to be from the top. Then this text will be added to every page of your document and every new page you add after that. To remove a header or footer simply delete one of them on any page and it will delete the rest on all of the other pages.

Figure 3.70

Page numbers work the same way, and you have a few choices as to where the numbers are placed on the page and if you want the first page to not be numbered at all. As you add pages, they will be automatically numbered for you.

Figure 3.71

Chapter 3 – Google Docs

Importing Charts From Sheets

Sheets is Google's version of Microsoft's Excel spreadsheet program. If you have any charts that you have created in Sheets, then you can import them into your document as well as link them so when changes are made, your document will be updated as well.

To insert a Sheets chart go to the *Insert* menu, choose *Chart,* and then *From Sheets*. You will be prompted to choose one of your existing Sheets files to import into Docs.

Figure 3.72

Once you choose one don't forget to decide if you want the data in your document to be updated whenever your spreadsheet is updated. If so, then leave the box for *Link to spreadsheet* checked, and if not, uncheck it.

Figure 3.73

Formatting a Document
Now that we have some text and images in our document it's time to format it to make it look a little more presentable and professional. There are many upon many ways to format your document to suit your tastes, but for this section I will be going over the most common formatting procedures that you will most likely be using.

Editing Text
Let's begin by adding a title to the document and have that title text use the Title style for the document. I decided to call my document *My Exciting Document*. After I type in the title, I will highlight it (as shown in figure 3.74).

Figure 3.74

Then from either the *Format > Paragraph* styles menu item or the Styles toolbar option, I will choose *Title* as the style and have Docs apply the style to my highlighted text.

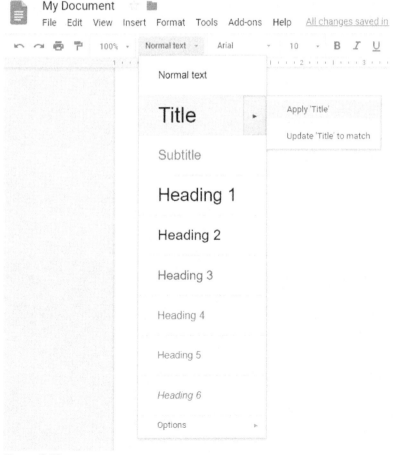

Figure 3.75

Now you can see my title is in *Title* style format, and now can also be used if I want to make a table of contents.

> # My Exciting Document
>
> Now that you know what all the menu items do it's time to create a new document and see how the process works. If you are using to using another word processing program like Microsoft Word then you will find the process very familiar.
>
> When you first open Docs it will give you options to create a new blank document or start with one of the available templates from the Template Gallery. For my example I want to start with a blank document so all I need to do is click on *Blank* under *Start a new document*.

Figure 3.76

I will now make some section headings called Section 1 and Section 2 and apply the Heading 2 style to the text, which can also apply to the table of contents if I add one later.

My Exciting Document

Now that you know what all the menu items do it's time to create a new document and see how the process works. If you are using to using another word processing program like Microsoft Word then you will find the process very familiar.

Section 1

When you first open Docs it will give you options to create a new blank document or start with one of the available templates from the Template Gallery. For my example I want to start with a blank document so all I need to do is click on *Blank* under *Start a new document*.

The first thing you will want to do is give your document a name unless you don't plan on keeping it then you can just leave the default Untitled document name as is. To change the name simply click on Untitled document and it will become highlighted and you can then change it to whatever you like. I will change mine to Notes.

Section 2

Now you can click within the blank page to get a cursor to start typing your text. Docs will automatically place the new text you type at the upper top most section of the page so if you want to start a few lines down you can press the Enter key on your keyboard as many times as you need. I am assuming know how to type in text in a document otherwise you might need to get some practice before even using Docs. I am actually going to use the text from this chapter for my examples so if it looks familiar you will know why!

Figure 3.77

Now I will apply some basic text formatting to the title and section names to make them stand out a little better. I will first make the title bold and underlined so it stands out. To do so, I will simply highlight the text from the title and then click on the B in the toolbar (for bold) and then click the U in the toolbar (for underlined) and I will be all set. I can also go to the *Format > Text* menu and do the same thing from there.

Then I will make the section headings red by highlighting the Section 1 and Section 2 text, click on the underlined A in the toolbar (for text color), and choose red from the color choices. You can see the results from these changes in figure 3.78.

Figure 3.78

Next (for some reason) I want to have the first paragraph have all the words capitalized, but don't want to retype the whole thing. Once again, I will highlight the text I want to change, then go to the Format menu and then *Text > Capitalization > UPPERCASE.* (You might have noticed by now that I am using the Format menu a lot on this section on formatting!)

Chapter 3 – Google Docs

My Exciting Document

NOW THAT YOU KNOW WHAT ALL THE MENU ITEMS DO IT'S TIME TO CREATE A NEW DOCUMENT AND SEE HOW THE PROCESS WORKS. IF YOU ARE USING TO USING ANOTHER WORD PROCESSING PROGRAM LIKE MICROSOFT WORD THEN YOU WILL FIND THE PROCESS VERY FAMILIAR.

Section 1

When you first open Docs it will give you options to create a new blank document or start with one of the available templates from the Template Gallery. For my example I want to start with a blank document so all I need to do is click on *Blank* under *Start a new document*.

Figure 3.79

Text Alignment
Next, I want to center the title in the document and change the text alignment to left aligned rather than justified like it is currently. To do so, I will once again highlight the title text, and then either go to the align section on the toolbar or go to *Align & indent* on the Format menu, and choose the align center option (figure 3.80).

Figure 3.80

Now to change the alignment of the main document from justified to aligned left, I will highlight the text I want to change and do the same process, but this time I will choose *align left* rather than *centered*. When doing this you might have to do it in sections if there is other text you don't want changed in between the text you do want to change. You can see the results in figure 3.81. I will say I prefer justified over aligning the text to the left, and you might have noticed that's the format I used for this book!

My Exciting Document

NOW THAT YOU KNOW WHAT ALL THE MENU ITEMS DO IT'S TIME TO CREATE A NEW DOCUMENT AND SEE HOW THE PROCESS WORKS. IF YOU ARE USING TO USING ANOTHER WORD PROCESSING PROGRAM LIKE MICROSOFT WORD THEN YOU WILL FIND THE PROCESS VERY FAMILIAR.

Section 1

When you first open Docs it will give you options to create a new blank document or start with one of the available templates from the Template Gallery. For my example I want to start with a blank document so all I need to do is click on *Blank* under *Start a new document*.

The first thing you will want to do is give your document a name unless you don't plan on keeping it then you can just leave the default Untitled document name as is. To change the name simply click on Untitled document and it will become highlighted and you can then change it to whatever you like. I will change mine to Notes.

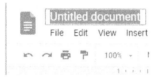

Section 2

Now you can click within the blank page to get a cursor to start typing your text. Docs will automatically place the new text you type at the upper top most section of the page so if you want to start a few lines down you can press the Enter key on your keyboard as many times as you need. I am assuming know how to type in text in a document otherwise you might need to get some practice before even using Docs. I am actually going to use the text from this chapter for my examples so if it looks familiar you will know why!

Figure 3.81

Word Art

If you are also a Microsoft Word user, then you might have used the Word Art feature to insert text with effects such as outlines or shadows. Docs has the same feature, and actually calls it Word Art as well, but the process varies a little from how it's done in Word.

Chapter 3 – Google Docs

In Docs you will need to insert your Word Art as a drawing, which means going to the Insert menu, selecting Drawing, and then New+. From the Actions menu choose Word art and type in your text. Then you can format the text the way you like in regards to colors and borders. The text is not as customizable as it is in Word, but it's good enough to get the job done. Once you are happy with your Word Art, click on Save & Close and it will be inserted into your document. (Just be sure to place the cursor where you want the text to be inserted before creating it so you don't have to move it afterward.)

Figure 3.82

Now that I have some text in my document I want to add an image between the third and last paragraph. To do so I will put my cursor in between the paragraphs as you can see in figure 3.46.

There are several ways to accomplish this task. I can copy and paste the image from this document over to my Notes document but for this example I will insert an image from my local computer by browsing to its location from the Insert > Image menu.

Figure 3.83

Line Spacing

Docs uses a default line spacing of 1.15, which is a little wider than single space and is fine for most people. But sometimes you might want to change that to increase or decrease the amount of space between each line of text. Figure 3.84 shows the difference between single and double spacing.

Single Spacing

Now you can click within the blank page to get a cursor to start typing your text. Docs will automatically place the new text you type at the upper top most section of the page so if you want to start a few lines down you can press the Enter key on your keyboard as many times as you need. I am assuming know how to type in text in a document otherwise you might need to get some practice before even using Docs.

Double Spacing

Now you can click within the blank page to get a cursor to start typing your text. Docs

will automatically place the new text you type at the upper top most section of the page

so if you want to start a few lines down you can press the Enter key on your keyboard

as many times as you need. I am assuming know how to type in text in a document

otherwise you might need to get some practice before even using Docs.

Figure 3.84

If neither single or double spacing works for you, then you can choose a custom spacing of your own to fine tune how your text looks. To set the spacing, highlight the text you want to change, go to the Format menu, then to Line spacing, and configure it the way you want.

There is also an option to add a space before or after the paragraph if you just need more or less space in between paragraphs rather than all of the lines of text. You can customize the paragraph space as well if the default doesn't work for you.

Numbered and Bulleted Lists
I went over numbered and bulleted lists when discussing the format menu, but want to spend a little time going into them in a little more detail since there are different ways to use this type of formatting in your document.

When creating a list in Docs, you can use this feature to have them be automatically numbered or marked with bullets or other characters so you don't have to do it manually. Your lists will also be easier to read and they'll look more organized.

For example, take a look at the *Sales Teams* list in figure 3.85. It gets the job done, but looks rather boring and not too organized. Now take a look at figure 3.86 where I added a little formatting to the text and made a bulleted list out of the teams. It's much easier to see the three teams and their members, and is easier on the eyes as well.

Sales Teams

Team 1
Sue
Dan
Johnny
Molly

Team 2
Ronald
Tisha
Kim
Beth

Team 3
Sal
Murr
Joe
Brian

Figure 3.85

Sales Teams

- **Team 1**
  - Sue
  - Dan
  - Johnny
  - Molly

- **Team 2**
  - Ronald
  - Tisha
  - Kim
  - Beth

- **Team 3**
  - Sal
  - Murr
  - Joe
  - Brian

Figure 3.86

If I don't like the style I used, I can simply highlight my list and go back to *Format > Bullets & numbering,* choose a new style, and it will be updated automatically.

Sales Teams

- Team 1
  - Sue
  - Dan
  - Johnny
  - Molly

- Team 2
  - Ronald
  - Tisha
  - Kim
  - Beth

- Team 3
  - Sal
  - Murr
  - Joe
  - Brian

Figure 3.87

Now let's say I want a numbered list rather than a bulleted list. All I need to do is highlight the list again and go back to *Format > Bullets & numbering*, choose one of the numbered lists, and once again it will be updated automatically.

Sales Teams

1. **Team 1**
    a. Sue
    b. Dan
    c. Johnny
    d. Molly

2. **Team 2**
    a. Ronald
    b. Tisha
    c. Kim
    d. Beth

3. **Team 3**
    a. Sal
    b. Murr
    c. Joe
    d. Brian

Figure 3.88

Page Setup
Page setup is where you can change things such as margins and paper size, and for many people, the default settings will work just fine. But if you plan on printing your document, you should check these settings before doing so in case you need to make changes so everything looks correct when printed.

The default Docs settings are 1 inch margins, portrait layout (tall), 8.5 x 11 inch paper size, and a white background.

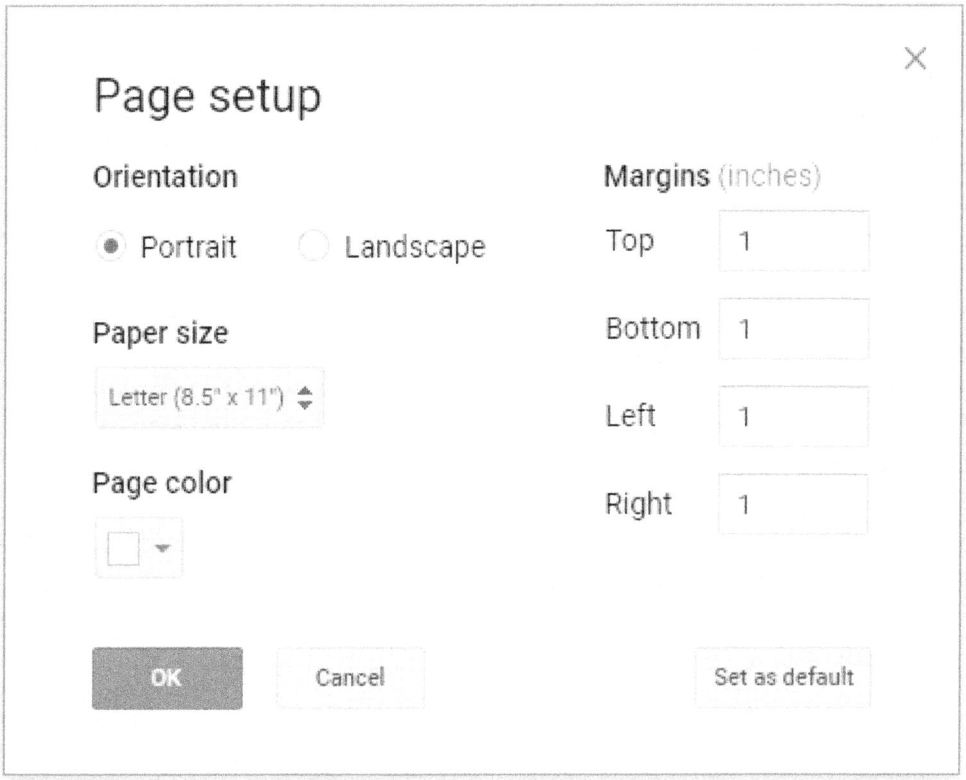

Figure 3.89

Most people print their documents on 8.5 x 11 paper, which is also known as letter size, but this can be changed if needed. Unfortunately, there is no custom size option in Docs like there is in Microsoft Word. You *can* enter a custom setting when printing your document though (discussed next).

If you change the margins to make them smaller, be sure that your printer can print that close to the edge of the paper without cutting off some text. It's always a good idea to print just one page to see how it looks before wasting paper and ink printing the entire document just to print it all over again.

I don't recommend changing the page color to anything else but white unless you like using a lot of ink, and after all is said and done it might not look as good on paper as it does on the screen after you print it.

If you change the settings of your document and want to use those exact same settings for future documents, then you can click the button that says *Set as default* to have it apply to new documents as you create them.

Keep in mind that over formatting a document can sometimes be worse than under formatting it. If you use too many fonts, colors, text sizes, and so on, your document can lose its consistency and look too "busy".

Printing and Publishing a Document

Now that you have your document completed and formatted the way you like, it's time to print it out on some paper, or maybe even publish it online so others can view your work for themselves.

To print your document, go to the *File* menu and then to *Print,* and you will be shown a preview of how your document will print, and also have some choices to make before actually printing your document. As you can see in figure 3.90, my document will require six sheets of paper, meaning it's six pages long.

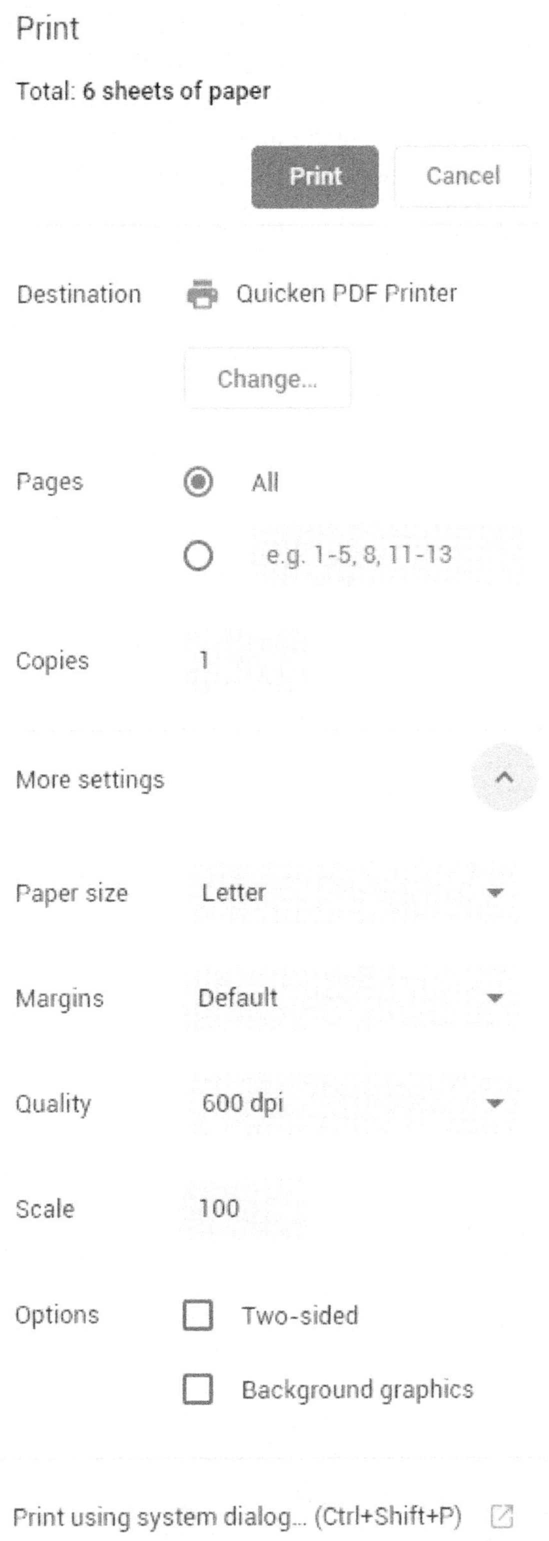

Chapter 3 – Google Docs

Print

Total: **6 sheets of paper**

[Print] [Cancel]

Destination   🖶 Quicken PDF Printer

[Change...]

Pages   ● All
           ○ e.g. 1-5, 8, 11-13

Copies   1

More settings ⌃

Paper size   Letter ▼

Margins   Default ▼

Quality   600 dpi ▼

Scale   100

Options   ☐ Two-sided
              ☐ Background graphics

Print using system dialog... (Ctrl+Shift+P) ↗

Figure 3.90

Chapter 3 – Google Docs

The *Destination* shows what printer the document will be sent to for printing, so if you need to change that to another printer or even a PDF printer, you can click on the *Change* button. As you can see in figure 3.91, I have many other options to choose from for printing. Also notice that it is showing destinations for the tsimms account, and if you have other Google accounts, you can choose one of them for things such as sending to a different Google Drive.

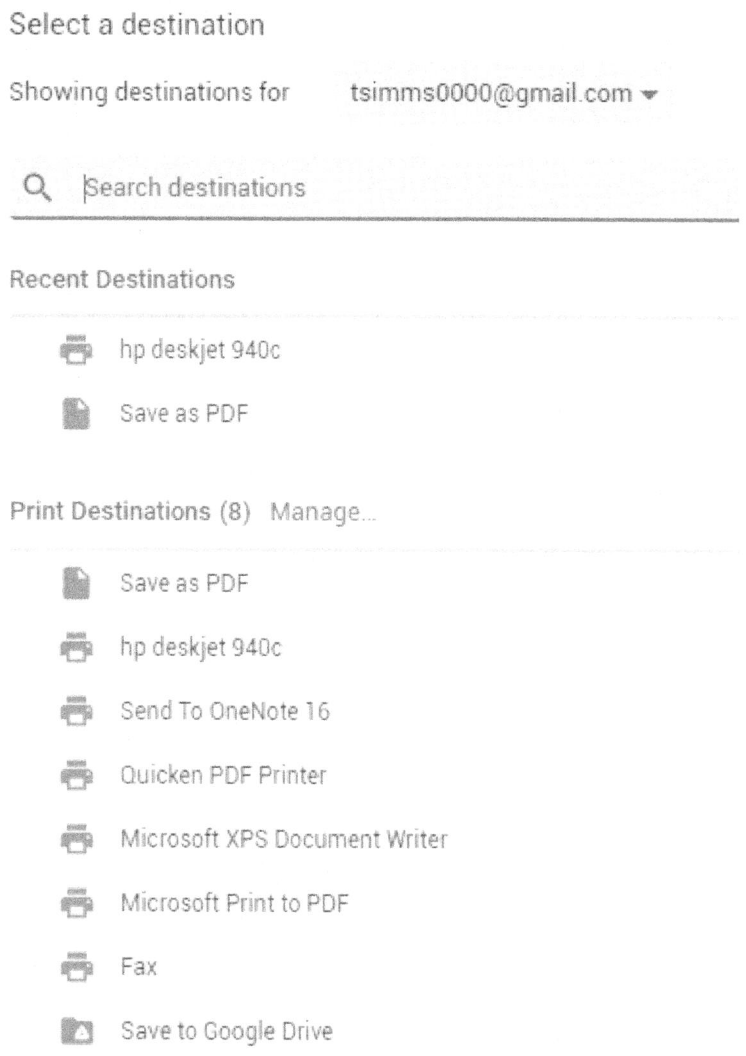

Select a destination

Showing destinations for   tsimms0000@gmail.com ▼

Q Search destinations

Recent Destinations

- hp deskjet 940c
- Save as PDF

Print Destinations (8)   Manage...

- Save as PDF
- hp deskjet 940c
- Send To OneNote 16
- Quicken PDF Printer
- Microsoft XPS Document Writer
- Microsoft Print to PDF
- Fax
- Save to Google Drive

Figure 3.91

By default, Docs will want to print the entire document, but you can change that by clicking the radio button under *Pages* to the second one and adding the pages you want to print. So, if you wanted to only print pages 1 through 3, you would enter *1-3* in the box. If you wanted to print pages 1,3, and 5, you would enter *1,3,5* in the box.

If you need multiple copies printed then change the *Copies* section from the default of 1 to however many copies you need. Just be sure things are the way you want before printing a bunch of copies so you don't have to do it again!

Under *More settings,* which can be accessed by clicking the down arrow next to it, there will be some additional formatting options that you can apply to your document before printing it. Here you can change the *paper size* to one of the included sizes, as well as enter in a custom page size of your own. You can also change the *margins* if they need to be adjusted to make things look correct on the page when printed. The default dpi (dots per inch) next to *Quality* is 600, which should be plenty for most print jobs (unless you are printing super high resolution pictures and your printer can actually *do* so). If things are a little too big for the paper you are printing on, you can *scale* them down from the default 100%, or even make them larger if needed. (Keep in mind that increasing the size might affect the quality of how images print out.) If your printer supports printing on both sides of the paper, you can choose the *Two-sided* option to save paper. Finally, if you have graphics\images in the background of your document, you can have those printed as well by checking the box next to *Background graphics*.

At the bottom of the print dialog window is a setting for *Print using system* dialog. If you click on this, Docs will open the print management interface that your operating system uses to print rather than use the web based one from Google Docs. If you take a look at figure 3.92, you can see that when I click on Print using system dialog, it brings up the Windows print interface (since I am using Microsoft Windows for my operating system). Using this method will give you more choices for fine tuning printer settings before printing.

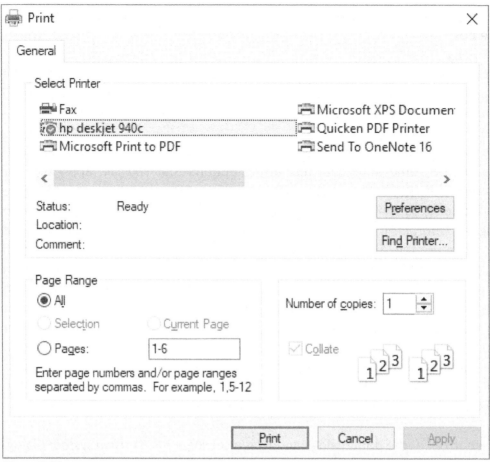

Figure 3.92

Publishing a Document

I mentioned publishing a document earlier in this chapter, but wanted to go through the process in a little more detail in case this is something you wish to do with your document.

To publish your document to the Internet you will go to the *File* menu and then choose *Publish to the web*.

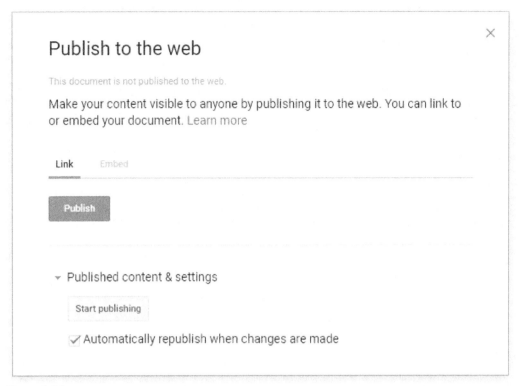

Figure 3.93

Then you will need to decide if you are going to make a link or get some HTML code to embed on your website.

- **Link** – Using this option will publish your document to the Internet, where others with the link will be able to view it. They will not be able to edit it or do anything else with it except print it. Once you click on *Publish* (as seen in figure 3.93) it will publish your document and give you a link (as shown in figure 3.94).

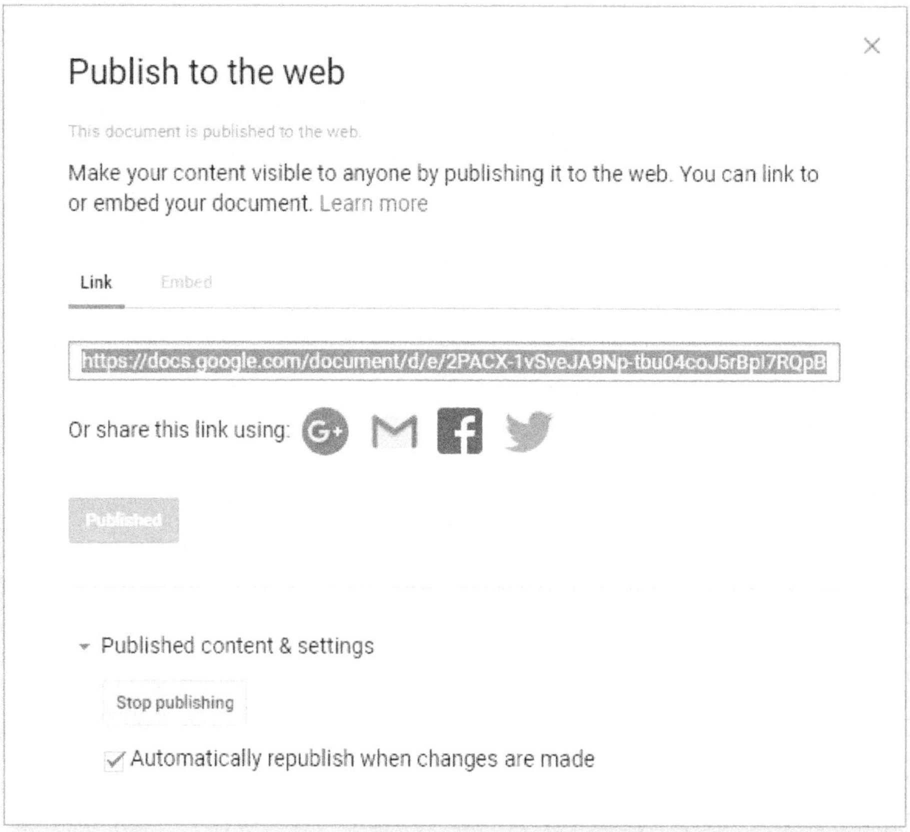

Figure 3.94

Then you can share that link via services such as Google+, Gmail, Facebook, and Twitter, or copy the link and email it to someone else so they can view your document. Figure 3.95 shows what my document looks like formatted as a web page when I paste the address into my web browser.

Chapter 3 – Google Docs

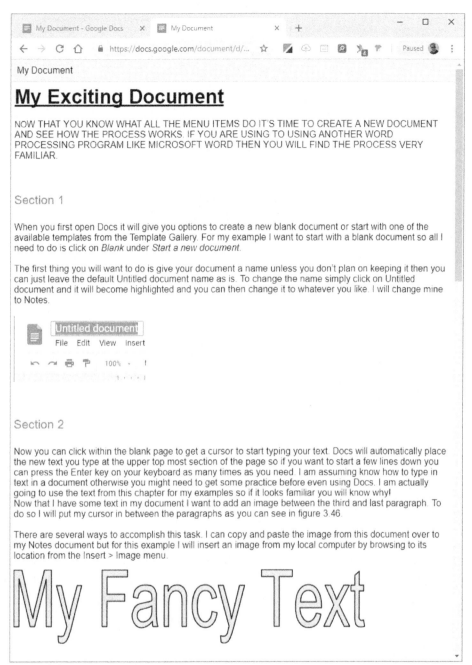

Figure 3.95

- **Embed** – Choosing this option will get you HTML code that you can use to embed your document into an existing webpage. By "embed" I mean place the actual document within the webpage so it looks like it's part of that page. A common example of embedding code is when someone places someone else's YouTube video on their website. This is done by embedding the code linked to that video.

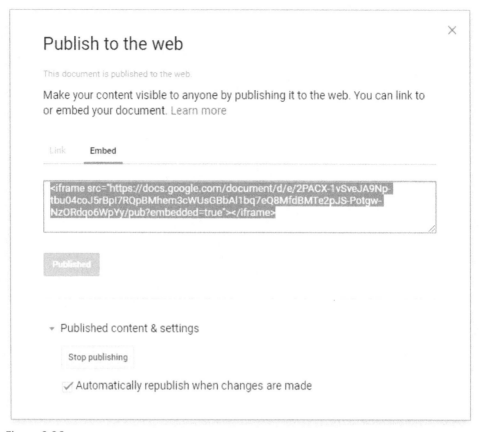

Figure 3.96

Once you click on *Start publishing,* you will be presented with the HTML code required to embed your document onto your website.

If you don't want your document published anymore, all you need to do is click on the *Stop publishing* button. If you want your published document to be updated online whenever you update the document itself, then you can check the box that says *Automatically republish when changes are made* (which should be checked by default).

Sharing a Document
Sharing a document is similar to publishing a document with the main difference being that it's actually opened with Google Docs, and you can give other people the right to edit your document. The sharing process works the same for other Google apps like Sheets and Slides, so I will only be going over the process in this chapter.

You can share your document by clicking the *Share* button next to your profile picture on the top right of the screen. Figure 3.97 shows the Share settings window after you click on *Advanced,* which gives you additional sharing options.

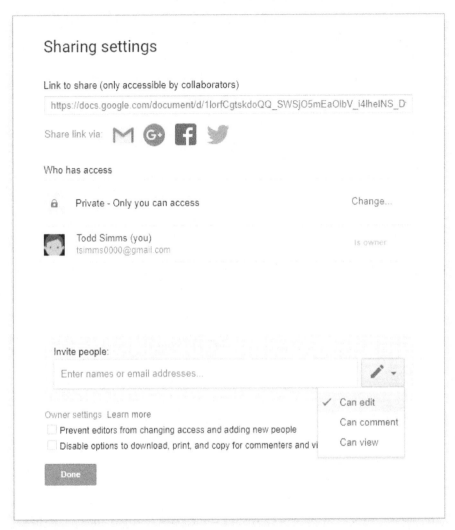

Figure 3.97

By default, your document is set to private so only you can access it, but it's easy to give others permission to view and even edit your document by clicking on *Change.*

There are three options you can set for link sharing:

- **On (public on the web)** – This will make your document public on the Internet and allow anyone to find it by searching for items contained in it.

If you choose this option you can set the permissions to be view only, comment, or edit.

- **On (anyone with the link)** – This option publishes your document on the web, but the only people who will be able to view it are ones who have the actual link that you create when sharing the document. You can still choose the view only, comment, or edit settings for your document.

- **Off (specific people)** – The Off option disables sharing of your document, but you can still publish it to the web for yourself if desired.

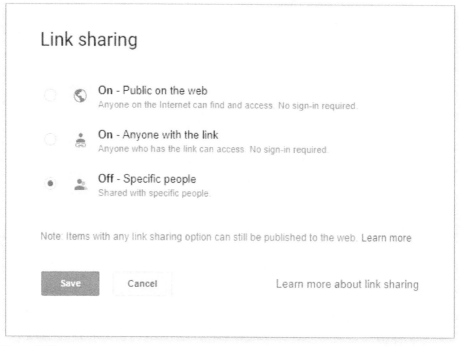

Figure 3.98

If you had your document shared with others, they would show up in the list of who has access, so now I am going to invite someone to access my document by putting their email address in the *Invite people* box (figure 3.97), and then give them the edit permission.

When you invite a person who doesn't have a Google account you will need to make a choice between *Send an invitation* or *Send the link* (as shown in figure 3.99). If the person you are sending the invitation to will need to edit the document, then they will need to sign in with a Google account. If they just need to view the document, then they can do so by clicking on the link they receive in the email that will be sent to them.

Chapter 3 – Google Docs

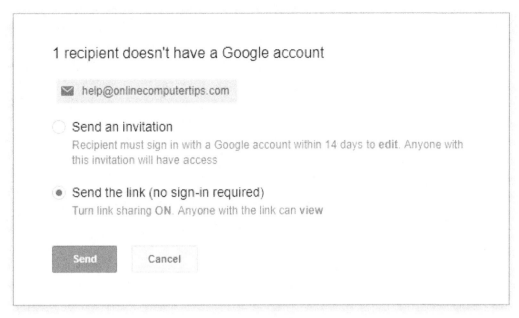

Figure 3.99

Figure 3.100 shows what the email they receive will look like. It has the document name and a button that they can click to open the document in Google Docs.

Chapter 3 – Google Docs

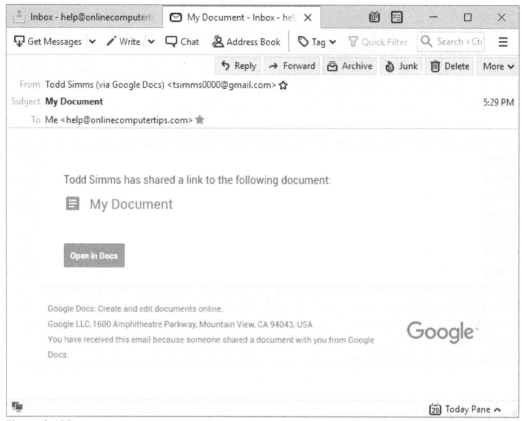

Figure 3.100

Once you share your document with a non-Google user, you should see a new icon on your toolbar next to the Share button. (It's usually some random animal showing you that there is an anonymous user accessing your document.)

Figure 3.101

Now I shared the same document with my Google account, and as you can see in figure 3.102, my name appears in the list of who has access, but the non-Google account does not.

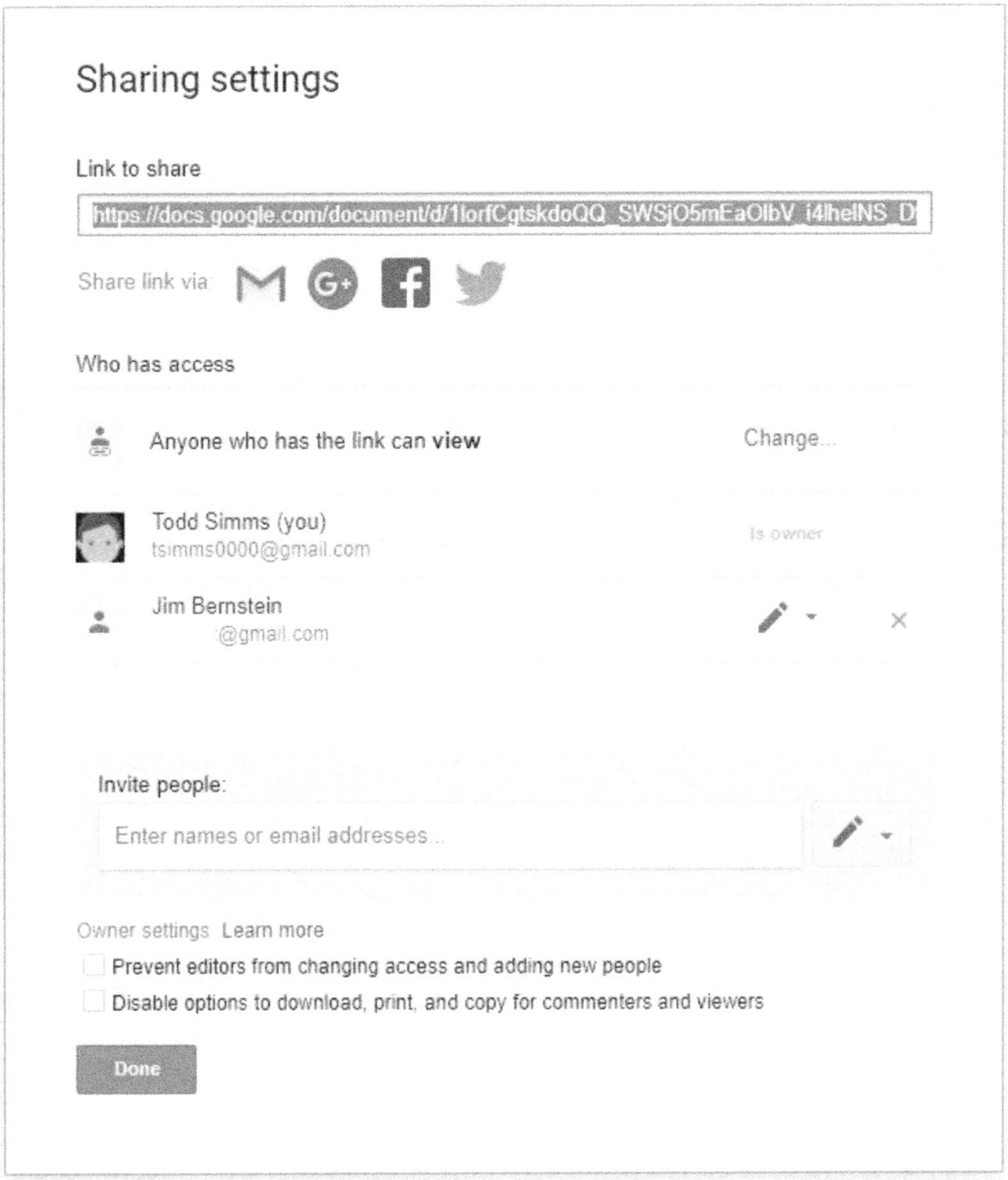

Figure 3.102

Now when I open Todd's document with my Google account, you can see that the document shows that I have access to it by showing my Google profile picture on the toolbar next to the Share button.

Chapter 3 – Google Docs

Figure 3.103

The last section of the Sharing settings I want to discuss is the *Owner* settings that you can see in figure 3.97 at the bottom of the window.

If you don't want anyone that you have assigned the editor right to change your sharing access or add other people without your permission, then you can check the box that says *Prevent editors from changing access and adding new people*.

The box that says *Disable options to download, print, and copy for commenters and viewers* will disable those features for other users. This comes in handy when you have sensitive information that you don't want shared or leaked. This option is also available for files stored in your Google Drive.

Chapter 4 – Google Sheets

Google Sheets is Google's answer to Microsoft's Excel spreadsheet software and looks and feels very similar to it. The purpose of a spreadsheet is to be used as a place to store data in rows and columns, allowing you to manipulate the data with things like formulas or links to other data.

Many people use spreadsheets for keeping information in a list type format, but there is much more that spreadsheets can do, so keep that in mind when you start using them. If you need something done, there is most likely a way to do it, but figuring it out may be a little tricky at times. But since the purpose of this book is to get you familiar with Google's apps, I'm going to stick with the basics.

Sheets Interface

Just like with Microsoft does with its Office suite, Google tries to keep things as consistent as possible between their apps so you don't have to start from scratch when you want to use a different application. (And this makes it easier for me because it's less that I have to write about for this section, and even some of the others!)

Just like with Docs, when you first open Sheets you will have the option to start a new blank spreadsheet, or open one of your existing spreadsheets that you have worked on in the past. Sheets will list your past spreadsheets under the templates, and you can also get to them from the folder icon (called the file picker) on the right side of the screen (as shown in figure 4.1).

Chapter 4 – Google Sheets

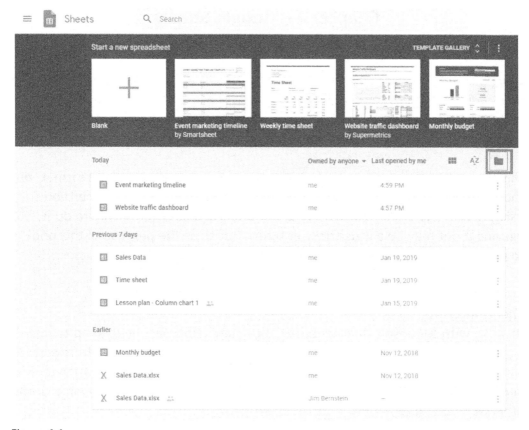

Figure 4.1

After clicking on the file picker, you will be shown files from your Google Drive and also have options to choose files that have been shared with you, marked as starred, recent, or you can upload a file from your local computer or other device. For this chapter, I will be using a template called *Event marketing timeline* that already has some data filled in. When I get to the formatting section, I will start with a new file so we can practice some of the formatting options available for Sheets.

Sheets Specific Menu Items
Just like with Docs, Sheets has many of the same menus and menu items, so for this section I will only go over the ones that are specific to Sheets since I went over the others in the last chapter on Docs. Even the toolbar has many of the same choices as it does when you are using Docs.

Chapter 4 – Google Sheets

Figure 4.2

File Menu

As you can see in figure 4.3 (assuming you remember), the only menu item that is new compared to what we have seen so far is the one called *Spreadsheet settings* at the bottom of the menu listings.

Figure 4.3

Within Spreadsheet settings there are two areas with options that you can change:

153

Chapter 4 – Google Sheets

General – Here you can change your locale, which is the country that you are in. When you change your country setting, Sheets will format you spreadsheet accordingly so your data looks correct.

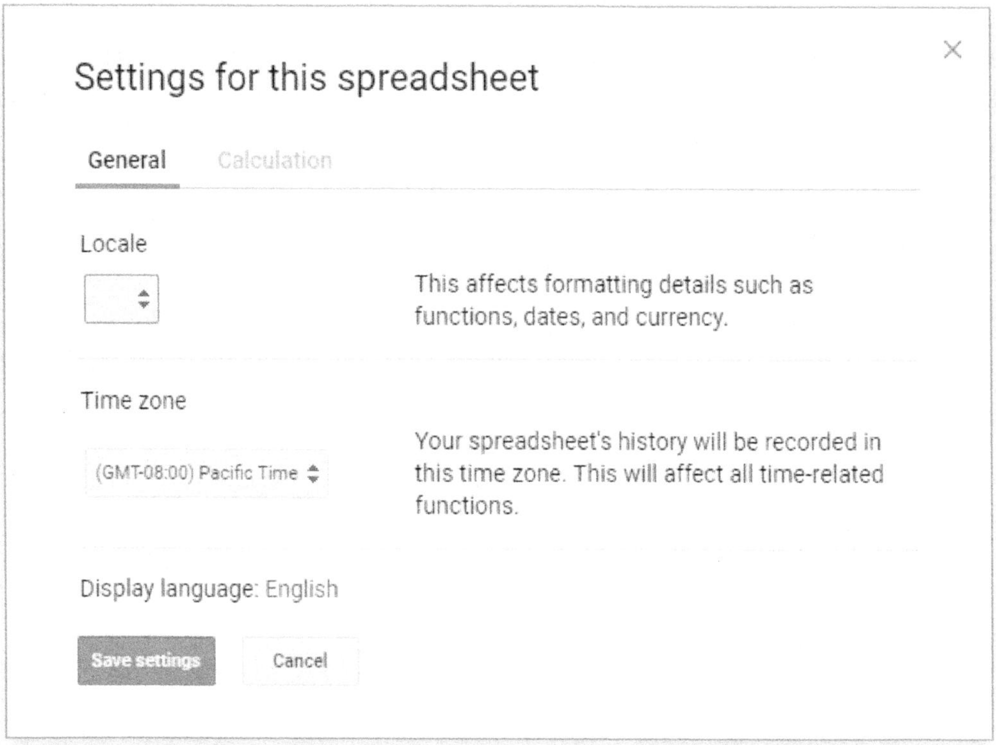

Figure 4.4

For example, if you went from the United States to the United Kingdom, the currency format would change from the Dollar ($) to the Pound (£) (as you can see in figure 4.5). One thing to note when changing the locale is that the Spreadsheet most likely will not update itself, and you will need to reapply the formatting to whichever cells need to be changed to reflect the new location.

Chapter 4 – Google Sheets

United States

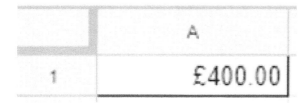

United Kingdom

Figure 4.5

Changing the time zone will affect how data that uses the time is displayed in your spreadsheet as well as revision history.

Calculation – You can have fields on a spreadsheet that can be updated, such as the current date and time.

Sheets offers you three choices of how you want these values to be recalculated and updated to reflect changes:

- **On change** – Only updates the value when it's changed.

- **On change and every minute** – Updates the value when changed and checks for updates every minute.

- **On change and every hour** - Updates the value when changed and checks for updates every hour.

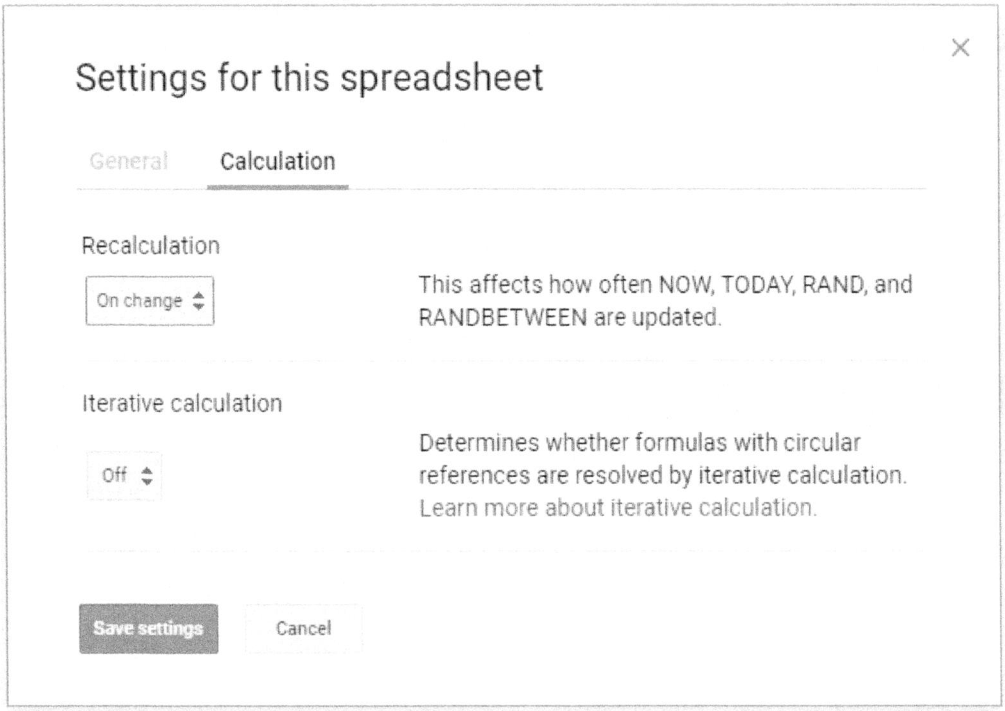

Chapter 4 – Google Sheets

Figure 4.6

Iterative calculation sets the number of times a formula with a circular reference can occur.

Edit Menu
The Edit menu in sheets has some familiar choices, but as you can see near the bottom of the menu items, there are some other options that are specific to Sheets, and this is what I will be discussing next.

Chapter 4 – Google Sheets

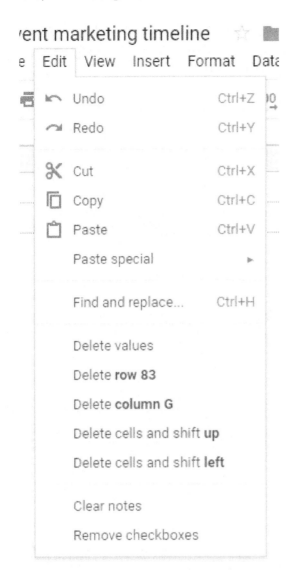

Figure 4.7

Before I get too into these choices on the Edit menu, I just want to point out that what you see next to some of the choices will vary based on what cell you have highlighted in your spreadsheet, so pay attention so you don't delete the wrong thing on accident. If you take a look at figure 4.7, you will see that I am in row 83 and in column G in my spreadsheet.

- **Delete values** – Using this option, you can delete the contents of cells while leaving columns and rows intact. Sometimes people like to delete a column or row in its entirety when trying to get rid of data, but if you just want to delete what is *in* the cells, you can use this option.

157

- **Delete row** – I just mentioned how you can delete a row to get rid of all the data in that row. This comes in handy if you want to move the data closer to existing data when you delete the particular row. For example, in figure 4.8 I want to get rid of all the Yellow Data because I don't need it anymore. If I were to use the *Delete values* option, I would end up with my spreadsheet looking like figure 4.9.

	A	B	C	D	E	F
1	Green Data	Green Data	Green Data	Green Data	Green Data	Green Data
2	Yellow Data	Yellow Data	Yellow Data	Yellow Data	Yellow Data	Yellow Data
3	Red Data	Red Data	Red Data	Red Data	Red Data	Red Data
4						
5						

Figure 4.8

As you can see, it removed the data, but the yellow cell coloring is still there and I have an extra row between my Green and Red data.

	A	B	C	D	E	F
1	Green Data	Green Data	Green Data	Green Data	Green Data	Green Data
2						
3	Red Data	Red Data	Red Data	Red Data	Red Data	Red Data
4						
5						

Figure 4.9

If I use the *Delete row* option instead, my results will look like figure 4.10. The extra row is now gone, and I only have the Green and Red data, which is exactly what I want. The numbers of the rows will update when doing this, so if you delete row 2, then row 3 will then be labeled as row 2 when it is moved up.

	A	B	C	D	E	F
1	Green Data	Green Data	Green Data	Green Data	Green Data	Green Data
2	Red Data	Red Data	Red Data	Red Data	Red Data	Red Data
3						
4						
5						

Figure 4.10

Chapter 4 – Google Sheets

- **Delete column** – This works the same way as the Delete row function, but does it for columns instead. The letters of the columns will update when doing this, so if you delete column A, then column B will then be labeled as column A.

- **Delete cells and shift up** – Choosing this option will delete whatever cell or cells you have highlighted and move the other data up. As you can see in figure 4.11, I have cell A2 highlighted, so when I choose *Delete cells and shift up,* it deletes cell A2 and I get the results shown in figure 4.12.

	A	B	C
	fx Yellow Data		
1	Green Data	Green Data	Green Data
2	Yellow Data	Yellow Data	Yellow Data
3	Red Data	Red Data	Red Data
4			

Figure 4.11

	A	B	C
	fx Red Data		
1	Green Data	Green Data	Green Data
2	Red Data	Yellow Data	Yellow Data
3		Red Data	Red Data
4			

Figure 4.12

- **Delete cells and shift left** – This will perform a similar process to *Delete cells and shift,* up except it will delete the data and move the contents of the other cells to the left, as shown in figures 4.13 and 4.14.

	A	B	C	D
1		Green Data	Green Data	
2		Yellow Data	Yellow Data	
3		Red Data	Red Data	
4				

Figure 4.13

159

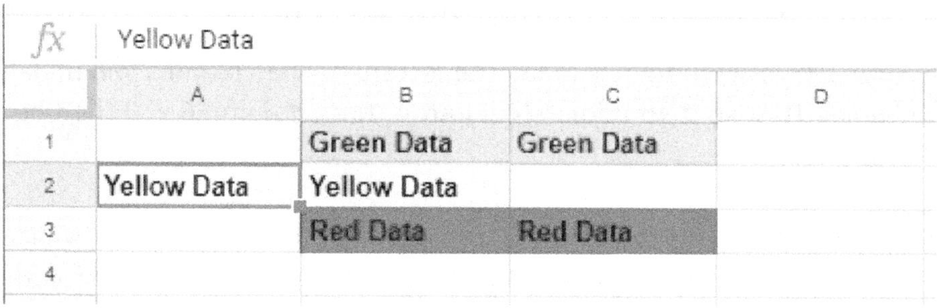

Chapter 4 – Google Sheets

![Figure 4.14 spreadsheet showing Yellow Data selected with Green Data, Yellow Data, and Red Data cells]

Figure 4.14

- **Clear notes** – Sheets allows you to add notes to specific cells in case you need to add some pertinent information to that cell for you or others to view. To add a note to a cell, all you need to do is right click on it and choose *Insert note*, and then type in what you want the note to say (figure 4.15).

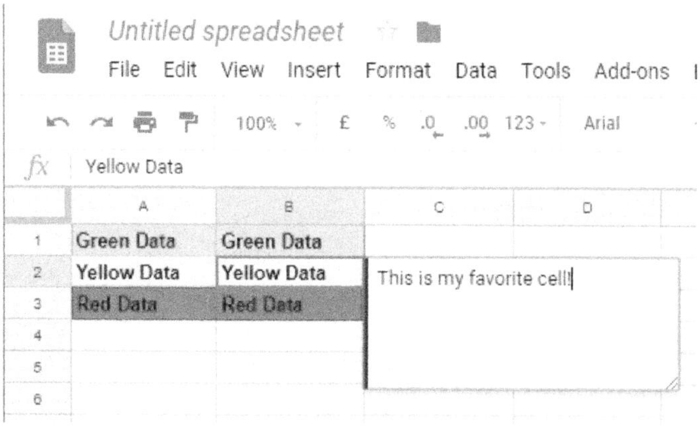

![Figure 4.15 showing a spreadsheet with a note "This is my favorite cell!" attached to a cell]

Figure 4.15

You will notice in figure 4.16 that cell B2 has a black triangle in the upper right hand corner, indicating that there is a note there. To read the note, all you need to do is hover over the triangle to have it display the note for you (which will look similar to figure 4.15).

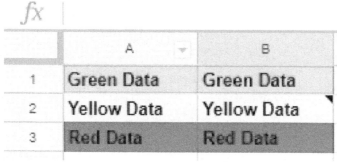

Figure 4.16

160

Chapter 4 – Google Sheets

If you need to erase the note for any reason, all you need to do is click within that cell, go to the Edit menu, and choose *Clear notes*. The note will then be removed.

- **Remove checkboxes** – Checkboxes can be used to put checkmarks in certain cells, for example, if you were creating some type of form that could make use of them. I will get into how to create them shortly, but if you need to remove them, simply go to the Edit menu and choose *Remove checkboxes*.

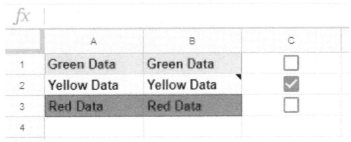

Figure 4.17

Insert Menu
The Sheets Insert menu has some spreadsheet specific items as well as some of the standard items such as the ability to insert an image, drawing, link, and so on (figure 4.18).

Chapter 4 – Google Sheets

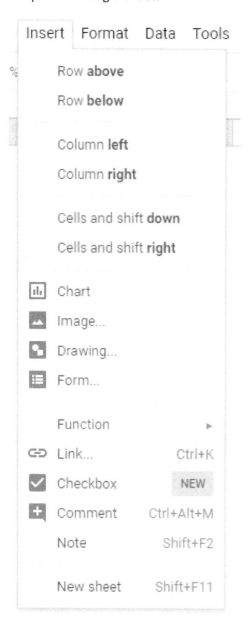

Figure 4.18

Most of the choices on this menu should be easy to understand, but there are a few that might not be, so I will now go over all the Sheets-specific menu items.

- **Row above** – This option will add a new row above whatever cell you happen to be in. So, if I'm in cell A2 (as shown in figure 4.19), and choose the *Row above* menu item, it will add a new row above cell A2. This new row will take over the number 2 row position (as shown in figure 4.20). It will

162

will insert as many rows as you have highlighted, so if you have three rows highlighted, it will insert three new rows.

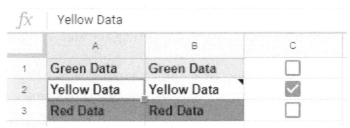

Figure 4.19

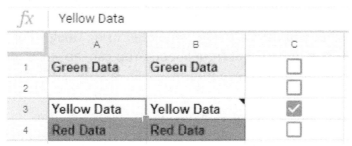

Figure 4.20

I purposely left the cell color fill and checkboxes to show you that when you create a new row, it will take the formatting of the existing row and apply it to that new row. If I didn't have cell color fill applied or the checkboxes, then it would just be a blank, empty row.

- **Row below** – This does the same thing as the *Row above* option, but will put the row *below* the cell or row you have highlighted.

- **Column left** – This will do the same thing as the *Row above* or *Row below* option, but will do so with columns instead of rows. It will insert a new column to the left of the cell or column you are in and move the cells and their data to the right. It will insert as many rows as you have highlighted, so if you have three columns highlighted, it will insert three new columns.

- **Column right** – This will do the same thing as the *Column left* option, but will insert a new column to the *right* of the cell or column you are in and move the cells and their data to the left.

- **Cells and shift down** – Once again, this option is similar to the others, and will insert a cell and shift the existing data *down*. It will insert the number of cells to match how many cells you have highlighted. So, if you have three cells highlighted, it will insert three more new cells.

- **Cells and shift up** – It's the same as the *Cells and shift down* option, except it will shift the cells up. (Hopefully you are getting the idea by now!)

- **Chart** – Sheets has the ability to create custom charts based on the information contained within your spreadsheet. (I will be going over how to create a chart when I get to creating a spreadsheet.)

- **Form** – I will be going over Google Forms in Chapter 6. For now just know that you can insert a form into your spreadsheet, but unfortunately can't insert a form that you have already completed using Google Forms. You have to create one on the spot from Sheets. You can, however, open the responses to the questions on your form in a Sheets spreadsheet.

- **Function** – Functions are used in Sheets to calculate data such as adding up a column of numbers, or getting the average from the data in specific cells within your spreadsheet. (I will be going over this topic in more detail later in this chapter.)

- **Checkbox** – I went over how to *remove* checkboxes, but if you want to *add* a checkbox, you would do it from this option in the Insert menu.

- **Note** – I discussed how to add and remove Notes earlier in this chapter.

- **New sheet** – Spreadsheets can contain multiple sheets within them that can be used to separate data and help you keep things organized. Plus, you can still link the data within the sheets the same way you can in a single sheet. Going back to the Time sheet file I was working on, you can see in figure 4.21 that there are two sheets. One is called *Time sheet,* which is the one we were working on, and the other is called *Stats*.

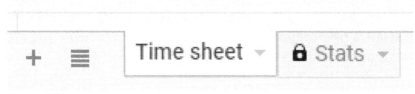

Figure 4.21

Chapter 4 – Google Sheets

You can add additional sheets from the Insert menu and also by clicking on the + sign to the left of the sheets themselves. When you add a new sheet, it will put it to the right of whatever sheet you happen to be on at the moment and give it a generic name (as you can see in figure 4.22).

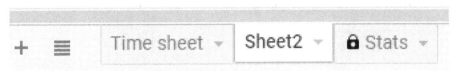

Figure 4.22

If you click on the down arrow next to the sheet name, you will be presented with several options that you can choose from to do things such as rename, copy, delete the sheet, and so on.

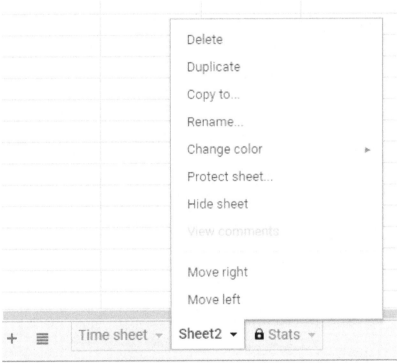

Figure 4.23

You might have noticed how the sheet called *Stats* has a lock icon by it, and that means that is has been protected from being changed by the creator of this spreadsheet. If you try and make a change to a protected sheet, you will get an error message similar to figure 4.24.

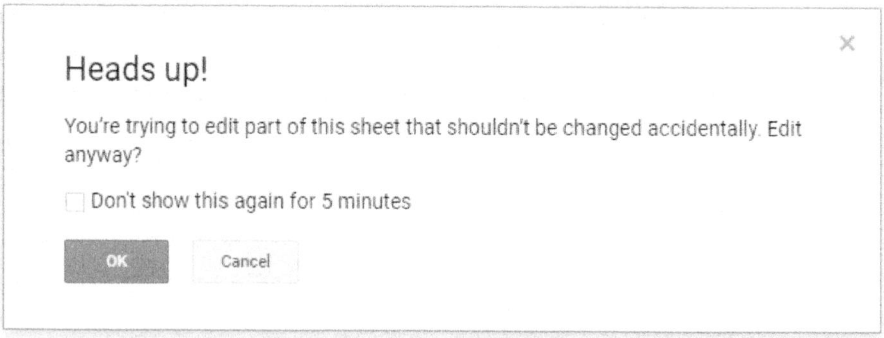

Chapter 4 – Google Sheets

Figure 4.24

In case you were wondering, you can set specific levels of sharing to your sheets and control who can and can't edit them.

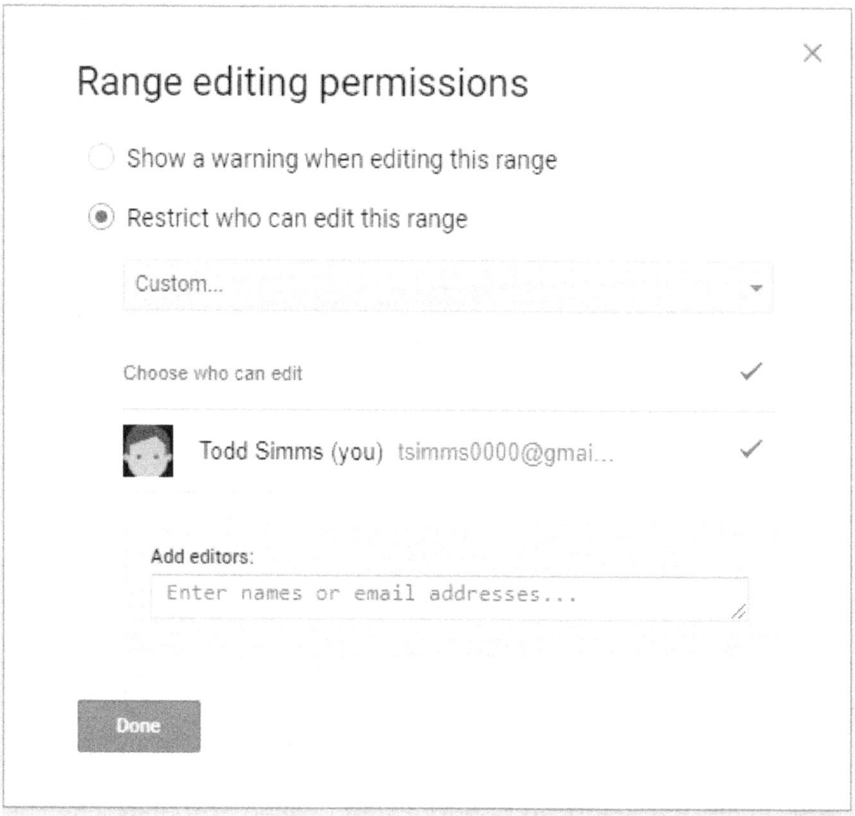

Figure 4.25

If you choose the *Hide sheet* option it will make it so the sheet is not visible within the Sheets file. To see your hidden sheets, you will need to go to the *View* menu and then to *Hidden sheets* to unhide them.

Chapter 4 – Google Sheets

Format Menu

Since I will have an entire section on formatting a spreadsheet, I won't spend too much time on this menu, but rather just point out the items that are specific to Sheets. Then for the formatting section I will go over some of the more real world formatting that you are more likely to use.

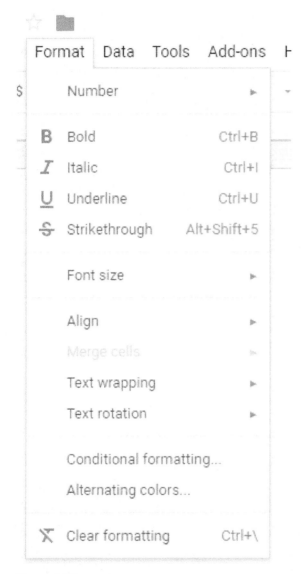

Figure 4.26

You can perform many of the same text formatting as you can with Docs, but there are also some Sheets specific formatting tasks that you can do on the cells themselves.

Chapter 4 – Google Sheets

- **Number** – This menu item can be used to format how your numbers are displayed within their cells. For example, if you are using currency for your numbers, then you can have them with your currency symbol. So, whenever you type in a number, such as 523, it will format it to look like $523.00. You can also have it do things like format your dates, as well as apply other number formatting.

- **Text wrapping** – When adding data to your spreadsheet you will only have so much room in a cell, so many times your text or numbers won't fit properly. When this happens, you can change how the text is displayed to make things easier to read.

    The default setting is to have text *overflow,* where it is displayed in the other cells even though it's really only in one cell. You can choose the *wrap* option, which will make the text fit within the cell by "wrapping" it to the shape of the cell and putting it on more than one line. Finally, you can use the *clip* option, which will simply cut off how the text is displayed at the end of the cell, but not actually cut off the text itself. Figure 4.27 shows all three of these options and how they look.

	A	B	C
Overflow 1	The text in this cell is too long so it doesn't fit		
2			
Wrap 3	The text in this cell is too long so it doesn't fit		
4			
Clipping 5	The text in this c		

    Figure 4.27

- **Text rotation** – Another cell formatting option you can choose is text rotation. Here you can rotate the text within the cell and have it tilt up or down, rotate up or down, stack vertically, or choose a specific tilt degree of your own.

Figure 4.28

- **Conditional formatting** – If you want to really get into formatting cells and have the same formatting apply to multiple cells, then this is where *Conditional formatting* comes into play. Here you can change things such as text color and format, as well as cell color.

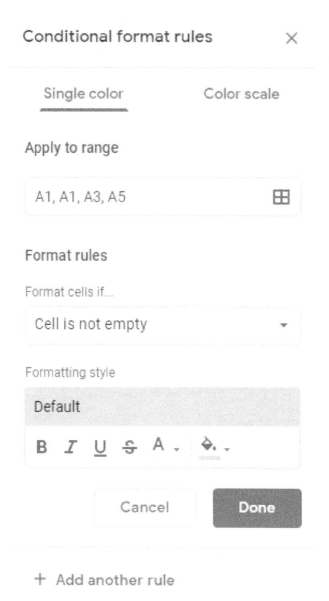

Figure 4.29

The Color scale section allows you to apply a scaled color pattern to the cells to make them really stand out, and will base the color on the value of the cell.

Chapter 4 – Google Sheets

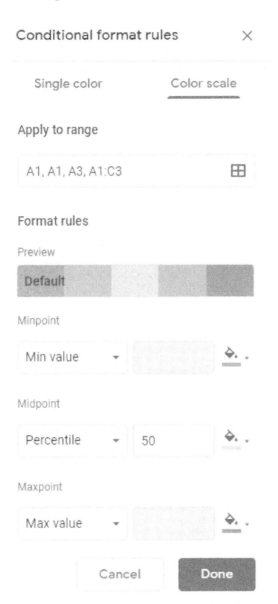

Figure 4.30

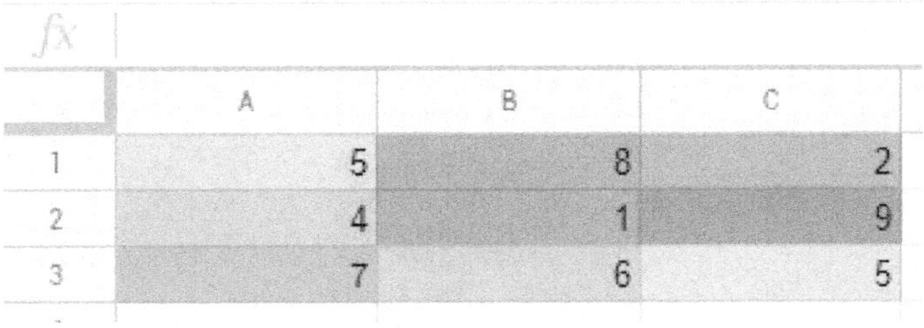

Figure 4.31

- **Alternating colors** – Here you can make each row a different color to differentiate between the two and make things easier to read. You can also make the header or footer a unique color to make it stand out.

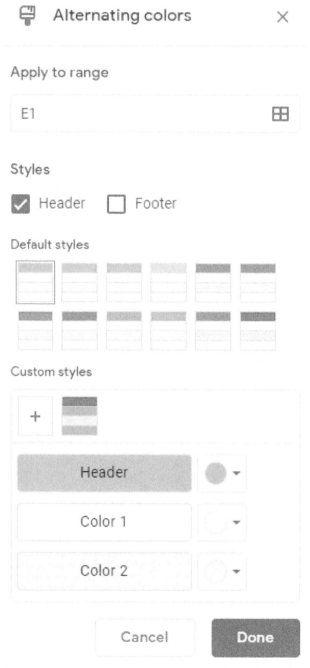

Figure 4.32

Chapter 4 – Google Sheets

	A	B	C
1	First score	Second score	Third score
2	5	8	2
3	4	1	9
4	7	6	5

Figure 4.33

- **Clear formatting** – If you just want things back to the basics and want to get rid of all the formatting changes you have done, simply highlight the cells you want to revert back to normal and then choose the *Clear formatting* option.

Changing cell colors is a great way to make the cells stand out and can be used to categorize your data as well. For example, you can make all of your sales numbers a different color for each month etc.

Data Menu

The Data menu will be used to manipulate data within your spreadsheet, so if you plan on doing some number crunching within Sheets, then you will find yourself using the items here (figure 4.34). If you are only going to be making spreadsheets that are more like lists, then probably not so much.

Chapter 4 – Google Sheets

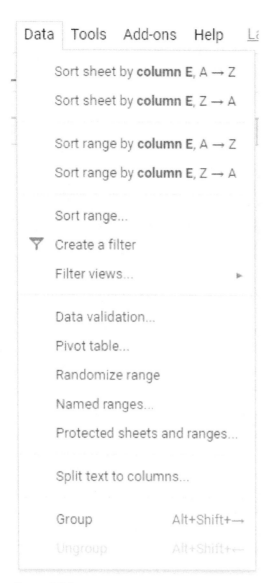

Figure 4.34

All of the items in the Data menu items are unique to Sheets, so let's go over them now. Keep in mind that some may be greyed out if you don't have a range of data to work with selected in your spreadsheet.

- **Sort sheet by column X, A → Z** – One of the more common things to do with the data in your spreadsheet is to sort it, making it easier to understand. In figure 4.35 I have a list of team members with their associated sales calls and the resulting number of sales.

Chapter 4 – Google Sheets

	A	B	C
1	Team member	# of calls	# of sales
2	Bill	45	24
3	Danny	57	33
4	Evan	22	14
5	Taylor	57	42
6	Cindy	46	38
7	Margaret	102	72
8	Carlos	78	55
9	Janet	67	39
10	Kim	25	15
11	Maria	58	31
12	Darren	81	62

Figure 4.35

Now let's say I want to sort the list by Team Member in alphabetical order. If I choose the *Sort sheet by column X, A → Z* option, notice how it sorts the names in alphabetical order, but also sorts the Team Member cell, which is not what we want.

	A	B	C
1	Bill	45	24
2	Carlos	78	55
3	Cindy	46	38
4	Danny	57	33
5	Darren	81	62
6	Evan	22	14
7	Janet	67	39
8	Kim	25	15
9	Margaret	102	72
10	Maria	58	31
11	Taylor	57	42
12	Team member	# of calls	# of sales

Figure 4.36

To get around this we simply highlight the range we want to sort, so in our case it would be cells A1-C12 because we want all of the data in the # of calls and # of sales columns to match up with their respective team member and get sorted along with the names.

	A	B	C
1	Team member	# of calls	# of sales
2	Bill	45	24
3	Danny	57	33
4	Evan	22	14
5	Taylor	57	42
6	Cindy	46	38
7	Margaret	102	72
8	Carlos	78	55
9	Janet	67	39
10	Kim	25	15
11	Maria	58	31
12	Darren	81	62

Figure 4.37

From the *Data* menu choose *Sort range*. Then you just check the box that says *Data has a header row* and choose the header name in the *Sort by* section. In our case, you would choose *Team member* as the header row name because we are sorting by team member name. If we were sorting by # of calls, then that would be what you would choose from the *Sort by* section. Also notice on the right of figure 4.37 that you can choose between sorting from A → Z or Z → A.

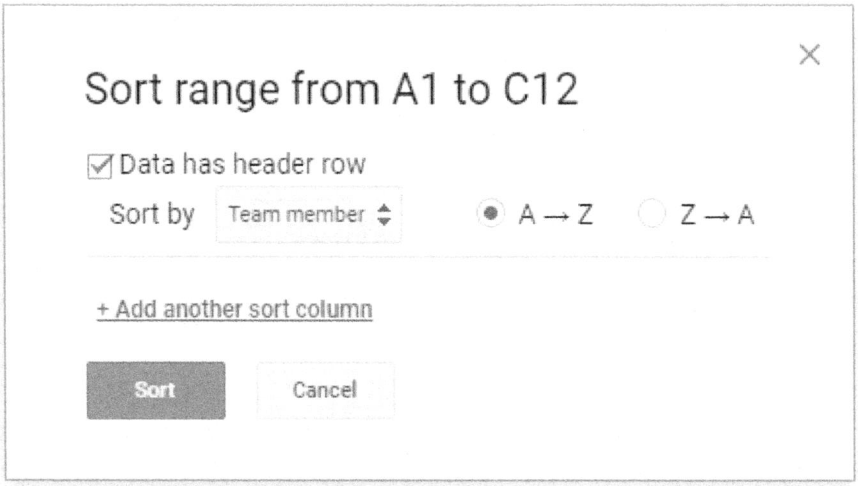

Sort range from A1 to C12

☑ Data has header row

Sort by [Team member ▾]   ● A → Z   ○ Z → A

+ Add another sort column

[Sort]   Cancel

Figure 4.38

Chapter 4 – Google Sheets

Then, after you click on the *Sort* button, you will see the names in alphabetical order while the Team member header is still at the top of the list and the # of calls and # of sales data still matches up with the correct name.

	A	B	C
1	Team member	# of calls	# of sales
2	Bill	45	24
3	Carlos	78	55
4	Cindy	46	38
5	Danny	57	33
6	Darren	81	62
7	Evan	22	14
8	Janet	67	39
9	Kim	25	15
10	Margaret	102	72
11	Maria	58	31
12	Taylor	57	42

Figure 4.39

Figure 4.40 shows what the table looks like after sorting by # of sales. Notice how the # of sales is in numerical order, but the names are not in alphabetical order anymore.

	A	B	C
1	Team member	# of calls	# of sales
2	Bill	45	14
3	Carlos	57	15
4	Cindy	22	24
5	Danny	57	31
6	Darren	46	33
7	Evan	102	38
8	Janet	78	39
9	Kim	67	42
10	Margaret	25	55
11	Maria	58	62
12	Taylor	81	72

Figure 4.40

Chapter 4 – Google Sheets

- **Sort sheet by column X, Z → A** – This works the same way as the previous option, just that you are sorting in the opposite direction.

- **Sort range** – I just went over how to sort a range in the *Sort sheet by column X, A → Z* section.

- **Create a filter** – Filters are used to have Sheets only display the data that applies to that filter. To apply a filter, simply highlight the range of cells you would like to filter on, and then choose *Create a filter* from the *Data* menu. I highlighted cells C2 through C12, which is the column that contains the number of sales for each team member. Then I chose to filter by condition and chose *Greater than or equal to* from the available choices. Then for the condition I entered the number 39, meaning my filter will show results that are greater than or equal to 39.

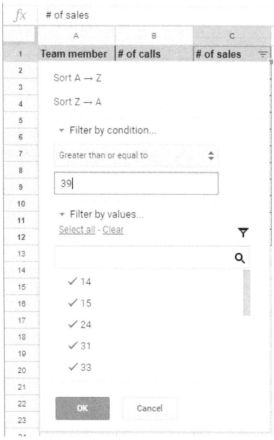

Figure 4.41

Figure 4.42 shows what the table looked like before applying the filter.

	A	B	C
1	Team member	# of calls	# of sales
2	Bill	45	24
3	Carlos	78	14
4	Cindy	46	15
5	Danny	57	31
6	Darren	81	33
7	Evan	22	38
8	Janet	67	39
9	Kim	25	42
10	Margaret	102	55
11	Maria	58	62
12	Taylor	57	72

Figure 4.42

Figure 4.43 shows what the table looks like after applying the filter. Notice how the filter symbol is showing in cell C1 after # of sales, and that column C is highlighted and the cell numbers on the left are missing some numbers. This means that rows 2, 3, 4, 5, 6, and 7 don't contain any data that is equal to or greater than 39 for the number of sales.

	A	B	C
1	Team member	# of calls	# of sales ▼
8	Janet	67	39
9	Kim	25	42
10	Margaret	102	55
11	Maria	58	62
12	Taylor	57	72
13			
14			

Figure 4.43

You can edit the filter criteria by clicking on the filter symbol in the cell, or you can also filter by values. If you look back at figure 4.41 you will see that you can check or uncheck the values for number of sales from the list and have Sheets only show results with the values you choose. Filtering comes in handy for larger sets of data compared to what I have shown you in my example. If you want to clear the filter, you can go to Data and then *Turn off filter*.

- **Filter views** – *Filter views* are used to create filtered views that you can use for yourself compared to views that everyone can see when you use the *Create a filter* option. And when I say "views that everyone can see", I mean others that you have shared your spreadsheet with.

You can also save multiple filter views that you can reuse later when needed. Figure 4.44 shows an example of a filter view which only shows the data between 20 and 70 in column C.

	A	B	C
	Name: Between 20 & 70		Range: C1:C12
1	Team member	# of calls	# of sales
2	Bill	45	24
5	Danny	57	31
6	Darren	81	33
7	Evan	22	38
8	Janet	67	39
9	Kim	25	42
10	Margaret	102	55
11	Maria	58	62
13			

Figure 4.44

Now when I go back to Filter views, my *Between 20 & 70* view is there so that I can apply it to my spreadsheet later if needed.

Chapter 4 – Google Sheets

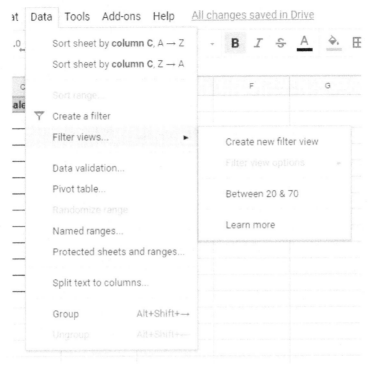

Figure 4.45

- **Data validation** – If you want to control how data is entered into your spreadsheet, you can use Data validation to only allow data based on a specified criteria. Once you highlight a range of cells and go to *Data* and then *Data validation*, you will be prompted to enter your criteria. In my example, the criteria is that the numbers in the cells must be between 20 and 50. There is an option to show a warning or reject the data input altogether.

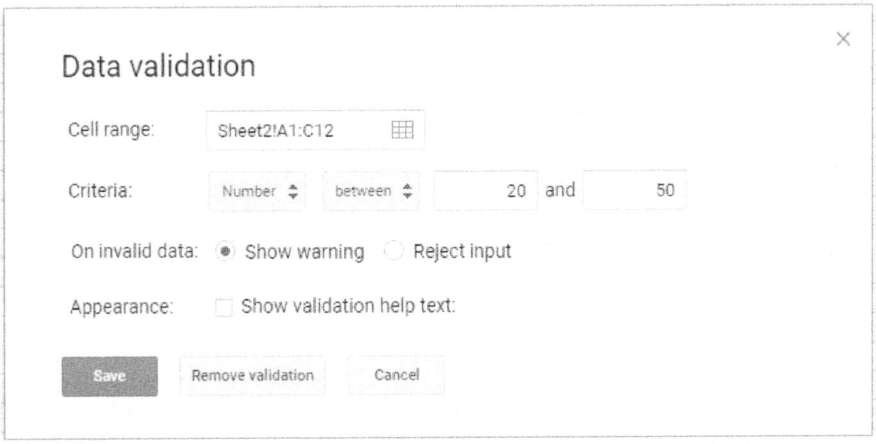

Figure 4.46

Figure 4.47 shows the results of the data validation. Notice the small triangle shape at the top right corner of every cell that doesn't have a value between 20 and 50. (Of course the names in column A will all fail because they are not even numbers.)

	A	B	C
1	Team member	# of calls	# of sales
2	Bill	45	24
3	Carlos	78	14
4	Cindy	46	15
5	Danny	57	31
6	Darren	81	33
7	Evan	22	38
8	Janet	67	39
9	Kim	25	42
10	Margaret	102	55
11	Maria	58	62
12	Taylor	57	72
13			

Figure 4.47

If I used the option to *reject input,* then whenever I tried to enter data in a cell that was part of this data validation I would get a message similar to the one shown in figure 4.48.

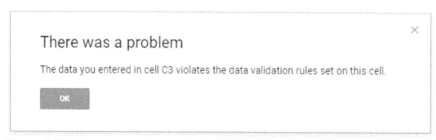

Figure 4.48

To remove the data validation from your spreadsheet, simply highlight the affected cell range and then go back to *Data* and then *Data validation* and click on *Remove validation*.

- **Pivot table** – Pivot tables can be used to narrow down a large data set or see relationships between data points. For example, you could use one to analyze which team member had the most sales for a specific month. (Pivot tables can be rather complex, and are beyond the scope of this book.)

- **Randomize range** – If for some reason, you want to randomize the order of the data in your spreadsheet, you can highlight the range and then go to *Data* and choose *Randomize range*. As you can see in figure 4.49, I have highlighted cells A2 through C12 and then chose the *Randomize range* option.

	A	B	C
1	Team member	# of calls	# of sales
2	Bill	45	24
3	Carlos	78	14
4	Cindy	46	15
5	Danny	57	31
6	Darren	81	33
7	Evan	22	38
8	Janet	67	39
9	Kim	25	42
10	Margaret	102	55
11	Maria	58	62
12	Taylor	57	72

Figure 4.49

Now, as you can see, the data has been randomized within the table, yet all the values for # of calls and # of sales still match with their respective team member.

Chapter 4 – Google Sheets

	A	B	C
1	Team member	# of calls	# of sales
2	Bill	45	24
3	Janet	67	39
4	Margaret	102	55
5	Maria	58	62
6	Darren	81	33
7	Danny	57	31
8	Evan	22	38
9	Cindy	46	15
10	Kim	25	42
11	Taylor	57	72
12	Carlos	78	14

Figure 4.50

Named ranges – Named ranges can be used to create shortcuts to a range of data. For example, suppose you want to use the # of calls column range in a bunch of formulas in the future. What you can do is highlight that range of cells (B2-B12), and then select *Named ranges* and give it a name (figure 4.52). Just be sure not to use any spaces in your name or you will get an error.

	A	B	C
1	Team member	# of calls	# of sales
2	Bill	45	24
3	Carlos	78	14
4	Cindy	46	15
5	Danny	57	31
6	Darren	81	33
7	Evan	22	38
8	Janet	67	39
9	Kim	25	42
10	Margaret	102	55
11	Maria	58	62
12	Taylor	57	72

Figure 4.51

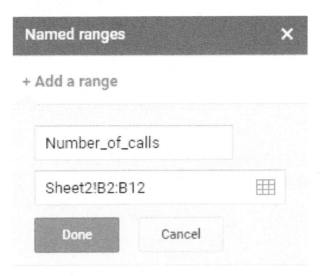

Figure 4.52

Then, when you go back to Named ranges, your named range will be there, along with any others you have created. When you go to create a formula, you can simply click on your range name and it will be input into the formula.

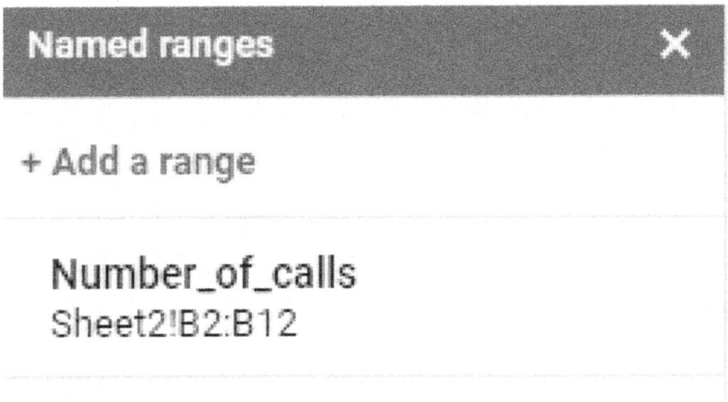

Figure 4.53

Chapter 4 – Google Sheets

Protected sheets and ranges – If you need to prevent others from changing data within your cells or even an entire sheet, then you can protect them from being changed with the *Protected sheets and ranges* option.

In figure 4.54 I have protected a range in Sheet 2 that includes B2 through C12 and named it "Not to be changed!"

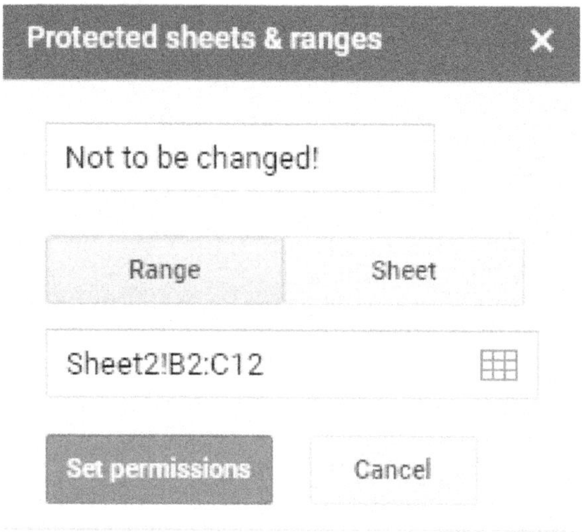

Figure 4.54

When I click on *Set permissions*, I will have options as to who can edit the range and what happens when people try to edit the range.

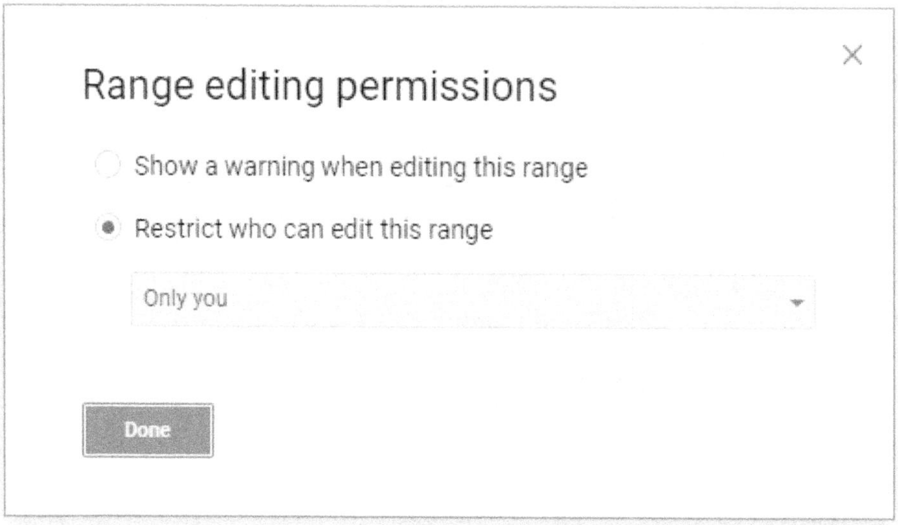

Figure 4.55

Now when another user who does not have permission to change the data in that range (or sheet) tries to do so, they will see an error message similar to figure 4.56.

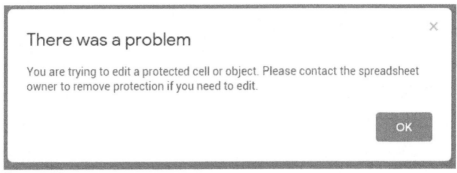

Figure 4.56

To remove the protection from a range or sheet, go back to your protected sheets and ranges and click on the trash can next to the name you created.

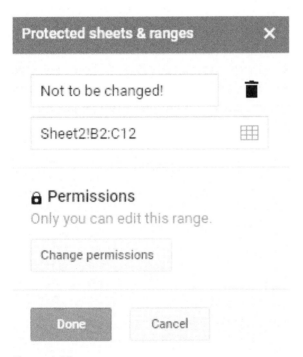

Figure 4.57

- **Split text to columns** – Often when using a spreadsheet application, you will have the need to paste in some data from a different source or have some existing data that is in one cell, but should really be split up into more than one. If you take a look at figure 4.58, you will see that there are four names in the last name, first name format. I need to have the first and last names separated into different columns, but I really don't want to retype them into new cells, especially if you have a really long list.

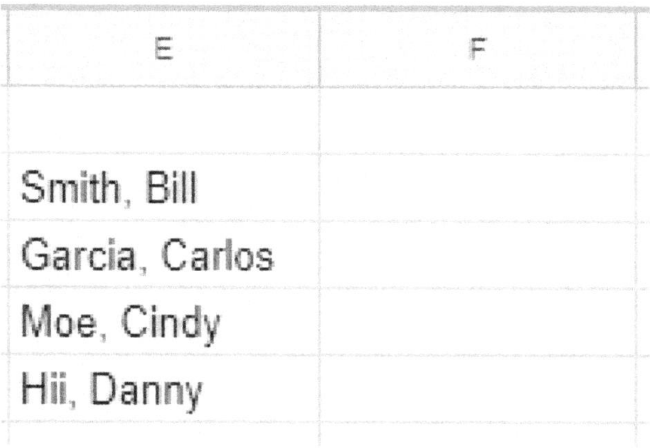

E	F
Smith, Bill	
Garcia, Carlos	
Moe, Cindy	
Hii, Danny	

Figure 4.58

To fix this problem I simply highlight the cells with the names in them and choose the *Split text to columns* option. The names are then automatically split into two separate columns, and you will get an option as to what the character separating the data was. In my case it was a comma between the first and last name. Sheets will try and detect this character automatically, but you can also specify this separator manually if the *detect automatically option* doesn't work correctly.

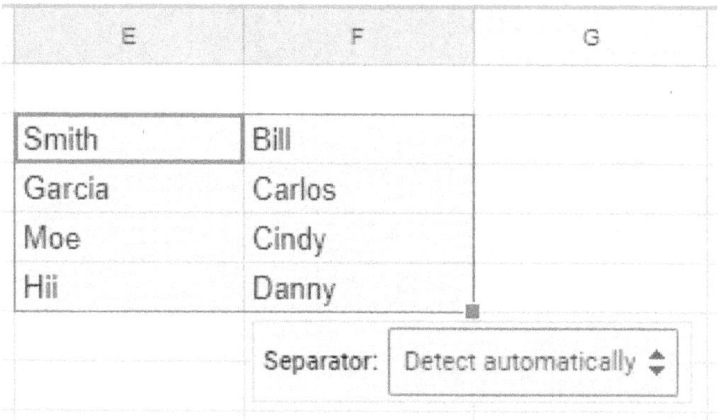

E	F	G
Smith	Bill	
Garcia	Carlos	
Moe	Cindy	
Hii	Danny	

Separator: Detect automatically

Figure 4.59

- **Group** – The Group feature is fairly new to Sheets, and has been something they needed to add for quite some time since Excel users find it so useful. You can group rows or columns together making easier to display your data and get rid of unwanted clutter. It doesn't actually group or manipulate the data in the cells, but rather treats them as one unit that you can then hide when it's not needed.

If you take a look at figure 4.60, you can see that I have highlighted rows 4 through 8, then clicked on the *Group* option from the Data menu, and now there is a minus sign to the left of the rows I have highlighted.

	A	B	C
1	Team member	# of calls	# of sales
2	Bill	45	24
3	Carlos	78	14
4	Cindy	46	15
5	Danny	57	31
6	Darren	81	33
7	Evan	22	38
8	Janet	67	39
9	Kim	25	42
10	Margaret	102	55
11	Maria	58	62
12	Taylor	57	72

Figure 4.60

Then when I click on the minus sign, those highlighted rows are now hidden, and if I want to get them back I just click on the + symbol.

	A	B	C
1	Team member	# of calls	# of sales
2	Bill	45	24
3	Carlos	78	14
9	Kim	25	42
10	Margaret	102	55
11	Maria	58	62
12	Taylor	57	72

Figure 4.61

- **Ungroup** – To remove a grouping you need to have the rows or columns showing, and then go back to the Data menu and choose *ungroup*.

Tools Menu
Finally, I want to discuss the Tools menu for Sheets since it contains some interesting options that you can use while working with your spreadsheets.

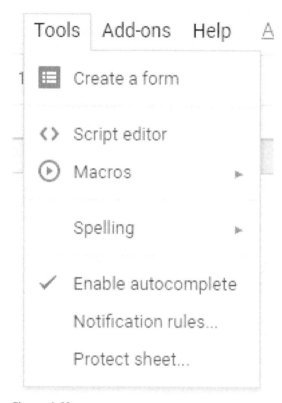

Figure 4.62

All of the choices from the Tools menu are different from what we have seen with Docs except for Spelling, so let's go over these choices now.

- **Create a form** – This is the same thing you saw when we went over the *Insert form* earlier in the chapter.

- **Script editor** – Scripting is used to do things such as create custom functions, interact with users, and other techy things like that. Once again, scripts are beyond the scope of this book, so you can check them out later for yourself when you are ready.

Chapter 4 – Google Sheets

- **Macros** – Macros are used to record a series of data entry manipulations that can then be saved and used again later by running the macro. For example, let's say you wanted to record the process that is involved in creating a table that is 8 rows by 4 columns, and then format each row with a different color. You can select *Record macro* and go through the table creation process, and when you are done click on *Save* (as seen in figure 4.63).

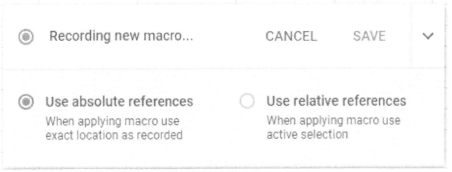

Figure 4.64

When saving your macro, you can assign it a shortcut so that when you want to run it, all you have to do is press the shortcut key combination. In my case this key combination is Ctrl-Alt-Shift-5.

Figure 4.65

Then your macro will be listed under *Macros* in the Tools menu, where you can click on it to run it or use your keyboard shortcut.

You can also manage your macros from the Macros menu item and do things such as edit them or delete them.

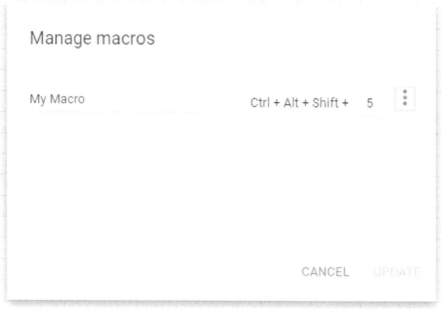

Figure 4.66

- **Enable autocomplete** – Autocomplete is used to help you fill in your cells faster by suggesting information based on data you have already typed into your spreadsheet. So, if you've used the word "hamburger" before and started typing in the first few letters (ham), Sheets will automatically complete the rest of the word for you so you don't have to type it. But if it's not the word you were meaning to type, then you can simply keep typing over it and do not have to accept its suggestion.

- **Notification rules** – Notification rules are used to let you know when someone else makes changes to your spreadsheets when sharing them with other users. As you can see from figure 4.67, there are options to notify you when changes are made or when a user submits a form. You can also set the notification to email you a daily summary of changes if any are made, or send you an email right away when something is changed.

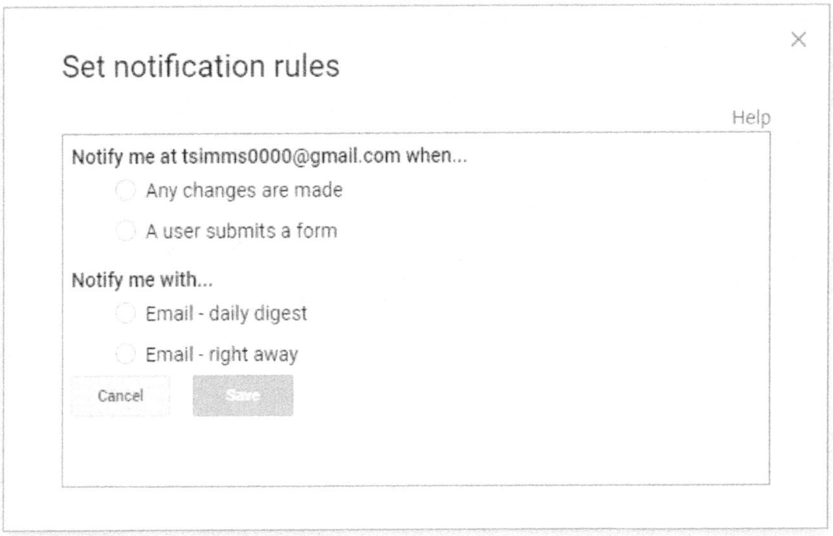

Chapter 4 – Google Sheets

Figure 4.67

- **Protect sheet** – I have discussed protecting your spreadsheet earlier in the chapter, but here is another place you can do the same thing.

Creating a Spreadsheet

Now that all the boring stuff is out of the way, it's finally time to create a spreadsheet and start entering some data that we can manipulate later on. Just like with Docs, Sheets has many built-in templates that we can use from calendars to invoices to timesheets and so on. But rather than use one of those, let's begin with a blank spreadsheet so we can start from scratch.

If you have Sheets already open, you can go to the *File* menu and then *New* and choose *Spreadsheet*. If you are just opening Sheets, then you can click on *Start a new spreadsheet – Blank*.

Figure 4.68

Chapter 4 – Google Sheets

Then you will be presented with a completely blank spreadsheet with no data in any of the cells and no formatting applied. This is when you will begin entering your data (assuming you have data to enter and have an idea of where it needs to go). How you enter data will be determined by the type of data and how you want it displayed or laid out.

Most people start in the upper left hand corner in cell A1. The cells get their names based on their location, so cell A1 is in column A and row 1.

Figure 4.69

To enter data in a cell, all you need to do is click on it and start typing. You can also copy and paste data from another source such as a document, website, or other spreadsheet. All of the same keyboard shortcuts for copying (Ctrl-C), cutting (Ctrl-X), and pasting (Ctrl-V) will work in Sheets.

When you type the data in the cell, you will notice that it also appears in the fx bar (formula bar). If you need to edit or delete the data in the cell, you can do so from the fx bar, or the cell itself. (When I get to formulas you will see how the fx bar comes into play.)

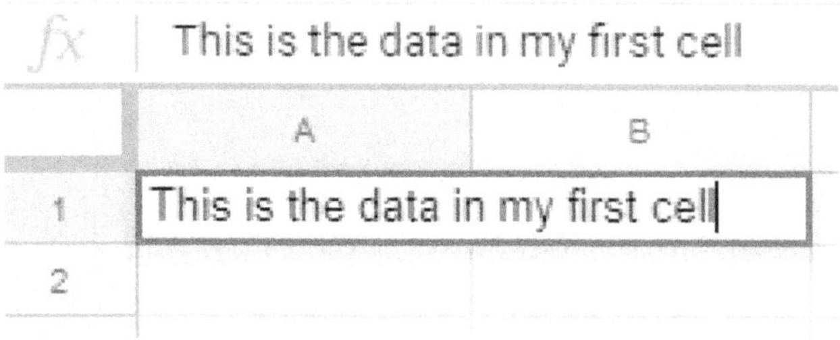

Figure 4.70

Once you type your data in a cell, you can simply press the Enter key on the keyboard to go to the next cell down, or use the arrow keys to go to the next cell up, left, or right (assuming you can move that way). When in cell A1, you can't go up or left because there is nowhere to go.

Chapter 4 – Google Sheets

You might have noticed how the data runs over into cell B1 in figure 4.70. I talked about how to change this earlier in the chapter, but I will go over it again here. Just because the data runs over into cell B1 doesn't mean it's actually *in* B1, and we can prove that by clicking in B1 and see how there's nothing in the fx bar.

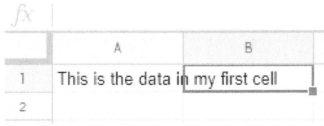

Figure 4.71

This might be confusing at first, but you have the option to apply the clip option from the *Format > Text wrapping* menu so the data doesn't overflow. Just keep in mind that if you want to see all of the data in that cell, you will need to click on it to display it in the fx bar.

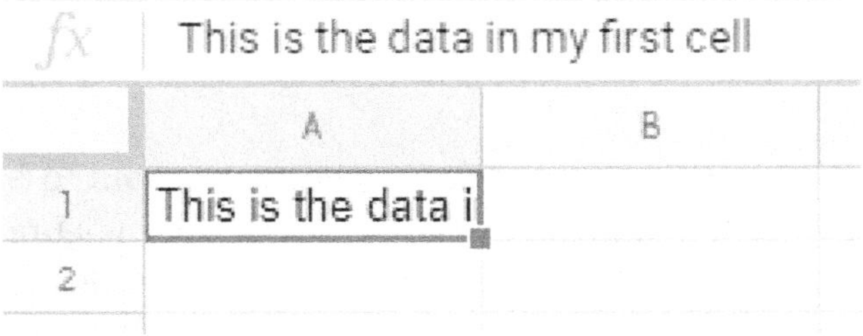

Figure 4.72

Or you can use the *text wrap* option to have the extra text go down to the next line (not cell).

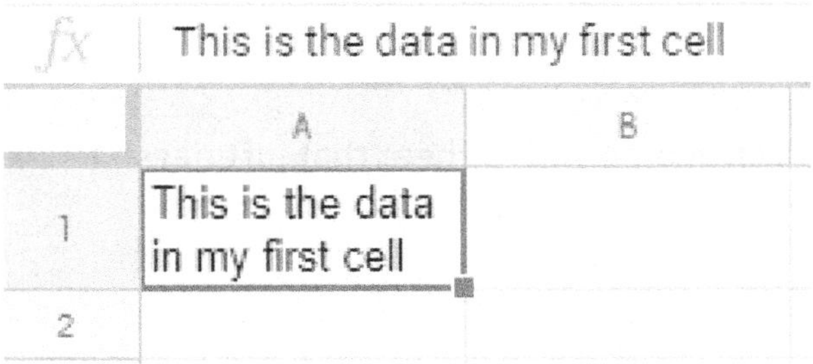

Figure 4.73

One thing to be aware of is that if you have a *lot* of data and use the text wrapping method, you will end up with a large row, and things might look a little funky.

195

Chapter 4 – Google Sheets

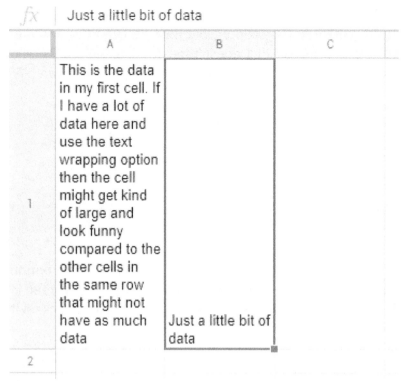

Figure 4.74

Another method you can use to help you display your data the way you want to is to stretch out the column (or row) size to make things fit. As you can see in figure 4.75, column A is much wider than it used to be, and is larger than columns B and C.

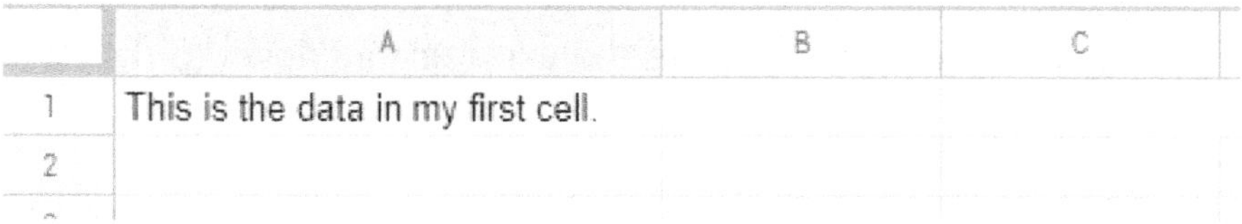

Figure 4.75

Once again, if you *overdo* this, you will end up with a sheet that just doesn't look right and will be wasting space trying to fit everything on the screen.

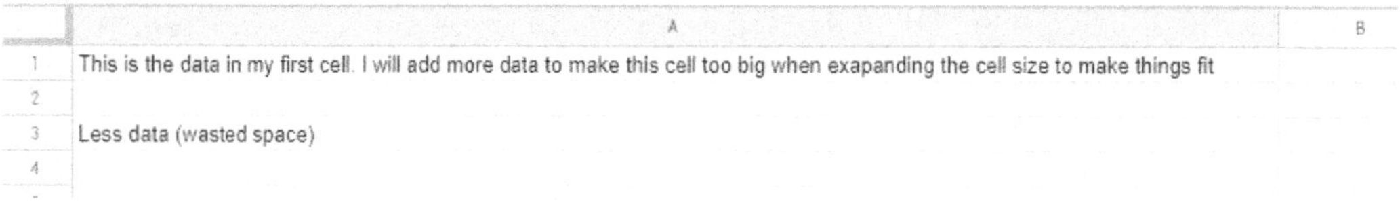

Figure 4.76

Chapter 4 – Google Sheets

So, now that we have an idea of how to get our data to display correctly and the options we have to do so, it's time to start adding some information to the cells. I am going to create a simple table with basic information in the cells. It will contain information about a group of employees and how many hours they work each day of the week. Then, once the data is in the cells, I will get into some formatting to make everything look more presentable, and then use some simple formulas to help make analyzing the data easier.

To create this table I will put the days of the week down the left hand side of the table in column A, and then the names of the employees across the top in row 1. One shortcut you will find yourself using often is the auto populate feature, where Sheets can finish a series of values for you. In my sheet I will type *Monday* in cell A2, but rather than having to manually type in the rest of the days, I can have Sheets do it for me.

As you can see in figure 4.77, when I have the cell highlighted that contains the word *Monday*, there is a little box at the lower right corner of the cell. To use the auto populate feature you need to hold your mouse pointer over the little box until it makes a cross (+) symbol (figure 4.78).

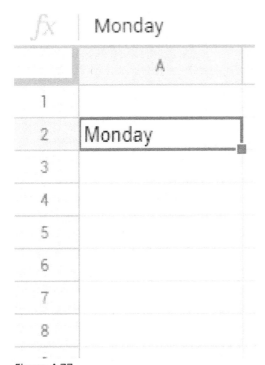

Figure 4.77

Chapter 4 – Google Sheets

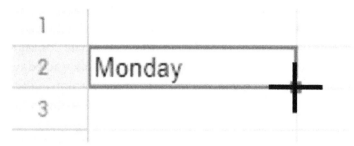

Figure 4.78

Then you will click on the cross symbol and drag your mouse down, in our case six more cells to make a total of seven days, and then release the mouse.

1	
2	Monday
3	
4	
5	
6	
7	
8	
9	

Figure 4.79

Then you will have the rest of the days filled in for you.

1	
2	Monday
3	Tuesday
4	Wednesday
5	Thursday
6	Friday
7	Saturday
8	Sunday

Figure 4.80

Chapter 4 – Google Sheets

This feature will work with other things such as dates and numbers if there is a pattern that Sheets can see emerging as you fill in cells. For example, if you were to start numbering cells down 1, 2, 3, 4, and so on, it can finish the job for you. However, if you tried it with just the number 1 in a cell, Sheets won't know that you are going for consecutive numbers, but rather just repeat the number 1 in all of the other cells.

Here is what I have so far after filling in the data for the table. It's not super exciting looking, but you should be able to make sense of it pretty easily.

	A	B	C	D	E	F	G
1		Cathy	Joe	Lisa	Maria	Steve	Allen
2	Monday	7	8	9	6	8	6
3	Tuesday	8	8	4	8	8	5
4	Wednesday	5	9	5	7	8	3
5	Thursday	6	5	8	7	9	5
6	Friday	9	6	8	8	7	7
7	Saturday	3	0	2	0	5	0
8	Sunday	0	2	2	0	0	3
9							

Figure 4.81

In order to make it easier to read and make it a little more appealing and professional looking, all I need to do is perform a little formatting.

Formatting a Spreadsheet

There are many ways to format your spreadsheet, and how you do it is completely up to you. Just keep in mind that if other people will be viewing or using your spreadsheet, you will want to keep your formatting subtle so they can do what they need to do and not be distracted by neon colors and hard to read fonts.

The first thing I will do is add some borders around the cells of the table to make it look more like an actual table. By default, Sheets will have light grey gridlines separating the cells. It is possible to get rid of the gridlines altogether if you like, but that might make things harder to read.

To create borders around the cells, simply highlight the range of cells you want to apply the border to. You can do this by clicking on the first one and dragging the mouse to highlight the ones you want. Or you can click on the first one, hold down the Shift key, and then click on the last one to highlight them all. Or you can hold down the *Crtl* key and click on individual cells to highlight them one at a time. Figure 4.82 shows the highlighted cells that I will be adding borders to.

Chapter 4 – Google Sheets

	A	B	C	D	E	F	G
1		Cathy	Joe	Lisa	Maria	Steve	Allen
2	Monday	7	8	9	6	8	6
3	Tuesday	8	8	4	8	8	5
4	Wednesday	5	9	5	7	8	3
5	Thursday	6	5	8	7	9	5
6	Friday	9	6	8	8	7	7
7	Saturday	3	0	2	0	5	0
8	Sunday	0	2	2	0	0	3
9							

Figure 4.82

Next, I will go up to the toolbar and find the *Borders* button and click on it to see my available border choices. There are several default styles you can use, which will be black in color, or you can change the border to any color you like and even change the line type to something like dashed or dotted.

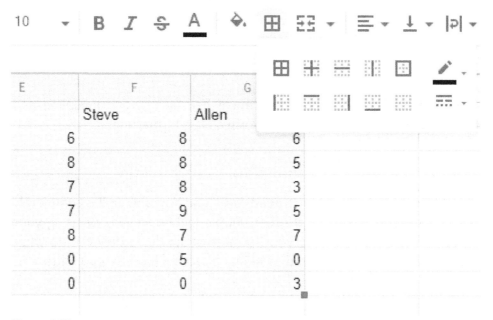

Figure 4.83

I am going to stick with the basic all-sides border, which is the choice on the upper left when you click the Borders button. Figure 4.84 shows the results.

Chapter 4 – Google Sheets

	A	B	C	D	E	F	G
1		Cathy	Joe	Lisa	Maria	Steve	Allen
2	Monday	7	8	9	6	8	6
3	Tuesday	8	8	4	8	8	5
4	Wednesday	5	9	5	7	8	3
5	Thursday	6	5	8	7	9	5
6	Friday	9	6	8	8	7	7
7	Saturday	3	0	2	0	5	0
8	Sunday	0	2	2	0	0	3

Figure 4.84

For my next formatting task I am going to make the employee names bold, then change the font and make them larger so they stand out. To do so I will highlight the names in row 1, and from the toolbar change the font size from 10 to 14, change the font to Oswald, and click the B for **bold**. Figure 4.85 shows the results.

Figure 4.85

	A	B	C	D	E	F	G
1		**Cathy**	**Joe**	**Lisa**	**Maria**	**Steve**	**Allen**
2	Monday	7	8	9	6	8	6
3	Tuesday	8	8	4	8	8	5
4	Wednesday	5	9	5	7	8	3
5	Thursday	6	5	8	7	9	5
6	Friday	9	6	8	8	7	7
7	Saturday	3	0	2	0	5	0
8	Sunday	0	2	2	0	0	3

Figure 4.86

For the days of the week, I want to have them use alternating colors so it's easier to look down each row and keep track of what day we are on. For this I will highlight the range of A1 through G8, go to the Format menu, choose *Alternating colors* (discussed earlier), and will choose the orange theme for this example.

Chapter 4 – Google Sheets

	A	B	C	D	E	F	G
1		Cathy	Joe	Lisa	Maria	Steve	Allen
2	Monday	7	8	9	6	8	6
3	Tuesday	8	8	4	8	8	5
4	Wednesday	5	9	5	7	8	3
5	Thursday	6	5	8	7	9	5
6	Friday	9	6	8	8	7	7
7	Saturday	3	0	2	0	5	0
8	Sunday	0	2	2	0	0	3

Figure 4.87

One thing I now want to add to my table is a title header since I forgot to do that before I entered in my data. So now I need a row above row 1, but obviously there is no row above row 1 since that is the first row. There are a couple of ways I can go about getting a blank row above my table.

The first way involves highlighting the entire table and dragging it down a row so the name Cathy will be in cell B2 and so on. Once the range is highlighted, place your cursor on the edge of the highlighted range until it turns into a hand, and then click and hold while dragging the table down to the next row. Then you can release the mouse button.

D	E	F	G
Lisa	Maria	Steve	Allen
9	6	8	6
4	8	8	5
5	7	8	3
8	7	9	5
8	8	7	7
2	0	5	0
2	0	0	3

Figure 4.88

An easier way to do this would be to right click on the row number you want to add a row above (in this case row 1), and then choose *Insert 1 above*. If you are following along, you might have noticed that the alternating colors stayed at row 1 instead of moving down to row 2.

Chapter 4 – Google Sheets

	A	B	C	D	E	F	G
1							
2		Cathy	Joe	Lisa	Maria	Steve	Allen
3	Monday	7	8	9	6	8	6
4	Tuesday	8	8	4	8	8	5
5	Wednesday	5	9	5	7	8	3
6	Thursday	6	5	8	7	9	5
7	Friday	9	6	8	8	7	7
8	Saturday	3	0	2	0	5	0
9	Sunday	0	2	2	0	0	3
10							

Figure 4.89

I did this to show you that you will need to watch out for things like this when formatting your spreadsheet, and if I were to have made the heading before I started, I wouldn't have this problem. Fortunately, the first method I mentioned will move the alternating colors, so I will undo the last operation by pressing Ctrl-C on my keyboard (Command-Z on a Mac), or I could also go to the Edit menu and choose Undo or even click the left curved arrow on the toolbar.

Now that I have my new blank row above my table, it's time to make the table header. I am going to name this table *Employee Hours*, and will begin by typing that in cell A1. I will then make the text bold and increase the size to 18 pt.

Next, I want to center the table name across the top of the table itself rather than have it in the left hand corner. To do that, I will highlight all of the cells above the table in row 1, then click on the *merge cells* button in the toolbar and choose *Merge all*.

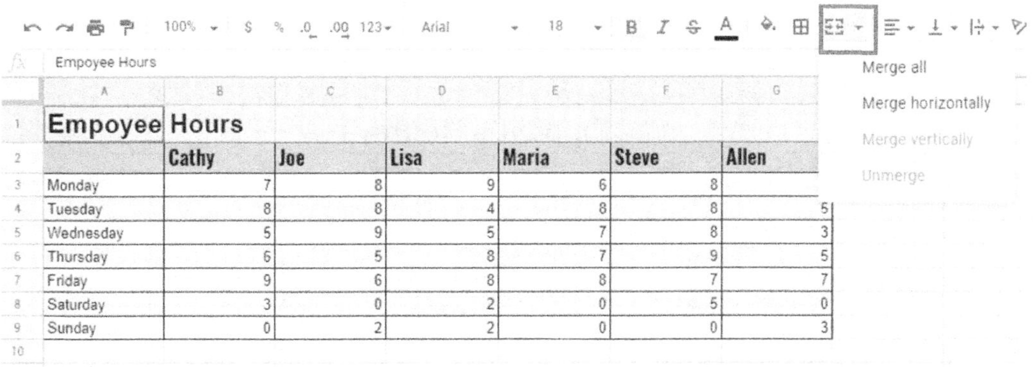

Figure 4.90

Notice how all the gridlines in row 1 are missing? That is because cell A1 has merged across the area that I had highlighted, making it one large cell.

Chapter 4 – Google Sheets

	A	B	C	D	E	F	G
1	Empoyee Hours						
2		Cathy	Joe	Lisa	Maria	Steve	Allen
3	Monday	7	8	9	6	8	6
4	Tuesday	8	8	4	8	8	5
5	Wednesday	5	9	5	7	8	3
6	Thursday	6	5	8	7	9	5
7	Friday	9	6	8	8	7	7
8	Saturday	3	0	2	0	5	0
9	Sunday	0	2	2	0	0	3
10							

Figure 4.91

Now all I need to do is center the text from the *Horizontal align* button on the toolbar, or go to the *Format* menu and choose *Align > Center* as shown in figure 4.92. Figure 4.93 shows the results, and I also decided to fill the header cell with a color to make it stand out a little better.

Figure 4.92

	A	B	C	D	E	F	G
1				Empoyee Hours			
2		Cathy	Joe	Lisa	Maria	Steve	Allen
3	Monday	7	8	9	6	8	6
4	Tuesday	8	8	4	8	8	5
5	Wednesday	5	9	5	7	8	3
6	Thursday	6	5	8	7	9	5
7	Friday	9	6	8	8	7	7
8	Saturday	3	0	2	0	5	0
9	Sunday	0	2	2	0	0	3
10							
11							

Figure 4.93

Performing Calculations and Using Formulas

Now that we have our table looking good and have all the data in there, it's time to start doing some calculations to see how our data is looking in order to make comparisons between employees and get an overall picture of what is really going on with their work.

The first thing I want to do is get the weekly totals for each employee's hours worked. I will begin by adding the word *Totals* to cell A10 since that will be the row where I want my totals to show up. I will also make it bold and apply the bold text format to the rest of the row by highlighting cells A10 through G10 and clicking on the B for bold in the toolbar. Even though there is no text in the other cells yet, I can make them bold for when I do add text.

Since I used the alternating colors row formatting, Sheets will continue the theme each time I add data to a new row, so if that is not what you want, you can manually clear the color for that row or change it to a different color. I am going to change it to the same color I used for my title bar. (And yes, I do realize that if you are reading the paperback version of this book, you won't see the colors, but you can trust me that they're there!)

Another thing I did was highlight cells A10 through G10, went to the *Borders* button on the toolbar then, then to the *Borders style* button and changed it to a double line. This sets the border line style for any borders I make after checking it. Then I choose the top border so it will only apply this double line style to the top of the cells. The result can be seen in figure 4.94. It may be a little hard to tell it's a double line from the image, but you can take my word for it.

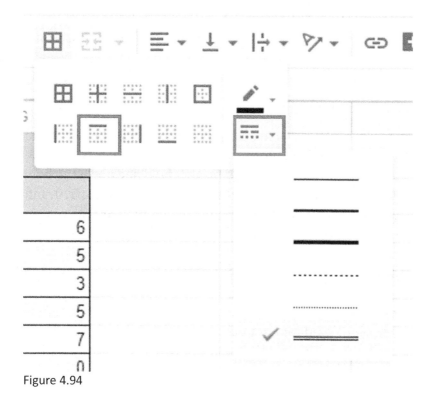

Figure 4.94

	A	B	C	D	E	F	G
1		\multicolumn{6}{c}{Empoyee Hours}					
2		Cathy	Joe	Lisa	Maria	Steve	Allen
3	Monday	7	8	9	6	8	6
4	Tuesday	8	8	4	8	8	5
5	Wednesday	5	9	5	7	8	3
6	Thursday	6	5	8	7	9	5
7	Friday	9	6	8	8	7	7
8	Saturday	3	0	2	0	5	0
9	Sunday	0	2	2	0	0	3
10	Totals						
11							

Figure 4.95

Now that I have everything looking the way I want, it's time to add up the hours for each employee, starting with Cathy. To do this, I am going to use the *SUM* function, which is one of the more commonly used functions in Sheets. First, I will highlight the range of numbers I want to add up, so in this case it will be cells B7 through B9. Then I will go to the *Functions* button on the toolbar and choose *SUM*.

Chapter 4 – Google Sheets

Figure 4.96

Sheets will then show you what it is going to do. In our case it's going to add up cells B3 to B9, and the formula will look like **=SUM(B3:B9),** which you can also see in the fx bar in figure 4.97. You don't have to use the SUM function to do this, and can actually type it in manually if you like. Just be sure to always start your formulas with the = sign.

Chapter 4 – Google Sheets

	A	B	
fx		=SUM(B3:B9)	
		A	B
1			
2			Cathy	J(
3		Monday	7
4		Tuesday	8
5		Wednesday	5
6		Thursday	6
7		Friday	9
8		Saturday	3
9		Sunday	38 × 0
10		Totals	?=SUM(B3:B9)
11			

Figure 4.97

If you like what you see, simply press Enter and you will have the numbers added up for you. If you make any changes to the values, the total will be automatically updated.

	A	B
1		
2		Cathy	J
3	Monday	7
4	Tuesday	8
5	Wednesday	5
6	Thursday	6
7	Friday	9
8	Saturday	3
9	Sunday	0
10	Totals	38

Figure 4.98

Next, I need to do the same thing for each of the remaining employees, but rather than go through that same process again for each one, I am going to copy the formula over to the other cells where I want the formula to go. Once again, I am going to use the autopopulate feature, where I highlight the main cell and click on

Chapter 4 – Google Sheets

the little box in the lower right corner, then drag it across the other cells in row 10 to have it copy the function over. Figure 4.99 shows the results.

	A	Cathy	Joe	Lisa	Maria	Steve	Allen
1				Empoyee Hours			
2		Cathy	Joe	Lisa	Maria	Steve	Allen
3	Monday	7	8	9	6	8	6
4	Tuesday	8	8	4	8	8	5
5	Wednesday	5	9	5	7	8	3
6	Thursday	6	5	8	7	9	5
7	Friday	9	6	8	8	7	7
8	Saturday	3	0	2	0	5	0
9	Sunday	0	1	2	0	0	3
10	Totals	38	37	38	36	45	29
11							

Figure 4.99

For the next task I need to get the average hours worked per day for each employee, so I will add that in row 12 and do my formatting once again to make it look the way I want. Then I will start with Cathy again and click in cell B12 to get started. Once again, I will go to the Functions button, but this time I will choose AVERAGE. If you take a look at figure 4.100 you can see that it is asking me what data I want to get the average for. This is because I didn't select the cells in column B first, but that doesn't mean I can't get the job done.

	A	B	
1			
2		Cathy	Jo
3	Monday	7	
4	Tuesday	8	
5	Wednesday	5	
6	Thursday	6	
7	Friday	9	
8	Saturday	3	
9	Sunday	0	
10	Totals	38	
11			
12	Average	=AVERAGE( )	

Figure 4.100

Chapter 4 – Google Sheets

All I need to do is highlight the range I want (which is B3 through B9, in this case) and it will fill it in for me. If things look good, I just press Enter again and I will have my average (as shown in figure 4.101).

	A	Cathy	Joe
1			
2		**Cathy**	**Joe**
3	Monday	7	
4	Tuesday	8	
5	Wednesday	5	
6	Thursday	6	
7	Friday	9	
8	Saturday	3	
9	Sunday	0	
10	Totals	38	
11		5.428571429 ×	
12	Average	=AVERAGE(B3:B9)	

Figure 4.101

	A	B	
1			
2		**Cathy**	**Joe**
3	Monday	7	
4	Tuesday	8	
5	Wednesday	5	
6	Thursday	6	
7	Friday	9	
8	Saturday	3	
9	Sunday	0	
10	Totals	38	
11			
12	Average	5.428571429	
13			

Figure 4.102

Chapter 4 – Google Sheets

One thing I *don't* like is the number of decimal places that are displayed in the results. To fix that, I am going to click on cell B12 and go to *Format,* and then *Number > Number,* which will shorten the results down to two decimal places. Finally, I will use the autopopulate feature once again to drag my formula and formatting to all the other cells in row 12.

	A	B	C	D	E	F	G
1				Empoyee Hours			
2		Cathy	Joe	Lisa	Maria	Steve	Allen
3	Monday	7	8	9	6	8	6
4	Tuesday	8	8	4	8	8	5
5	Wednesday	5	9	5	7	8	3
6	Thursday	6	5	8	7	9	5
7	Friday	9	6	8	8	7	7
8	Saturday	3	0	2	0	5	0
9	Sunday	0	1	2	0	0	3
10	Totals	38	37	38	36	45	29
11							
12	Average	5.43	5.29	5.43	5.14	6.43	4.14
13							

Figure 4.103

There are many more functions you can do in Sheets, and they get way more advanced, but since this is not an advanced book, I will leave it at that, and you can feel free to try out some of the other functions yourself.

Creating a Chart

Now that we have some data, let's make a chart from it so we can see it in more of a top down graphical view. Charts can be created from the *Insert* menu, and then by choosing *Chart*. Figure 4.104 shows a closer view of the chart options. What you will see here will vary on your data and if you are on that data when you click on the Chart option from the Insert menu.

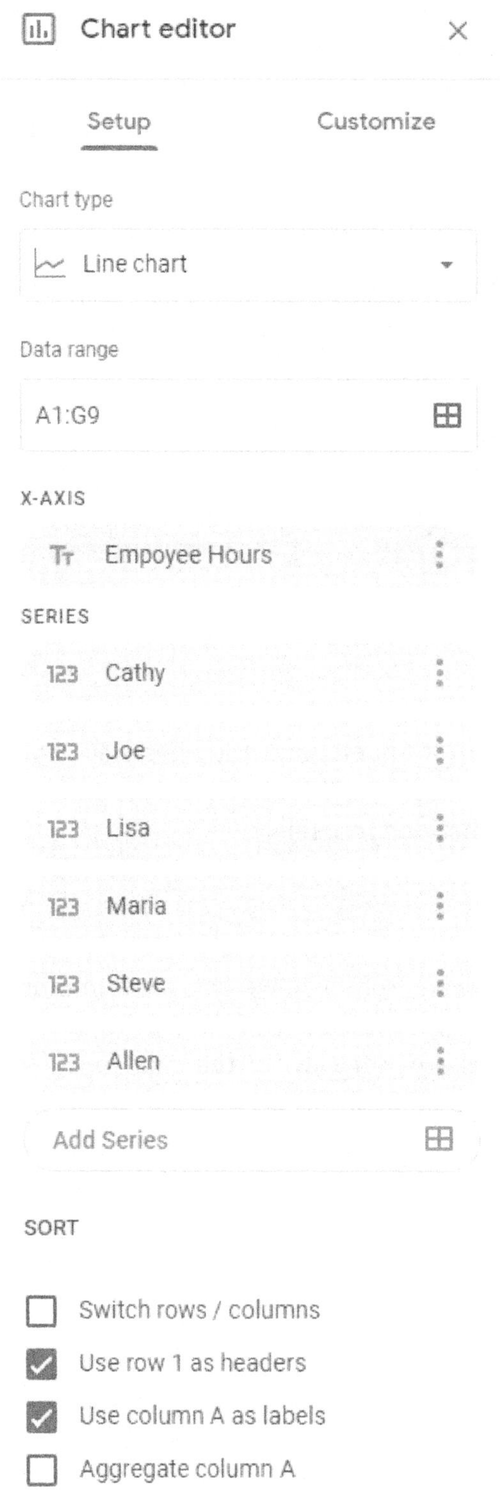

Chapter 4 – Google Sheets

📊 **Chart editor** ✕

Setup   Customize

Chart type

| ~ Line chart ▼ |

Data range

| A1:G9 ⊞ |

X-AXIS

Tr Empoyee Hours ⋮

SERIES

123 Cathy ⋮

123 Joe ⋮

123 Lisa ⋮

123 Maria ⋮

123 Steve ⋮

123 Allen ⋮

| Add Series ⊞ |

SORT

☐ Switch rows / columns
☑ Use row 1 as headers
☑ Use column A as labels
☐ Aggregate column A

Figure 4.104

Chapter 4 – Google Sheets

The Setup options allow you to change various configurations of the chart, such as the chart type and data range. As you can see in figure 4.105, there are many types of charts to choose from. I will be using a Column chart for my example.

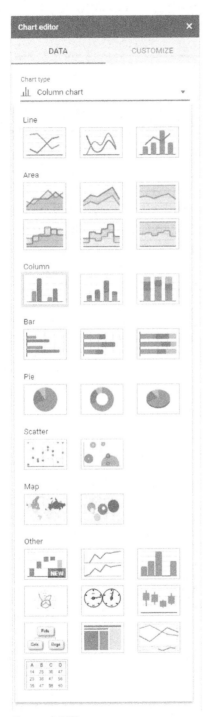

Figure 4.105

Tip: When creating charts, try out different types, but try to stick with a style that makes your data the easiest to read rather than going for the flashy, professional look. The people who have to read the chart will be thankful!

The *Data range* is what you need to focus on to get the right information into your chart. The easiest way to get the data range is to highlight the cells with the information that you want in your chart and Sheets will add it to the *What data* box, or you can just click on one of the cells and let Sheets choose the data for you and see if it selects what you like.

The *Sort* section allows you to change how the data is sorted in your chart. Figures 4.106 and 4.107 show what happens when you check and uncheck the box for *Switch rows/columns*. Can you see the difference between the two?

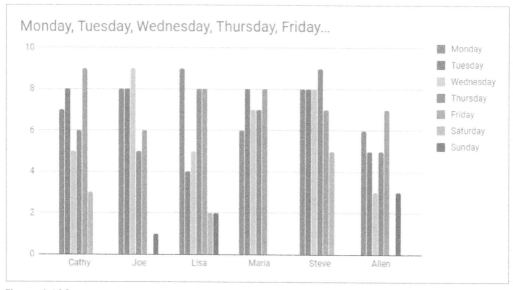

Figure 4.106

Chapter 4 – Google Sheets

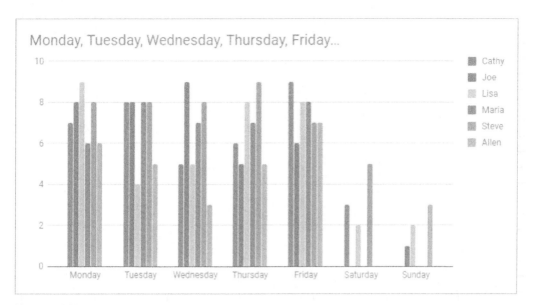

Figure 4.107

The *CUSTOMIZE* section is where you can apply formatting options to your chart (figure 4.108).

Chapter 4 – Google Sheets

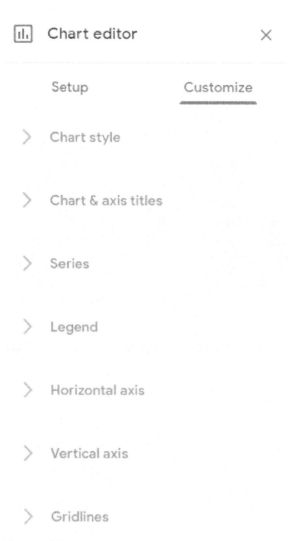

Figure 4.108

Here is a brief rundown of what each customization option will do. I will show you the finished chart after I configure all of the settings.

- **Chart style** – Here you can change things like the background color and chart font, as well as make your chart 3D or have it use compare mode if applicable. I will make the background light green and check the box for the 3D option for my chart.

- **Chart & axis titles** – In this section, you can do things like add a chart name and change the colors and fonts again. I will call my chart "Hours worked per employee" and center the title on the chart.

- **Series** – The *Series* section will let you apply things such as data labels and trendline bars to your chart. Trendlines are lines across the chart that will show increases and decreases in the data. (I won't use them for my chart because it will just make things look messy.) I will add data labels, though, even though it's not the best choice for my chart, but just so you can see how they look.

- **Legend** – Here is where you can customize your legend labels in regards to position, font, and format.

- **Horizontal axis** – If you need to change the formatting of the labels on the horizontal axis, you can do that here. I will make the labels red and italicize the type.

- **Vertical axis** – You can apply the same type of formatting here that you did for the horizontal axis.

- **Gridlines** – Gridlines can be added to the horizontal and\or vertical axis to make things easier to read. For my chart, I will leave only the horizontal gridlines on and not the vertical to keep things less cluttered. You can also change the color and count for the gridlines. For example, in my chart the numbers will be increments of 2 going up to 10.

Now that all my customization is complete, here is what my chart looks like (figure 4.109). I realize it's not the best data that can be used for a chart, but I just wanted to give you an idea of how it worked without making things too complicated. I also realize that if you are reading the paperback version of this book, you won't see the color changes, so you will just have to take my word for it!

Chapter 4 – Google Sheets

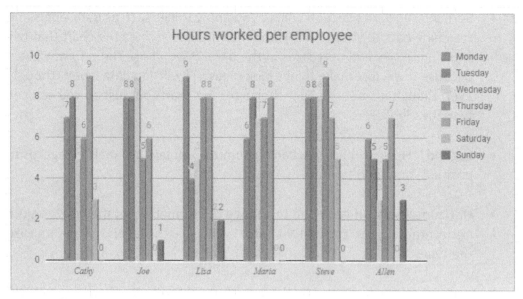

Figure 4.109

Sheets will place the chart inside of your spreadsheet, but you have the option to move it to its own sheet if you like by clicking on the three vertical dots at the top right of the chart and choosing *Move to own sheet* (figure 4.110).

Chapter 4 – Google Sheets

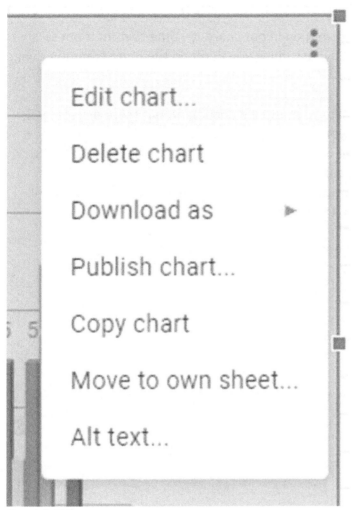

Figure 4.110

You can also do things such as download the chart as an image or PDF file and even publish it to the Internet for others to view. If you decide to publish your chart, it will work the same way as if you were publishing a document, where you will be given a link to that chart that you can send out to other people so they can view the chart.

Printing a Spreadsheet

Now that we have all the information in our chart, it's time to print it out so others can have their own copy (assuming you don't do the more common thing, which would be to email it).

Printing a spreadsheet is similar to printing a document, but there are some Sheets specific options that you can choose from when printing. The first one I want to mention is at the top where it says *Print* (as seen in figure 4.111). You have the choice to print the current sheet that you are on, or you can also choose to only print cells that you have highlighted, or the entire spreadsheet (workbook) if you have more than one sheet.

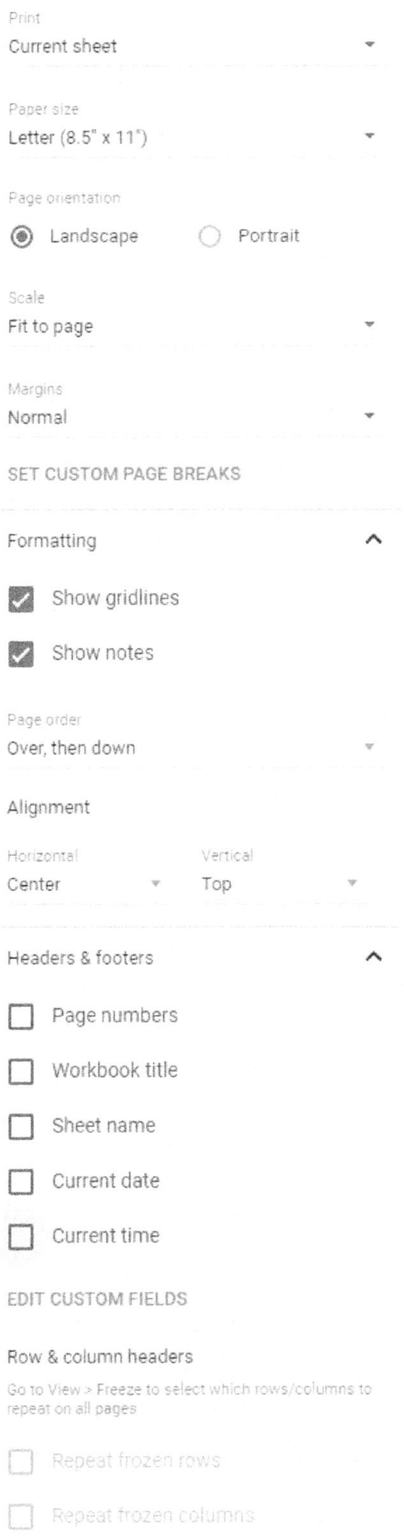

Chapter 4 – Google Sheets

Print
Current sheet

Paper size
Letter (8.5" x 11")

Page orientation
◉ Landscape   ○ Portrait

Scale
Fit to page

Margins
Normal

SET CUSTOM PAGE BREAKS

Formatting ˄

☑ Show gridlines

☑ Show notes

Page order
Over, then down

Alignment

Horizontal   **Vertical**
Center   Top

Headers & footers ˄

☐ Page numbers

☐ Workbook title

☐ Sheet name

☐ Current date

☐ Current time

EDIT CUSTOM FIELDS

Row & column headers
Go to View > Freeze to select which rows/columns to repeat on all pages

☐ Repeat frozen rows

☐ Repeat frozen columns

Figure 4.111

Chapter 4 – Google Sheets

Sheets will give you a print preview so you can see how your spreadsheet will look when printed. You might notice that your sheet doesn't fit correctly on one page and will be spilt into two separate pages for printing (figure 4.112). If that's the case, then you can go to the *Scale* section and choose to fit to the page height or width, or have it fit to the page itself, which will make it smaller on the paper but make everything fit on one page.

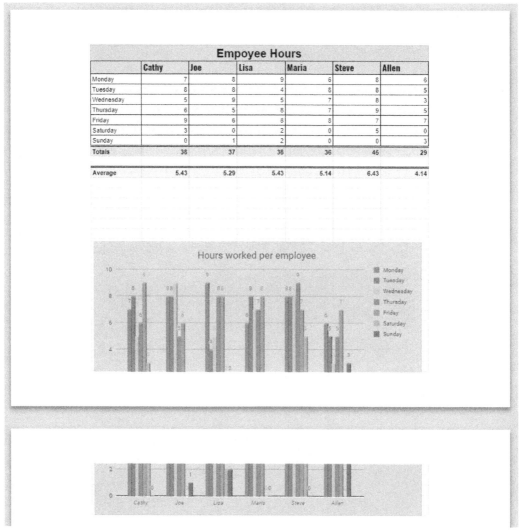

Figure 4.112

Under the *Formatting* section, you can choose whether or not to have gridlines or notes printed out with your spreadsheet. You can also change things such as the page order and alignment.

Chapter 4 – Google Sheets

If you have added things like headers, footers, or page numbers, you can have them printed as well by checking the appropriate boxes under the *Headers & footers section*. Many people also like to include things such as the date or workbook name in their printouts to make things easier to track, so those are options as well.

If you use any row or column headers that you have frozen to make things easier to read, then you can have those repeated on each page so that there is a header on every page. To freeze a row or column, all you need to is select the row or column, go to the *View* menu, and then click on *Freeze* and choose what you want to freeze.

Freezing comes in handy if you have a table with a large number of rows or columns and you want the headers\titles to stay visible when you scroll down or across the sheet. In my example it was not necessary, but I will freeze rows 1 and 2 to show you how it works.

If you take a look at figure 4.113, you will see the underline that starts under the number 2 of row 2 and goes all the way across. That is where I have frozen the rows on this sheet. Also, notice how it goes from row 2 to row 5 and Monday to Wednesday because I have scrolled the table up while the Employee Hours and name rows stay stationary. Just imagine how this would come in handy if you had hundreds of rows of data that you needed to scroll through while keeping track of which employees' data you were looking at.

	A	B	C	D	E	F	G
1		Empoyee Hours					
2		Cathy	Joe	Lisa	Maria	Steve	Allen
5	Wednesday	5	9	5	7	8	3
6	Thursday	6	5	8	7	9	5
7	Friday	9	6	8	8	7	7
8	Saturday	3	0	2	0	5	0
9	Sunday	0	1	2	0	0	3
10	Totals	38	37	38	36	45	29
11							
12	Average	5.43	5.29	5.43	5.14	6.43	4.14
13							

Figure 4.113

Chapter 5 – Google Slides

Slides Interface

If you have ever used Microsoft PowerPoint to create presentations, then using Google Slides should be pretty easy to get the hang of. If you have *never* used presentation software, then you may still find Slides easy to use since there's not a whole lot to it (unless your plan is to get super fancy and make a big production out of your presentation).

Slides is basically an app you can use to create a slide show presentation that you can show on things like a projector, website, or even email to someone else to view. Plus, you can also print out your slides if you want to have handouts for your audience to review later.

The Slides interface consists of the slide you are working on, plus a thumbnail view of the other slides within your presentation. And, of course, there are menu items and a toolbar with buttons that let you perform various actions.

Chapter 5 – Google Slides

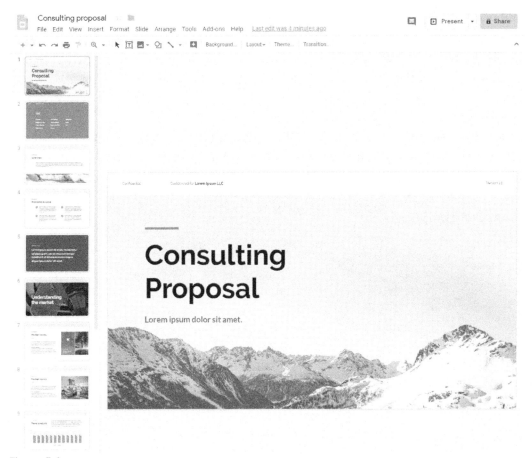

Figure 5.1

To navigate between slides, all you need to do is click on the thumbnail view of the one you want to work on, and it will become active in the main window.

There are various templates you can use as well as themes that you can apply to your presentation (which I will be going over when I get to the formatting section). And just like with the other Google Apps, you can share your presentation with other users and allow them to view it, as well as make changes to it.

Slides allows you to do things such as add pictures, videos, website links, charts, tables, animations, and so on to your presentation, which gives you the ability to keep people's interest rather than putting them to sleep with just plain old text. You also have the ability to view your slides as a full screen presentation at any time while working in Slides. You can use the mouse, keyboard, or even a remote to move through the slides during your presentation.

Chapter 5 – Google Slides

Slides Specific Menu Items

Once again, I would like to begin the chapter with the menu items that are specific to Google Slides, which will give you a much better understanding of what Slides is capable of creating.

File Menu

As you can see in figure 5.2, the File menu doesn't have anything new on it except for the *Import slides* option. Everything else is pretty standard, and I have discussed it already.

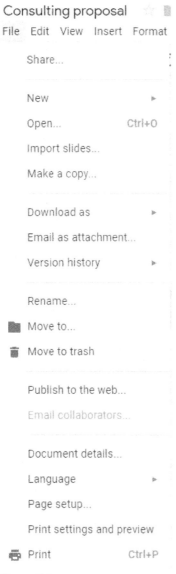

Figure 5.2

Chapter 5 – Google Slides

When you use the *Import slides* option, you will have the option to insert slides from one of your other presentations, upload an existing slide, or even a Microsoft PowerPoint presentation.

Figure 5.3

Once you choose a presentation to import, you will be able to select what specific slides you want to import, or you can just import all of them.

Edit Menu
The Edit menu does not contain anything new that we haven't seen before in Docs or Sheets.

View Menu
The View menu will allow you to change how your presentation is shown on the screen, which makes it easier to fine tune and perfect it before showing it to an audience (figure 5.4).

227

Chapter 5 – Google Slides

```
View   Insert   Format   Slide   Arrange
       Present                    Ctrl+F5

       Animations      Ctrl+Alt+Shift+B

       Master
       Grid view              Ctrl+Alt+1

       Zoom                           ▸
       Show ruler
       Guides                         ▸
       Snap to                        ▸

   ✓   Show speaker notes

       Full screen
```

Figure 5.4

Even though there are not a lot of choices here, you should still know what each of them is used for.

- **Present** – Choosing the *Present* option will start playing your presentation as a slide show, the same way you would see it if you were showing the finished product at a meeting (etc.).

- **Animations** – Here you can view the animations that you have applied to objects (such as pictures or text) in your presentation (figure 5.5). I will be going over how to create the animations later in the chapter.

Figure 5.5

- **Master** – The Master slide is responsible for keeping a consistent format and structure throughout your presentation (figure 5.6). If you want to edit this master slide, you can do so here, and then apply your new format to all of your slides.

Figure 5.6

- **Grid view** – If you want to have your slides displayed in a grid view, then that is easy to do with the *Grid view* option. This can make it easier to get an overview of all of your slides and how they are laid out. From here you can drag and drop your slides to rearrange their order. If you want to view or edit a specific slide, all you need to is double click it, and it will open in the normal view.

Chapter 5 – Google Slides

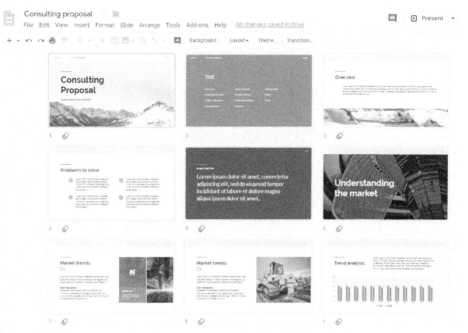

Figure 5.7

- **Zoom** – This feature lets you zoom in and out of your presentation when you need to get a closer look at something.

- **Show ruler** – Just like with Docs, you can have Slides show a ruler on the top and left hand side of your slides that can be used to measure things such as picture sizes and so on.

- **Guides** – Guides can be used to help you align text and images so that everything looks properly formatted within your slides. You can also change the guide colors if you need something that stands out a bit more. You can insert multiple vertical or horizontal guides and then move them around to wherever they are needed.

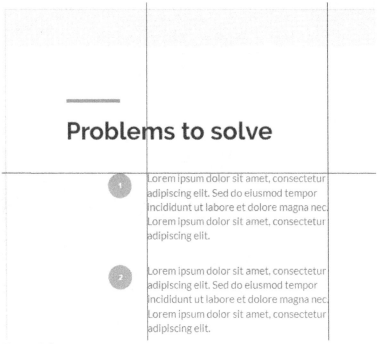

Figure 5.8

- **Snap to** – This feature will make your objects snap to their guidelines when moving them around, which allows you to place these objects exactly where you want them to be.

- **Speaker notes** – You can add *Speaker notes* to the bottom of individual slides so that you can remind yourself about things you want to say during your presentation. When you start your slideshow in presentation mode, you just need to click on the gear icon in the toolbar and choose *Open speaker notes* to have them displayed on your screen (figure 5.9).

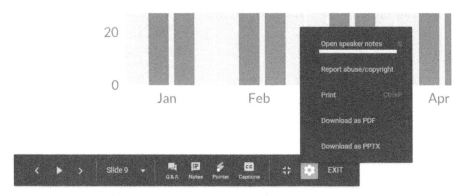

Figure 5.9

Chapter 5 – Google Slides

These notes will only be visible to you, so you don't need to worry about others knowing you needed notes for your presentation!

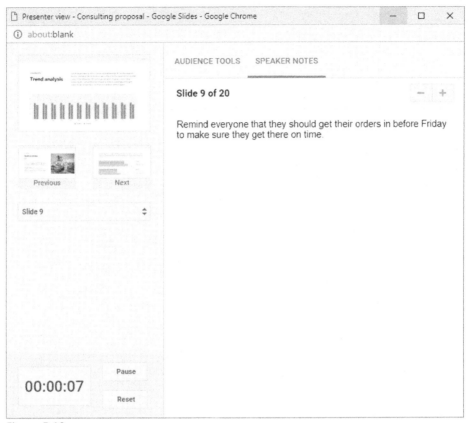

Figure 5.10

- **Full screen** – Full screen simply shows your slide in a larger view and hides the toolbar and menu items. To get back to the normal view, all you need to do is press the Esc key on your keyboard.

Insert Menu

The Insert menu in Slides contains quite a few things you can place into your slideshow to help give it a little more pizazz, and can be used to help keep people interested (figure 5.11).

Chapter 5 – Google Slides

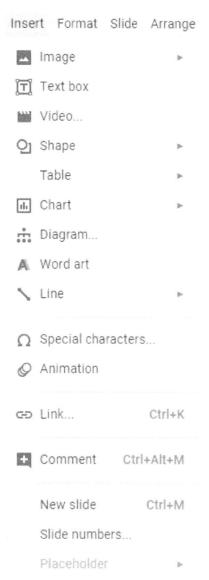

Figure 5.11

Most of these options are easy to use, and it doesn't take too much effort to make an exciting presentation. Now I would like to go over the Slides specific *Insert menu* choices.

- **Text box** – Slides doesn't work the same as other apps (like Docs) when you want to insert text. You can't just simply click where you like and start typing. Instead, you need to insert a text box and *then* enter your text within that box. Then you can drag your text box to any spot within your slide.

Chapter 5 – Google Slides

Figure 5.12

- **Video** – Slides makes it easy to insert videos within your presentation that you can then play within the slide itself while presenting. You can choose from YouTube videos, videos from other sites\URLs, and also videos from your Google Drive.

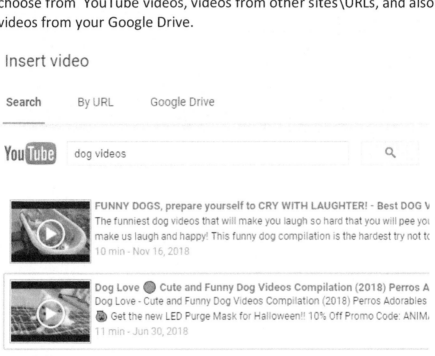

Figure 5.13

 To play most video clips during your presentation, you will need to have an active Internet connection, since Slides will be streaming the video from its online location.

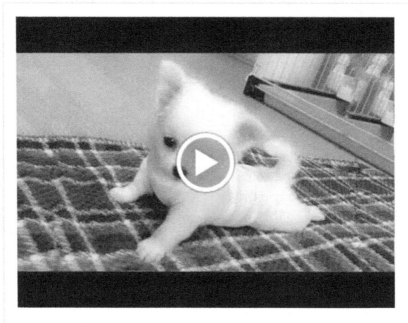

This is the text that I have typed within my text box.

Figure 5.14

- **Shape** – *Shapes* can be used to do things like add boxes around text and images, arrows to point at certain objects, smiley faces, and so on. There are four categories to choose from, and they are *Shapes, Arrows, Callouts,* and *Equations*.

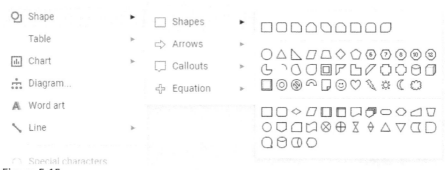

Figure 5.15

- **Diagram** – You can insert diagrams into your slides and then customize them with any text and colors you like to make them stand out even more. Sheets offers several types of diagrams, such as *grid, hierarchy, process, relationship,* and *cycle,* and within each category you will have several variations to choose from (figure 5.16).

Chapter 5 – Google Slides

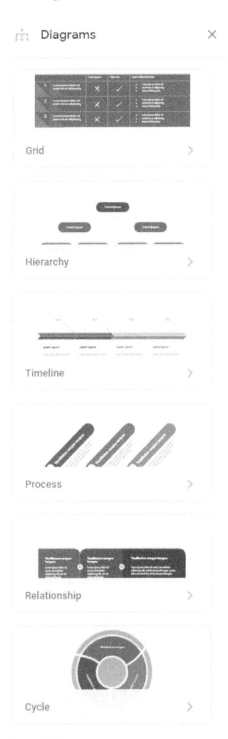

Figure 5.16

Once you add your diagram to your slide, all you need to do is edit it to suit your needs.

Chapter 5 – Google Slides

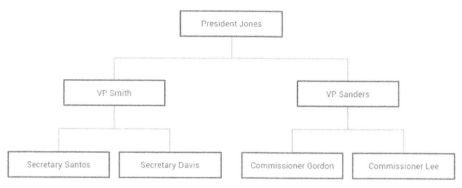

Figure 5.17

- **Line** – Inserting a *Line* is similar to inserting a shape, and Slides has several types to choose from. Once you insert your line, you can then edit it within the slide itself (which I will demonstrate later in the chapter).

Figure 5.18

- **Animation** – I discussed animations earlier in this chapter, and, once again, Slides will let you apply an animation to almost any object within your presentation. When using animations, you can have the process happen when you click the mouse, after the previous animation, or at the same time as the previous animation. There are several types of animations to choose from, plus you can control how quickly the objects move during the animation (figure 5.19).

238

Chapter 5 – Google Slides

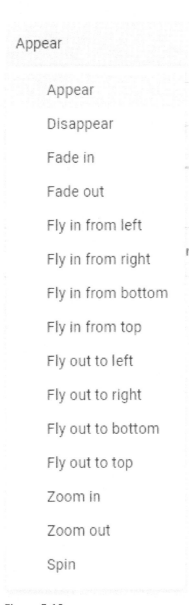

Figure 5.19

- **New slide** – This will insert a new slide after the slide that you're currently on.

- **Slide numbers** – If you want to have your slides numbered, then you can do so from the *Slide numbers* menu item.

- **Placeholder** – Placeholders can be used with your slide master to provide a place to do things such as suggesting where to add text when you add a new slide to your presentation.

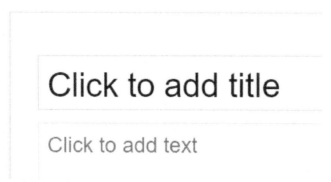

Figure 5.20

Format Menu

Even though I will have a section on formatting your presentation, I still want to go over the format menu itself since that will make the formatting section easier to follow.

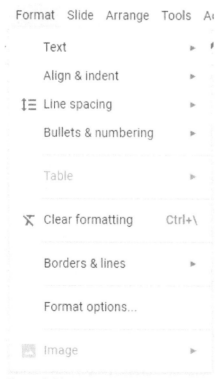

Figure 5.21

Chapter 5 – Google Slides

The Format menu in Slides is not too involved, but there are still a couple of Slides specific items that you should know about.

- **Borders & Lines** – I have discussed borders and lines before, but when you create things such as text boxes in Slides, you usually don't want a border around it at all, so here is where you can go to add or remove them by adjusting the options such as *Border color*.

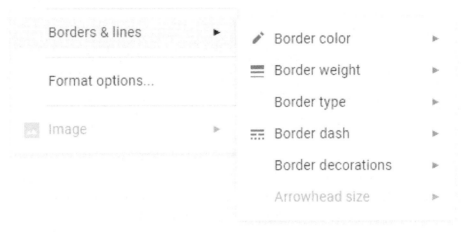

Figure 5.22

- **Format options** – Here you can change many of the formatting options for things such as Size & Position, Text fitting, Drop shadow, and Reflection (figure 5.23). Each of these categories has a variety of adjustments you can perform to fine tune the way your presentation looks. I will go over these in more detail when we create our own presentation from scratch.

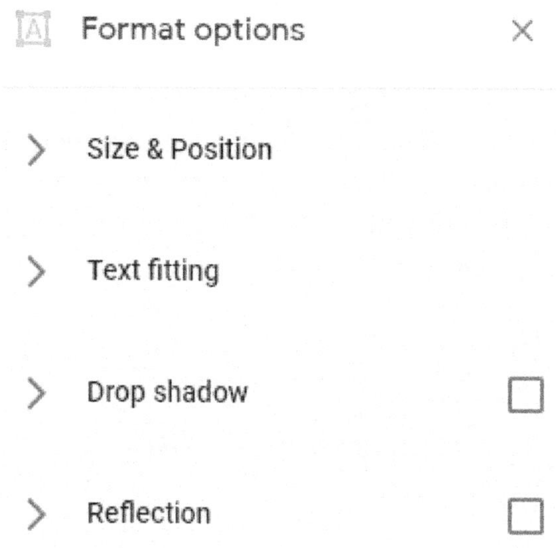

Format options	✕
› Size & Position	
› Text fitting	
› Drop shadow	☐
› Reflection	☐

Figure 5.23

- **Image** – You will most likely be adding images to your presentations, and need to be able to adjust them as needed. The Image option allows you to do this, and has other choices such as the ability to crop, replace, or reset your image. When you have an image selected, the Format options I just talked about will change as well (as you can see in figure 5.24).

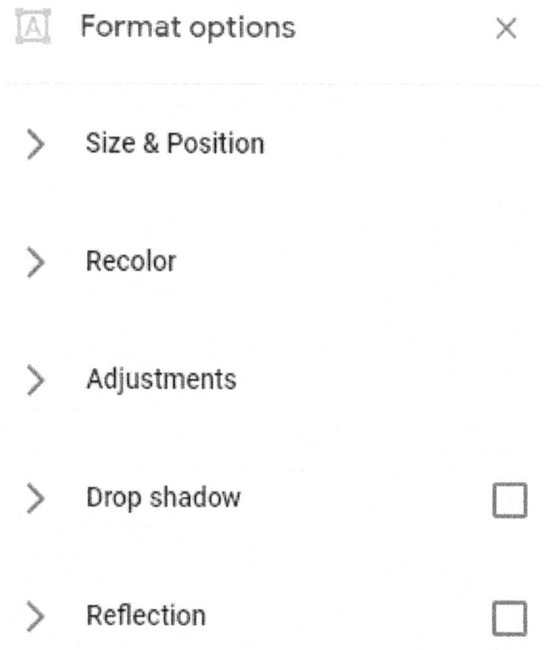

Format options	✕
› Size & Position	
› Recolor	
› Adjustments	
› Drop shadow	☐
› Reflection	☐

Figure 5.24

Chapter 5 – Google Slides

Slide Menu

This menu is obviously specific to Google Slides since it's called *Slides,* so I will be going over all of the items in this menu.

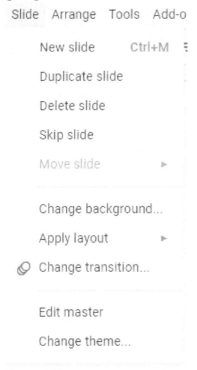

Figure 5.25

Figure 5.25 shows all of the available options, which I will now go over in more detail:

- **New slide** – This will insert a new slide after the slide that you are currently working on. It will be based on your master template, so if you are using the default, it will have a section called "Click to add title" and also a section called "Click to add subtitle". You can delete both of these sections if you don't need them.

- **Duplicate slide** – If you have created a slide and want an exact copy of that slide, then you can use the *Duplicate slide* option to make a copy of it. It will be placed after the existing slide.

- **Delete slide** – Choosing this option will delete the slide that you are currently on, so make sure you're on the one you want to delete before doing so!

- **Skip slide** – When it comes time to show your presentation, there may be some slides that you don't want to be shown or are not relevant to a particular audience. You can use the *Skip slide* option to have those slides be skipped when showing your presentation. To skip a slide, all you need to do is be on that slide and choose the Skip slide option, and it will put an icon of an eye with a cross through it telling you those slides will be skipped. If you take a look at figure 5.26, you will see that I set slides two and four to be skipped. To change the slide back to viewable, simply go back to the Slide menu and uncheck *Skip slide*.

Chapter 5 – Google Slides

Figure 5.26

- **Change background** – With Slide, you are not stuck with a boring white background, unless that's what you are looking for. You can change the background to be a different location, or even an image from your computer, Google Drive, or a website. I changed the background for my diagram slide to a cloudy sky image and then adjusted the colors of the text and lines to make things stand out a little better (figure 5.27).

Chapter 5 – Google Slides

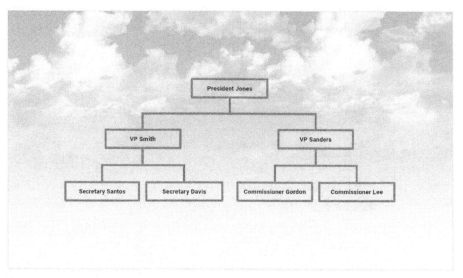

Figure 5.27

- **Apply layout** – Slides comes with a bunch of built-in layouts that you can apply to your slides, making it easier to keep them consistent and to give you some options as to how you can layout the information in your slides. When you choose the *Apply layout* menu item, you will be presented with your available slide layout choices. I like to use the *Blank* layout because I like to create my slides from scratch.

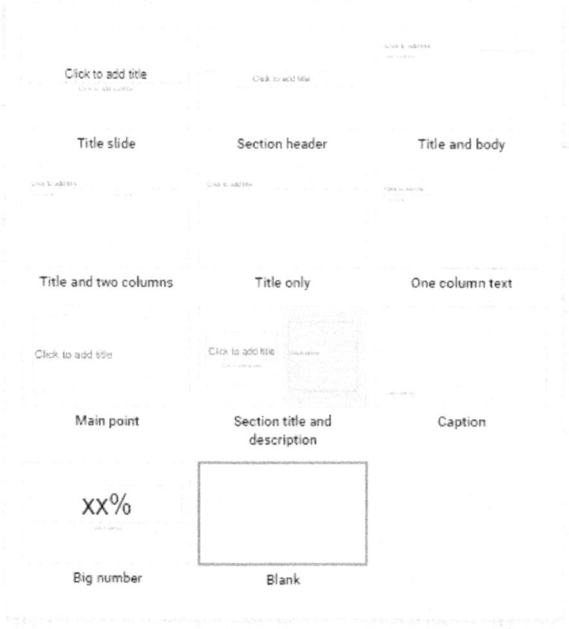

Figure 5.28

- **Change transition** – Transitions are used to apply effects between slides such as a slide in, fade, or flip and the Change transition option will let you add, remove, or edit your slide transitions.

- **Edit master** – I mentioned the master slide earlier in the chapter, and it is used to apply a standard and consistent format to the slides in your presentation. If you want to edit your master slide layout, then you can do so from here.

- **Change theme** – Themes are used to apply a particular look and feel to your presentation, and they can include things like custom colors, graphics, and text. You can use one of the many built in themes in Slides to apply to your presentation to give it a more professional look without a lot of extra work. Figure 5.29 shows some of the available themes that you can choose from.

Chapter 5 – Google Slides

Figure 5.29

Chapter 5 – Google Slides

 Just like I have mentioned with other Google Apps, you don't want to go crazy on the formatting, pictures, and colors because it will take away from the real content of your presentation.

Arrange Menu
When you have objects in your slides such as text, images, charts, and so on, they will need to be arranged in a certain order so everything looks correct. This is what you can do from the various options on the Arrange menu.

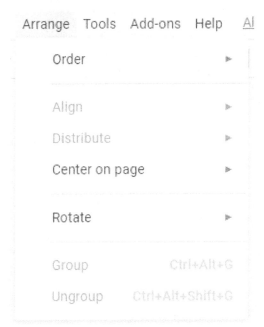

Figure 5.30

When using these menu items, you will notice that some are active and some are inactive (greyed out) depending on what you are trying to do.

- **Order** – The Order option will allow you to set objects forward and backward on your slide so certain objects are behind or in front of other objects. For example, I have set the text in figure 5.31 to the *Bring to front* setting so it will be on top of the picture.

249

Chapter 5 – Google Slides

Figure 5.31

There is also a setting called *Bring forward,* which will bring it one level forward rather than all the way to the front. This comes in handy when you have multiple "layers" of objects on top of each other. The same goes for sending objects to the back.

- **Align** – The *Align* option will let you arrange your objects to the left, center, right, top, middle, or bottom of each other when you have more than one object.

- **Distribute** – This option will let you distribute your objects either horizontally or vertically with each other when you have more than one object.

- **Center on page** – This option will let you distribute your objects either horizontally or vertically on the page\slide.

- **Rotate** – Slides will let you rotate your objects 90 degrees clockwise or counterclockwise as well as flip them vertically and horizontally. Figure 5.32 shows an example of an image being flipped horizontally.

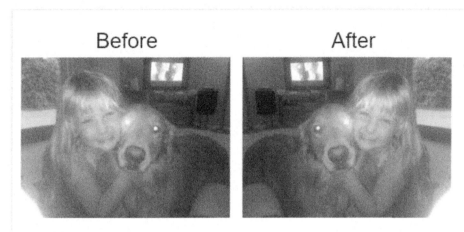

Figure 5.32

- **Group** – Many times you will have multiple objects (such as pictures and text boxes) that you would like to have grouped into one object to make them easier to move and resize (etc.). To do that, simply highlight all the objects you want to group using the mouse and Shift or Ctrl key, and then click on *Group* from the *Slides* menu.

- **Ungroup** – If you decided that you need to ungroup your objects, then highlight the grouped object and choose the Ungroup option.

Tools Menu
The Tools menu in Slides is pretty short, and has many of the same items I have already discussed, but does have a couple of interesting items (figure 5.33).

Chapter 5 – Google Slides

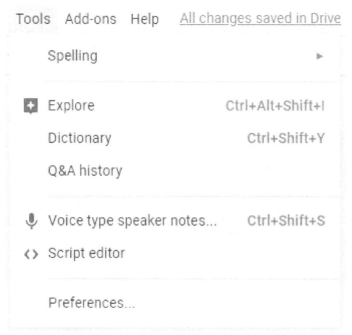

Figure 5.33

Out of the list of available options, there are two new ones that I will be discussing.

- **Q&A History** – This feature is used to answer questions submitted by people viewing your presentation as it's happening. If you decide to allow questions to be posted by viewers, you would simply send out a link that they can connect to and start posting their questions (as you can see in figure 5.34). You can also decide when you stop accepting questions and whether or not the audience can see the questions.

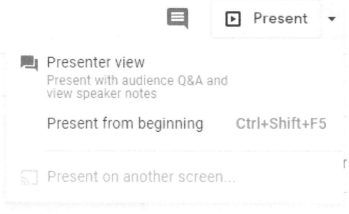

Figure 5.34

252

Chapter 5 – Google Slides

When you use *Presenter view* you will see questions that your viewers have submitted.

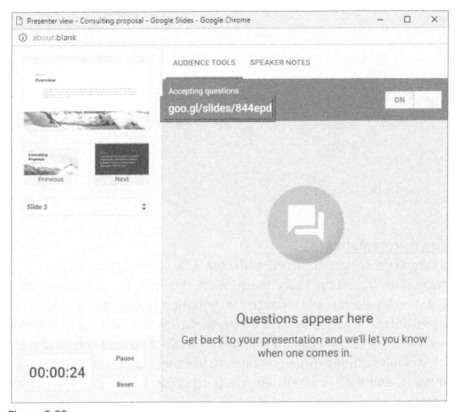

Figure 5.35

- **Voice type speaker notes** – If you have a microphone or are using Slides on your tablet or smartphone, you can use the *Voice type speaker notes* feature to speak into your device and type using the voice to text feature. You can also use various voice commands with this method, such as selecting text and formatting.

Chapter 5 – Google Slides

Figure 5.36

Creating a Presentation

It's finally time to get to work and create a presentation that will wow our audience and hopefully keep them awake! I will be starting with a blank presentation so we can add all of the information to see how it's done. To start a blank presentation, go to File > New > Presentation. You will see a new blank slide, although it's not really blank. It will have the *Click to add title* and *Click to add subtitle* default sections. You don't have to use these sections and can delete them if you want, and that is what I am going to do so I can start with a truly blank presentation.

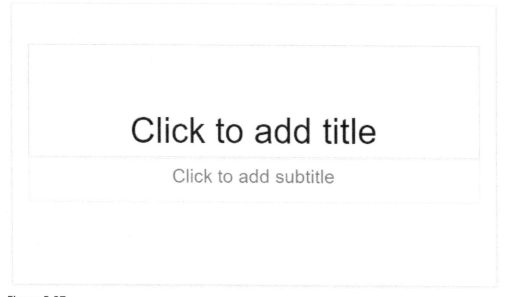

Figure 5.37

254

Chapter 5 – Google Slides

I am going to make the first slide my title slide, and will call it *July Sales Presentation*. To begin with, I will need to add a text box so I have somewhere to type. (Keep in mind that I also could have easily typed over the section called *Click to add title* and started from there.)

To create a text box, I can either go to the *Insert* menu and choose *Text box,* or click on the text box icon in the toolbar shown in figure 5.38. Then I will hold down the mouse button (if on a computer) and drag to draw out the approximate size of my text box. Then I can type in my title text (figure 5.39).

Figure 5.38

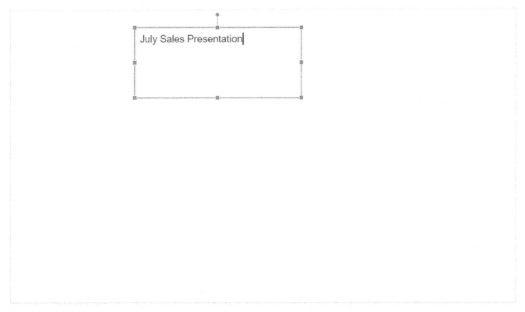

Figure 5.39

I am not going to worry about making it pretty until I get to the formatting section, which is coming up next.

Chapter 5 – Google Slides

Then I will make another text box at the bottom of the slide and add the text *"Presented by James Bernstein"*. Notice how the last word is put on the second line? That's because the text box is not wide enough to fit the whole line.

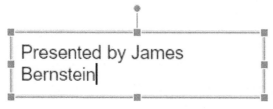

Figure 5.40

This is really easy to fix. All I need to do is click and hold on one of the squares to drag and resize the text box, and Slides will automatically adjust the text to make it fit.

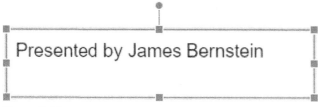

Figure 5.41

Now that I have the title slide complete, it's time to add another slide so I can start adding the information for my presentation. This can be done from the *Insert* menu by choosing *New slide,* or you can click on the + symbol above your slide list to add a new slide (figure 5.42).

Chapter 5 – Google Slides

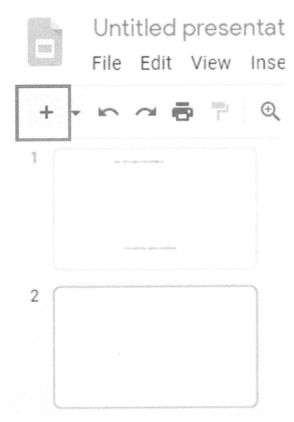

Figure 5.42

Slides will then insert a new slide below the current slide, and it will contain the *Click to add title* and *Click to add text* sections unless you were to choose *Blank* from the dropdown list, which is what I am going to do.

Next, I am going to insert a chart from a Sheets spreadsheet into the new slide showing some sales figures from three sales teams. To do so, I will go to the *Insert* menu, then choose *Chart,* and then select *From Sheets*. Then Slides will bring up a list of your available Sheets files (if you have any) and you can select the one you want to insert. In my case I will insert the one called *Sales Data* (figure 5.43).

Chapter 5 – Google Slides

Figure 5.43

Now I have my chart imported into my sheet. I chose the option to link it to the spreadsheet because that way it will update the chart in my presentation to match whatever changes I make on my spreadsheet.

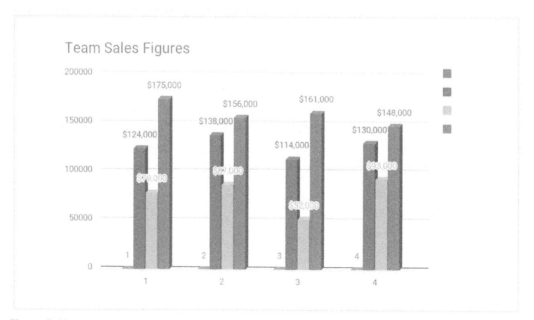

Figure 5.44

Chapter 5 – Google Slides

For my next slide, I will insert a video that can be played within the slide during the presentation. To start I will once again add a new blank sheet. Then I will go to the Insert menu and choose Video and search YouTube for a video on sales techniques. Finally, I will choose the one I was looking for and click on the Select button.

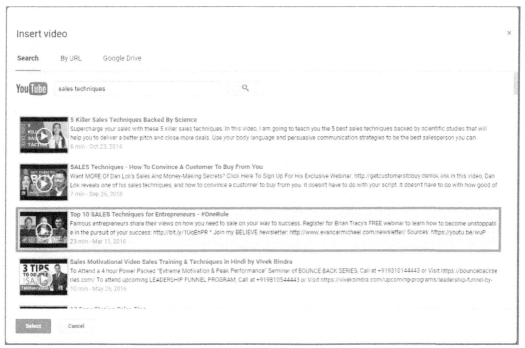

Figure 5.45

Remember that you can also paste in a URL (address) to another online video, or select one from your Google Drive if you have any stored there.

Now I will insert an arrow pointing to the video from the Insert > Shape menu and add some text that says "Very informative sales video". Then, just for fun, I want to insert a thumbs up image under the text. To do that, I go to *Insert* and then *Image* and choose *Search the web* since I don't have any thumbs up images on my computer or Google Drive.

Chapter 5 – Google Slides

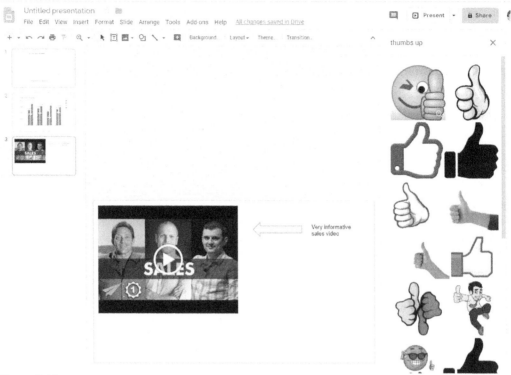

Figure 5.46

I will choose the very first image with the winking emoji and then click on *Insert* at the bottom of the screen. Here is what I end up with.

Figure 5.47

Chapter 5 – Google Slides

Finally, I will change the name of my presentation from *Untitled presentation* to *July Sales Presentation*, and as you can see in figure 5.48, I now have three slides in total. (In reality, you will most likely have more than three slides, but this is just for demonstration purposes.)

Figure 5.48

Formatting a Presentation
It is now time to take all of the work we have been doing on our presentation and make it look a little better so it doesn't look like it was created in five minutes. This is where formatting comes into play. There are several ways to format a presentation to make it look more professional, but the key is not to overdo it and make it look like you wanted to try every formatting option available.

261

Chapter 5 – Google Slides

I will begin by formatting the title text in slide one to make it fit the slide a little better and make it easier to read. The first thing I want to do is make it so the text is centered on the slide. One way to do this is to click and drag on the text box itself and move it to the center of the slide where a red vertical line will appear, allowing you to line up the center square on the text box with that vertical line.

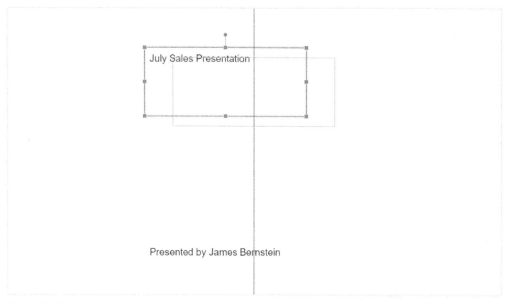

Figure 5.49

An easier way (in my opinion) is to make the text box the entire width of the slide and then center the text within the text box using the *Align* button on the toolbar, or the *Align and indent* option from the *Format* menu.

Chapter 5 – Google Slides

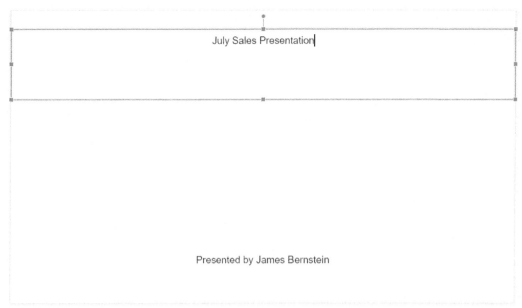

Figure 5.50

Next, I will change the font size and type for the title of the presentation.

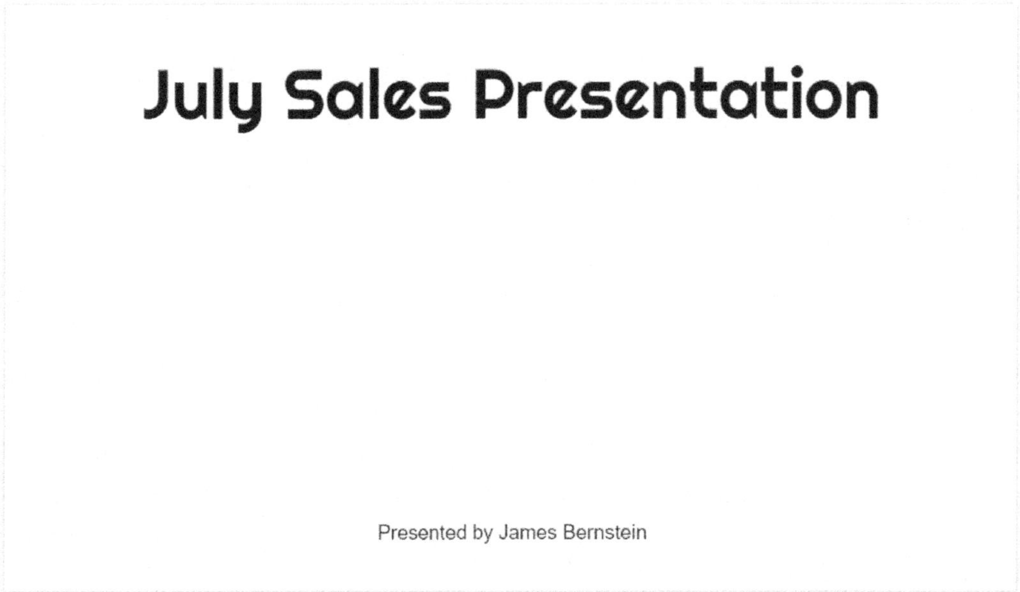

July Sales Presentation

Presented by James Bernstein

Figure 5.51

Now I will change the background color to green and add my company logo to the background of the first slide. To change the background color for all the slides at once, simply click on the first slide, hold down the Shift key, and click on the

Chapter 5 – Google Slides

last slide and they should all be highlighted. Next click on *Background* in the toolbar, then pick your color and click on *Done*.

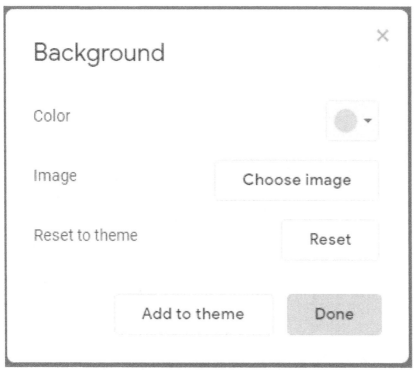

Figure 5.52

To add my company logo to the first slide, all I need to do is go to that slide and then to the *Insert* menu and choose *Image*. In my case, I'll choose *Upload from computer,* since that is where my logo file is located. Then I will browse my local hard drive to find the logo and click on *Open*.

From there I can format my logo image to make it look better on the slide. With the image highlighted, go to *Format options* on the toolbar or from the Format menu. As you can see in figure 5.53, there are many ways you can format your images. I will choose the *Transparency* option from the *Adjustments* section to make the image seem slightly transparent so it blends better into the background. You can see the results in figure 5.54.

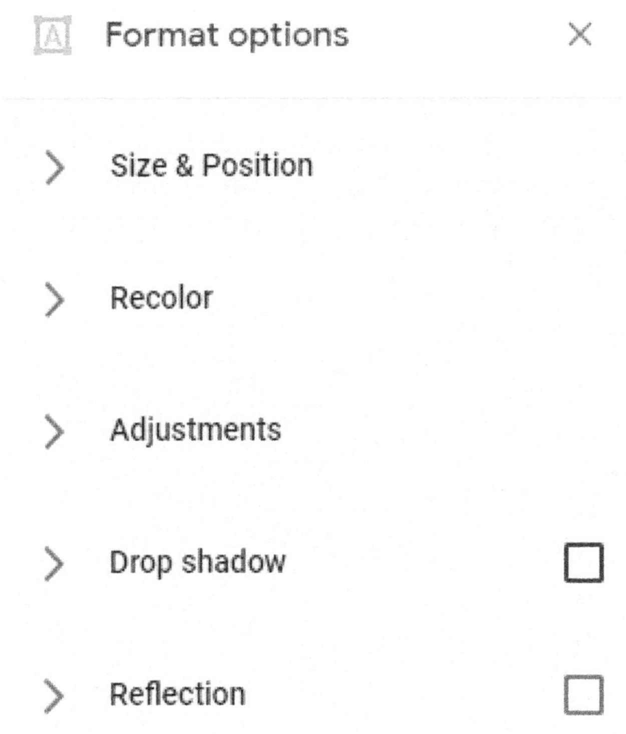

Chapter 5 – Google Slides

> [A] Format options   ✕

> Size & Position

> Recolor

> Adjustments

> Drop shadow   ☐

> Reflection   ☐

Figure 5.53

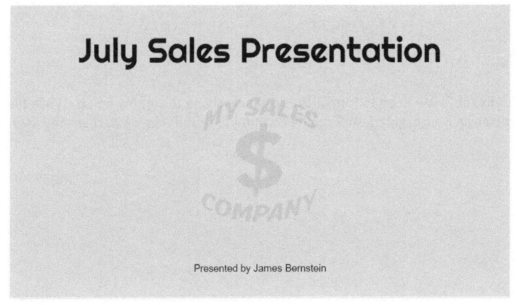

Figure 5.54

Applying a theme will add a little spice to your slides, but I find that many of them are a little overbearing and complicate the look of the slides with useless graphics.

However, I do think I want to add a border around the title slide just to make it stand out a little more. Slides will let you put borders around text and other objects, but I want a border around the entire slide itself, so to do that I am going to draw a box manually. I will go to the *Insert* menu and select *Shape,* and then choose a rectangle shape. Then I will draw the border around the inside of the slide using the mouse. As you can see, Slides will fill the border, which covers up the contents of the slide.

Figure 5.55

To fix this, I will need to format the rectangle shape to suit my needs. While the rectangle is highlighted, click on the *Format* menu and then on *Borders and lines*.

Chapter 5 – Google Slides

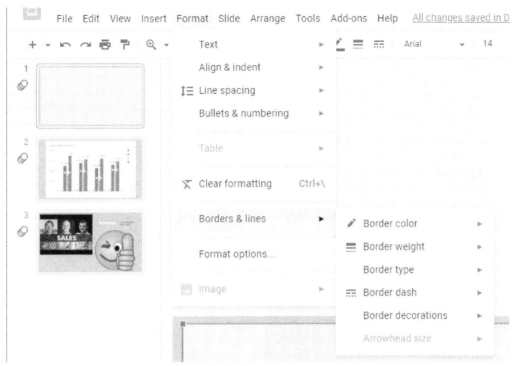

Figure 5.56

Next, I will change the *border weight* to 8 pt., the *border type* to thick-thin, and the *border decoration* to Round join. Then to make the box transparent, click on the *Fill color* toolbar icon and choose *Transparent*.

Chapter 5 – Google Slides

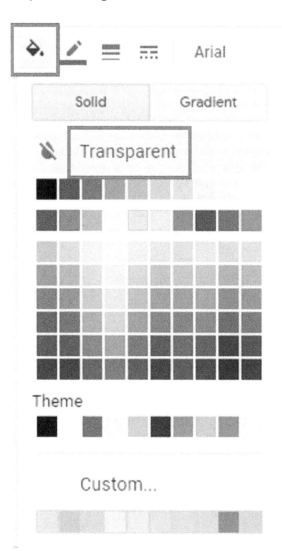

Figure 5.57

As you can see in figure 5.58, I now have a border around the inside of the slide. One downside to this is that the shape fill is technically still there, even though I made it transparent, so if you need to adjust anything inside of the border, you will need to drag the border out of the way first and then put it back in position when you are finished.

Chapter 5 – Google Slides

Figure 5.58

For the slide with the chart, I am going to add some fancy text to the top saying "Things are looking good!" and then add a gold star next to it, which is done the same way I added the thumbs up image from figure 5.47. I also copied and pasted the company logo image from slide one and made it smaller so it wouldn't overlap the chart.

Figure 5.59

Chapter 5 – Google Slides

Finally, for the last slide, I will need to do some cleanup so it doesn't look so cluttered.

Figure 5.60

This first thing I am going to do is move the video to the right side of the slide by dragging it over. Then I will resize it and make it larger by clicking on the image to highlight it, then placing my cursor over the square on the corner until it makes a double sided arrow and dragging it to enlarge it.

Figure 5.61

Now I will place a border around the video by clicking on it to select it, and then going to the *Format* menu and choosing *Borders and lines*, changing the border color to white, and the weight to 12 pt.

Figure 5.62

Next, I want to resize the thumbs up image and put the company logo over the thumb, but when I go to drag it on top of the thumb, it ends up behind it (as shown in figure 5.63).

Figure 5.63

To fix this I can either highlight the thumbs up image and go to the *Arrange* menu and choose *Order > Send backwards,* or highlight the company logo image and do the same except choose *Bring forward*. This can also be done by right clicking on the image and going to the *Order* option.

Now that I have the images where I want them and the size that I want them, I noticed that the company logo is too transparent or washed out to really be seen inside of the thumb.

Figure 5.64

To fix this, I will highlight the company logo image and go to the *Format* menu and choose *Format options*. Then I will go to the Adjustments section and move the slider for *Transparency* all the way to the left to remove the transparency effect. I will also move the *Contrast* slider to the right to try and darken the image up a little bit since it was light to begin with. You can see the results in figure 5.66.

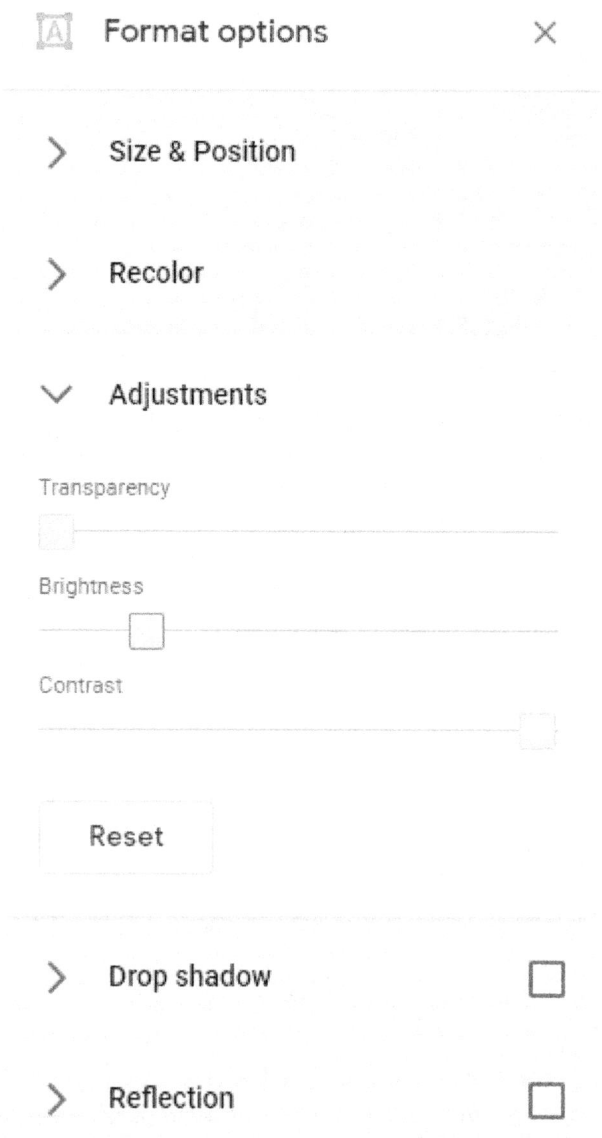

Format options

> Size & Position

> Recolor

∨ Adjustments

Transparency

Brightness

Contrast

Reset

> Drop shadow ☐

> Reflection ☐

Figure 5.65

Figure 5.66

Now I need to do something to make the "Very informative sales video" text look better and fix the arrow that is pointing the wrong way.

Figure 5.67

Chapter 5 – Google Slides

One option for fixing the arrow is to delete it and then go back to the Insert menu and add a new arrow shape that is pointing to the right. Or I can simply highlight the arrow shape, click and hold on the square box on the left side of the shape (at the arrowhead tip), and then drag it from left to right to invert the shape and have the arrow pointing the right direction.

One more thing I want to do to the arrow is make the arrowhead bigger. To do this I can click on the gold diamond shape on the object and drag to resize the arrowhead to the size I desire. The result can be seen in figure 5.69.

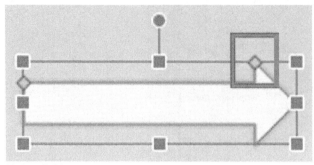
Figure 5.68

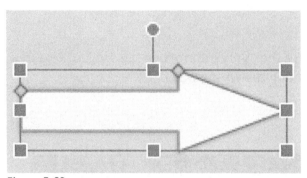
Figure 5.69

The final step in the formatting process for this slide is to fix the "Very informative sales video" text. I will highlight the text with my cursor and then choose the Oswald font and make it 18 pt. in size. Then I will make it bold and italicized. This can all be done from the font formatting buttons in the toolbar.

Figure 5.70

Chapter 5 – Google Slides

Finally, I want to make the text centered on two lines, so I will click on the *Align* button on the toolbar and then choose the *Center* option.

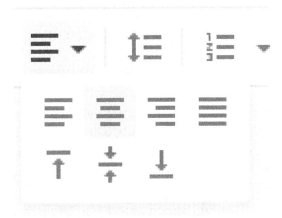

Figure 5.71

Now I have the finished result for the last slide.

Figure 5.72

Yes, I realize there is much more I could have done to make the slides even more presentable, but the point was to go over the basics of formatting to get you started so you can customize your own presentations.

Chapter 5 – Google Slides

Adding Animations and Transitions

One way to make your presentation stand out is by adding animations to objects within a slide and transition effects between slides. One thing I can't stress enough is that you should *never* overdo animations and transitions because it can be overkill and make you look like you just started using Slides and got a little too excited with the special effects!

Transitions

Let's begin with transitions, which are effects that you can add between slides as they advance from one slide to the next. Normally the next slide will just appear instantly when you are in presentation mode, but it can be nice to add a little something extra to make things stand out.

Normally you will have your title slide showing on the screen before you begin the presentation, so there is no need to add animations or transitions to this slide unless you *really* want to. So, to add a transition on the next slide, you will click on that slide in the thumbnail view on the left to select it. In my case, it will be slide number 2 as shown in figure 5.73.

Chapter 5 – Google Slides

Figure 5.73

With slide 2 selected, I will go to the *Slide* menu and click on *Change transition*. Then for the transition type I will pick the *Flip* transition. As you can see in figure 5.74, there are other types to choose from.

Chapter 5 – Google Slides

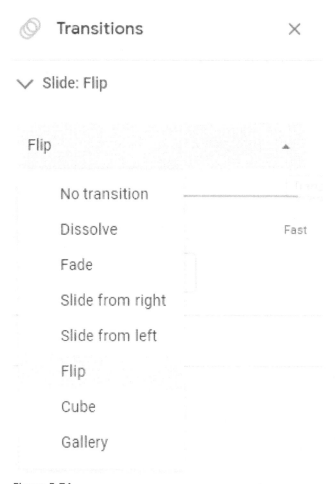

Figure 5.74

I will also set the speed to medium, which determines how quickly or slowly the slide will flip during my presentation (figure 5.75).

If I want to use this transition for all of the slides in the presentation, I can click the button that says *Apply to all slides*. To preview the transition effect, I can click on the *Play* button to have Slides show me what it will look like. Of course, I can't demonstrate that to you here, otherwise this would be one seriously high tech book!

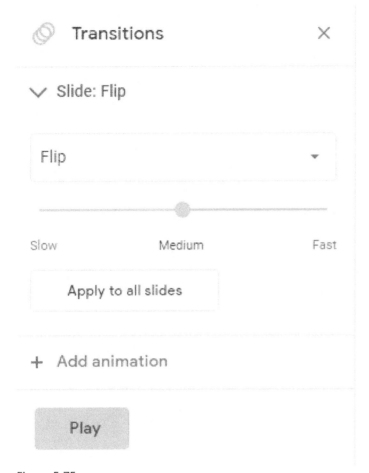

Figure 5.75

Animations
Animations are a little more involved than slides because you have to apply them to specific objects, such as text and images, and be aware of what order the animations occur so everything makes sense.

You can get to the animations from the same place as the transitions, but I like to right click on the object I want to add an animation to and choose *Animate* so I make sure I'm where I want to be. Once you choose the *Animate* option, you will have several different types of animations that you can apply to that object. I will be animating the chart from slide number 2.

Chapter 5 – Google Slides

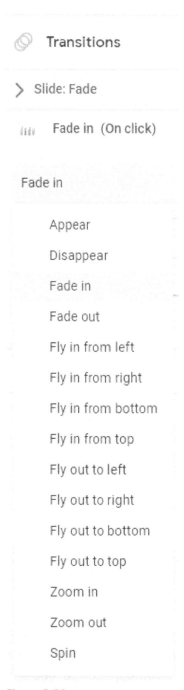

Figure 5.76

Once you choose the type of animation, you will need to choose if that animation occurs on the next click, *after* the previous animation, or *with* the previous animation. You can also select the speed that you want that animation to run at.

Chapter 5 – Google Slides

With Slides, you have the option to add additional animations to the same object by clicking on the *+ Add animation* button. If you look at figure 5.77, you can see that after my chart fades in, it will do a little spin. Once again, you can click the *Play* button to see how it will look during the actual presentation. To remove an animation click the X next to the animation name.

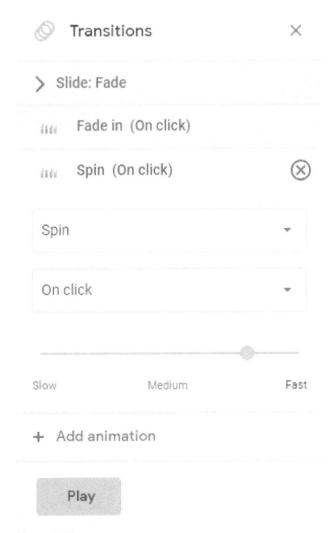

Figure 5.77

When you add animations to a lot of objects on a lot of different slides, then things can get complicated, so be aware of what order you are applying your animations and always be sure to preview them with the Play button, or even run the presentation itself from the Present button at the top of the screen to see how things will look.

Chapter 5 – Google Slides

Printing a Presentation
Although you typically don't print out presentations as often as you would a document or even a spreadsheet, it's still possible to do in case you want people to have their own copy to look at during your presentation or to take with them afterward.

If you go to the *File* menu and choose *Print settings and preview*, you can see the various choices you have for printing out your slides. Clicking on the choice next to *Close preview* will show you the various layouts you can use for printing.

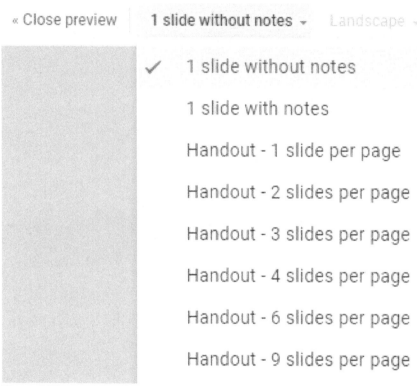
Figure 5.78

Figure 5.79 shows the *1 slide without notes* option, while figure 5.80 shows the *Handout – 3 slides per page* option.

Chapter 5 – Google Slides

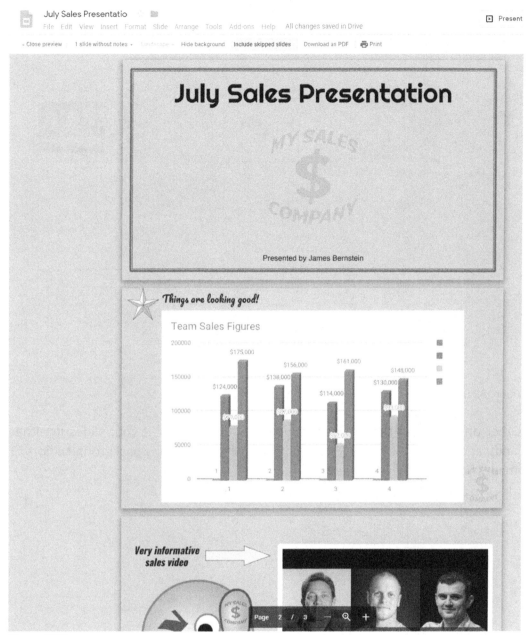

Figure 5.79

Chapter 5 – Google Slides

Figure 5.80

Other options from the top bar include the ability to print your slides in either landscape or portrait format, and also the ability to hide any background colors or images you might have applied.

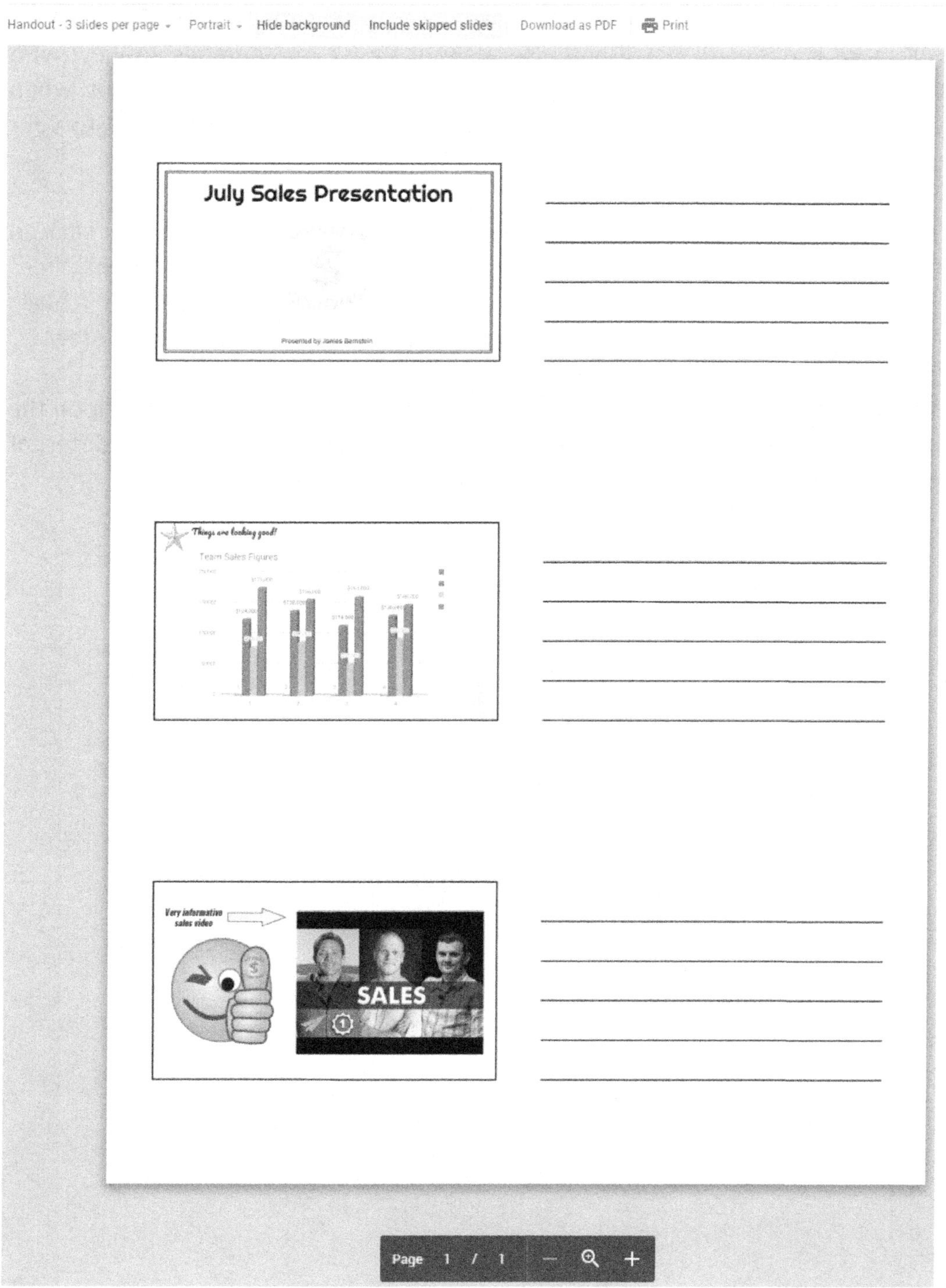

Chapter 5 – Google Slides

Figure 5.81

I discussed skipping slides earlier in this chapter where you can mark them as skipped and they won't show during your presentation. You can decide to have those skipped slides print or not print as well.

Chapter 5 – Google Slides

Finally, you have the option to download your presentation as a PDF file, which will make it easier to email and also make it easier for someone to view who doesn't use Google Slides and may not know how to open it otherwise. Plus, when you save it as a PDF file, people will not be able to make any changes to your presentation.

When you are ready to print out your slides, simply go to *File* and *Print,* or click on the *Print button* on the toolbar and select your printer as well as what pages\slides you want to print out. You can also choose to print out your presentation in black and white rather than color, and change the paper size to match your printer.

The *Scale* checkbox will come in handy when trying to make your slides fit on the page when printed, so you might find yourself having to play around with different percentage numbers to make things fit their best.

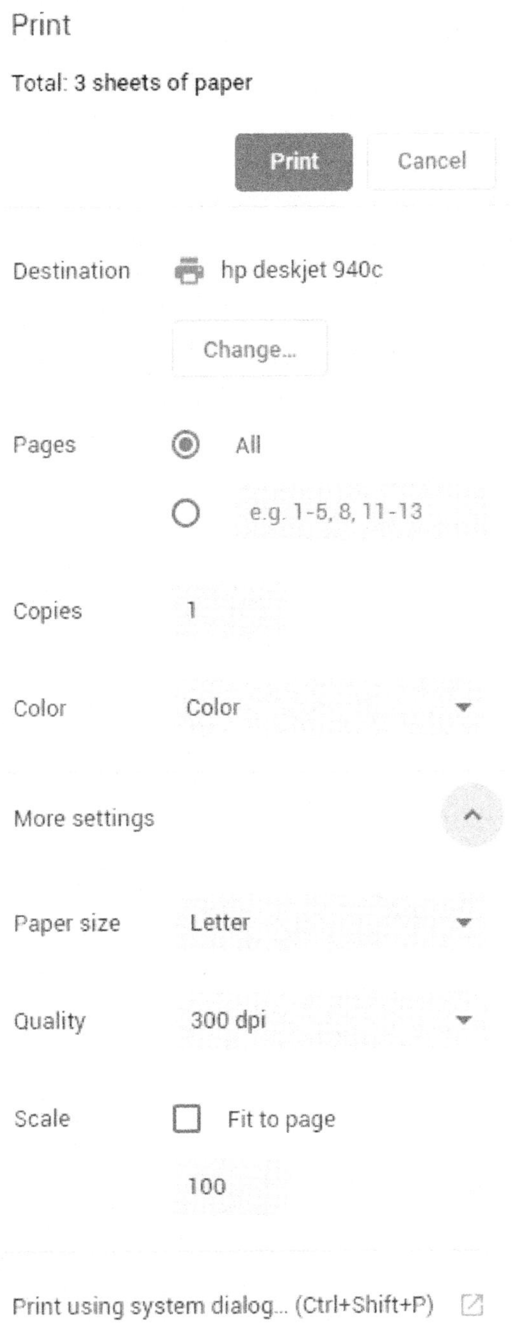

Chapter 5 – Google Slides

Print

Total: 3 sheets of paper

[Print] [Cancel]

Destination   hp deskjet 940c

[Change...]

Pages   ◉ All
      ○ e.g. 1-5, 8, 11-13

Copies   1

Color   Color ▼

More settings   ⌃

Paper size   Letter ▼

Quality   300 dpi ▼

Scale   ☐ Fit to page
     100

Print using system dialog... (Ctrl+Shift+P) ↗

Figure 5.82

Chapter 6 – Google Forms

Forms are a powerful tool that can be used to gather information on a variety of topics, or even used as a way to send out surveys to other people for things such as service or support satisfaction or suggestions to improve your business. Google Forms lets you create these types of forms from scratch, and also offers a variety of templates you can use to quickly create forms without a whole lot of work on your part. Figure 6.1 shows an example of a customer feedback form template you can use to quickly create your own form.

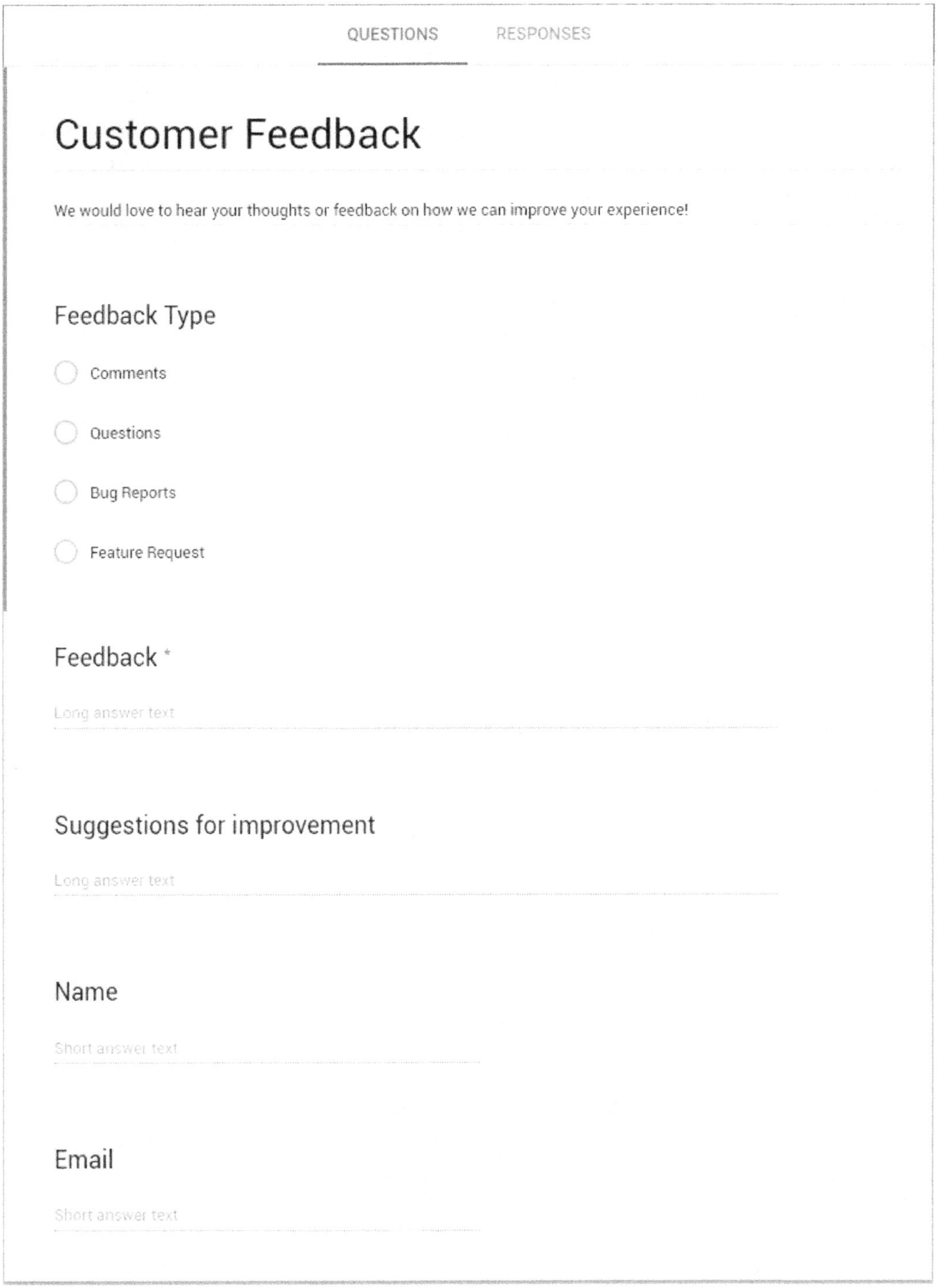
QUESTIONS
RESPONSES
Customer Feedback
We would love to hear your thoughts or feedback on how we can improve your experience!
Feedback Type
Comments
Questions
Bug Reports
Feature Request
Feedback *
Long answer text
Suggestions for improvement
Long answer text
Name
Short answer text
Email
Short answer text

Figure 6.1

Notice that there is also a *responses* section on the form that will allow you to view responses to the questions that people have entered after filling out your form (but I will get more into that later in the chapter).

Chapter 6 – Google Forms

Creating a Form

Since there are no menu items for Google Forms, I will get right into creating a form and showing you how to use your form once created. Once again, I will start from scratch rather than use one of the templates, since that is the best way to learn how to create and edit a form. It's a good idea to plan out what types of questions you will have on your form before starting so you don't end up doing too much rearranging or rewriting of the sections on your form.

When you open Forms and click to add a blank form, you will get a default looking form similar to figure 6.2.

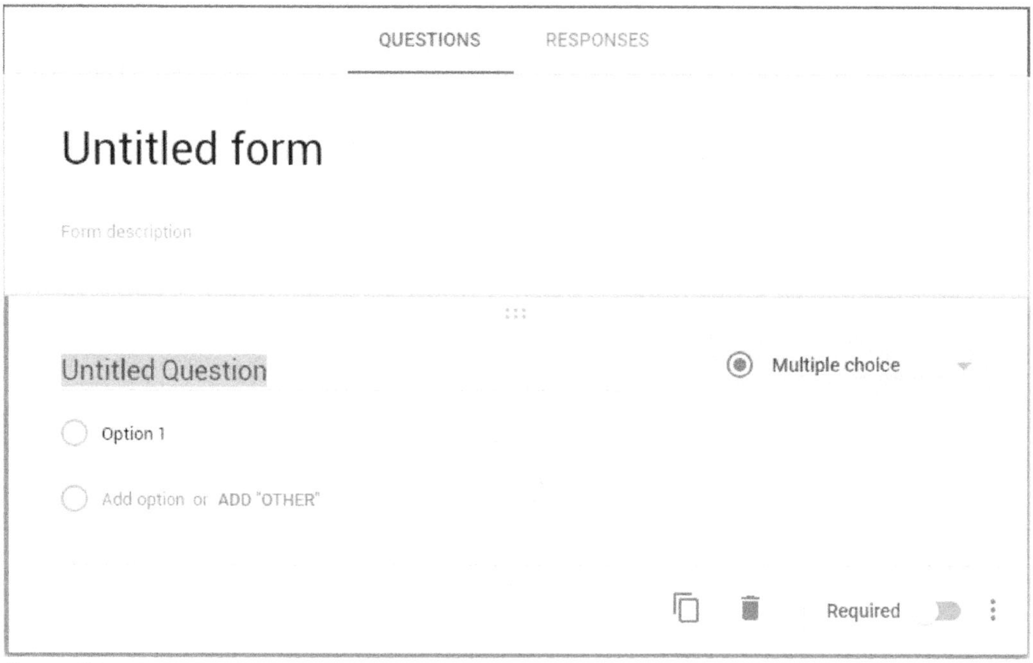

Figure 6.2

The first thing I am going to do is change the title of the form from *Untitled form* to *Mountain Bike Questionnaire* since that's the type of questions that will be on my form. To do so, all I need to do is highlight *Untitled form* and type in my new name. You can also enter in a description if desired.

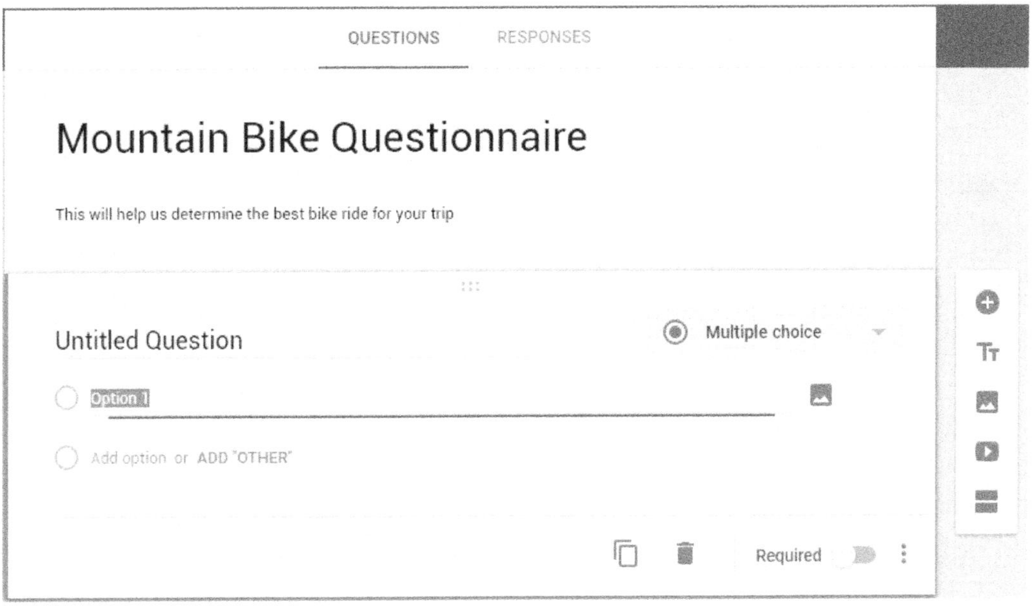

Chapter 6 – Google Forms

Figure 6.3

Now it's time to start adding some questions to the form. As you can see in figure 6.3, the question type is set to *Multiple choice,* but you also have the option of making it a variety of other types of questions (as shown in figure 6.4).

Chapter 6 – Google Forms

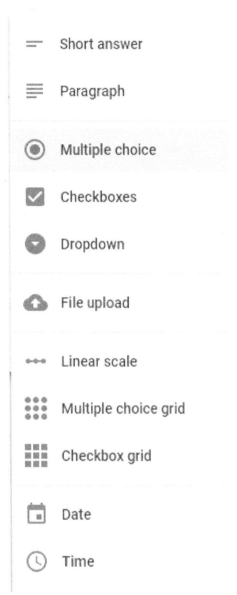

Figure 6.4

I will leave my first question as multiple choice to show you how that works. I will first enter my question in where it says *Untitled question*. Then where it says *Option 1* I will enter in one of the choices I will have for this question.

Chapter 6 – Google Forms

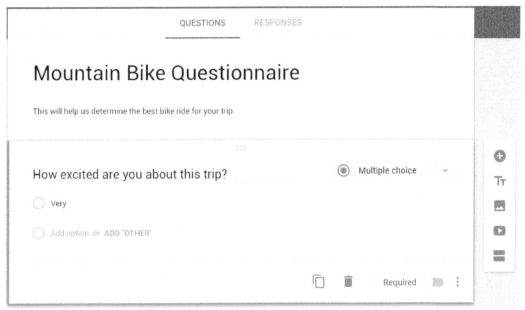

Figure 6.5

To add more choices for the question, you will click on where it says Add option and type in your next possible answer. There is also an option to add a picture next to each choice by clicking on the icon shown in figure 6.6.

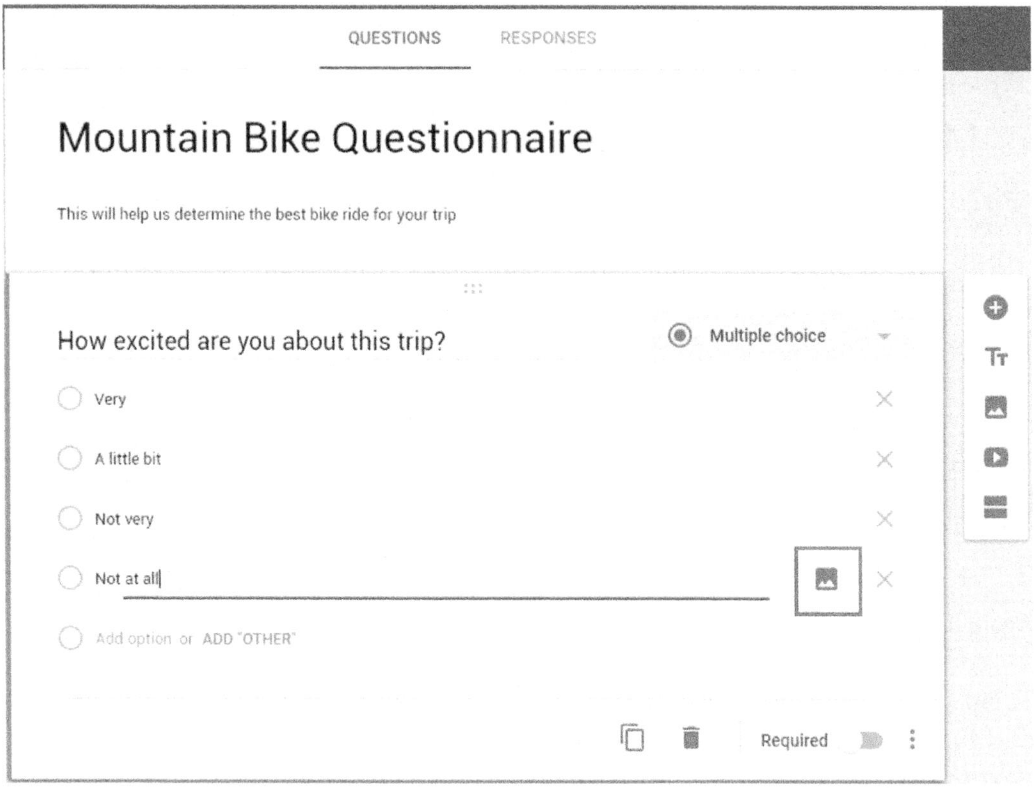
QUESTIONS
RESPONSES
Mountain Bike Questionnaire
This will help us determine the best bike ride for your trip
How excited are you about this trip?
Multiple choice
Very
A little bit
Not very
Not at all
Add option or ADD "OTHER"
Required

Figure 6.6

I added a frowny face for the *Not at all* choice just for fun.

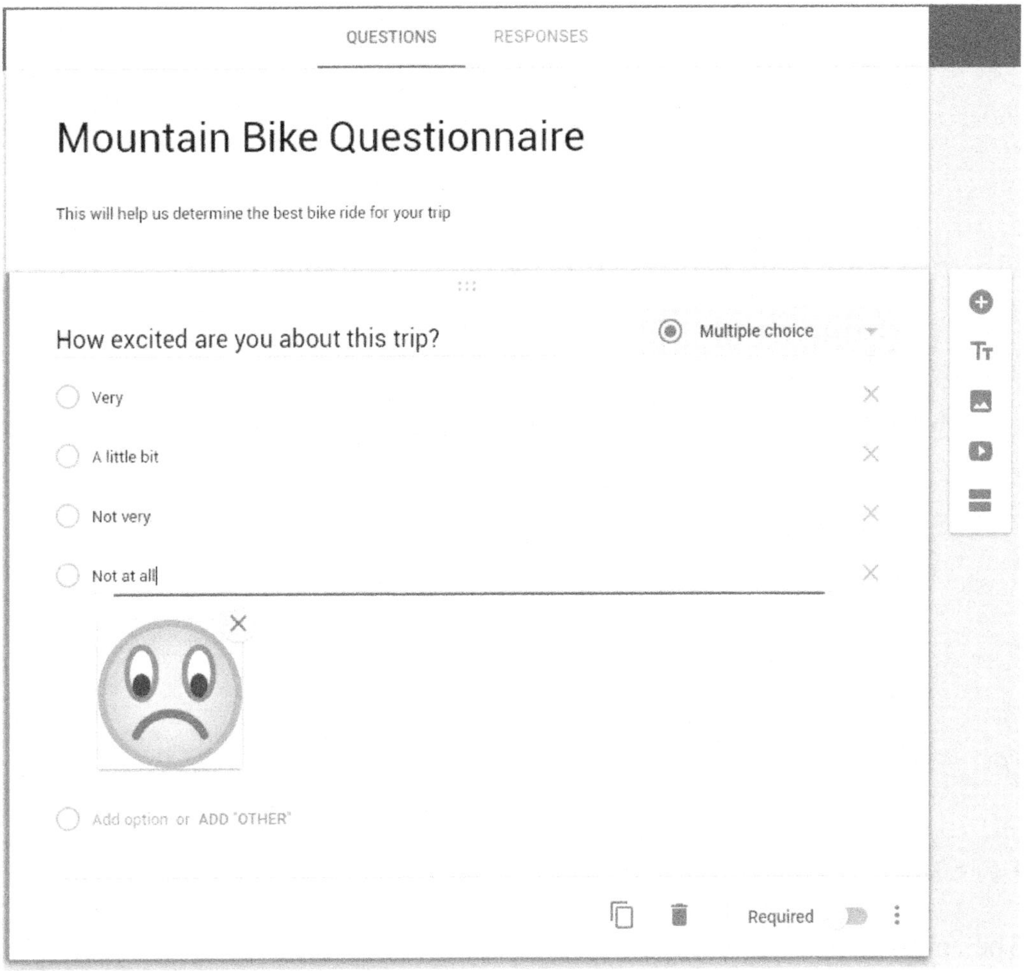

Figure 6.7

If you want to remove any of your answer choices, simply click on the X next to that question. If you want the question to be required, then move the slider next to *Required* at the bottom right over so it's highlighted.

You might have noticed the toolbar to the right of the question, so now would be a good time to go over what each one of these items does.

Chapter 6 – Google Forms

Figure 6.8

The option that looks like a + sign is used to add a new question to your form. The Tt choice is used to add a new title and description that can be used for the next question. The third one down is used to add an image to an answer (which I demonstrated earlier). The play button icon is used to add a video to your question and works the same way as adding videos to other Google apps. Finally, the last option that looks like = is used to add a new section to your form if you want to keep certain items more isolated from each other.

On the bottom of figure 6.7 you will also have a couple of icons. The first one is used to make a copy of that particular section\question, and the trash can icon is used to delete that question.

Next, I will click the + icon to add another question to my form. This time it will be a Dropdown type with a Yes and No answer. I will also make it a required answer by using the slider next to *Required* on the lower right corner.

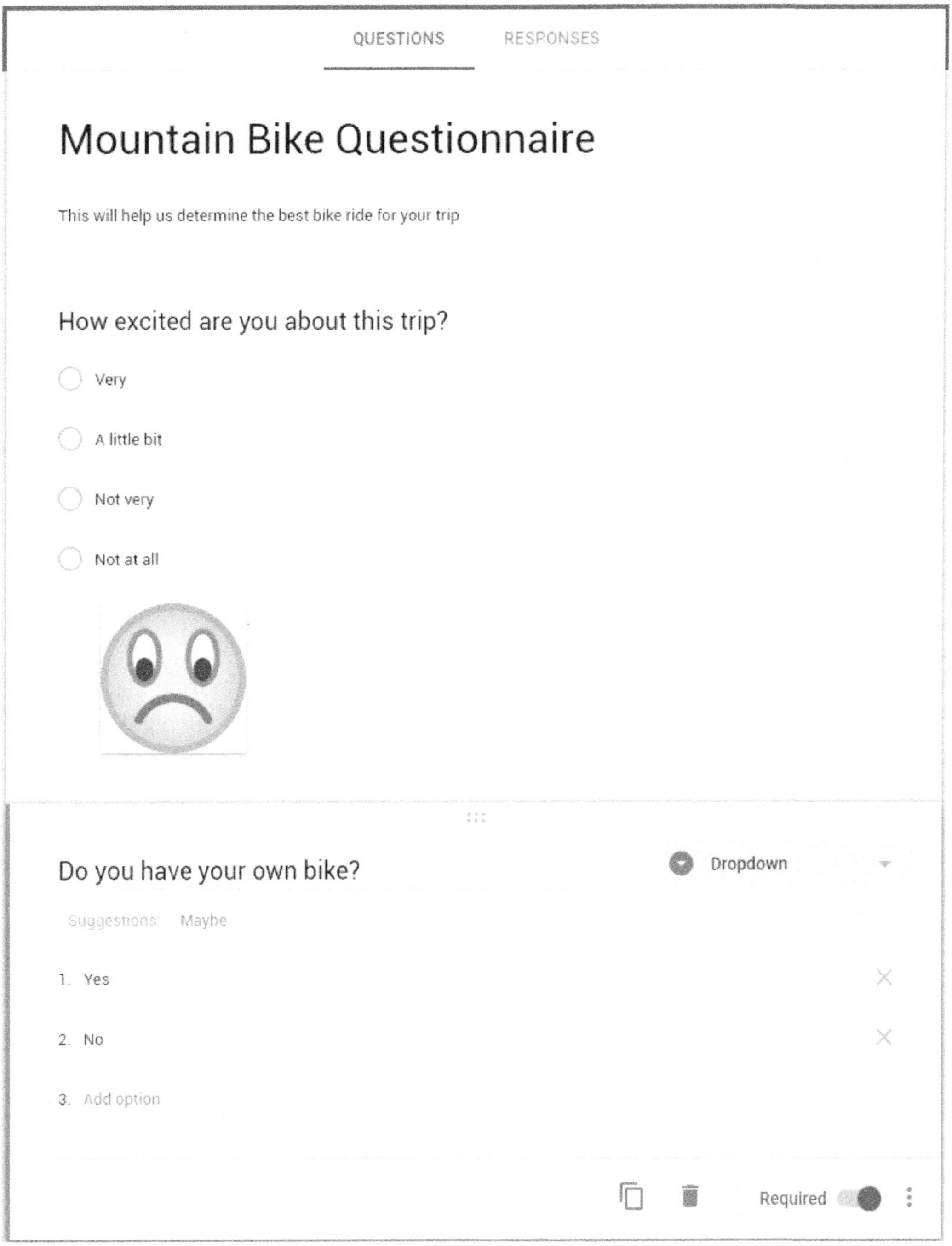

Chapter 6 – Google Forms

Mountain Bike Questionnaire

This will help us determine the best bike ride for your trip

How excited are you about this trip?

◯ Very

◯ A little bit

◯ Not very

◯ Not at all

Do you have your own bike?   Dropdown

Suggestions: Maybe

1. Yes
2. No
3. Add option

Required

Figure 6.9

I will now add a short answer question by selecting *Short answer* from the question type dropdown.

299

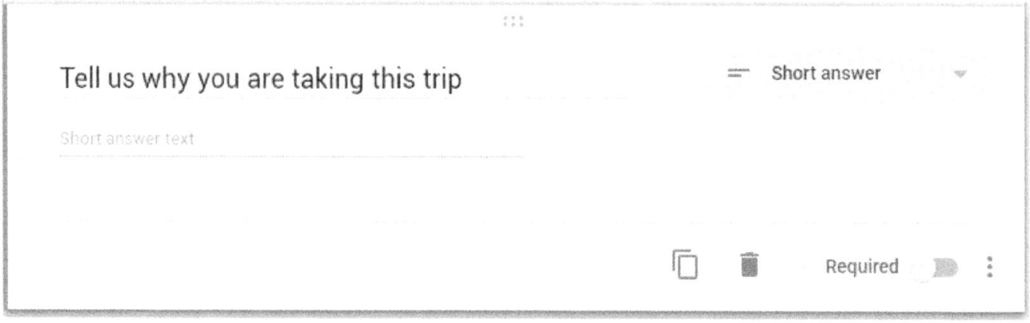

Chapter 6 – Google Forms

Figure 6.10

Now that I have my questions in order, I want to add a new section where I can place a video that the participants can watch to get more information about the trip. To do so, I will click on the = button on the toolbar and type in *Informational Video* for the section name. Then I will click on the insert video button and paste in the URL for a YouTube video that they can watch.

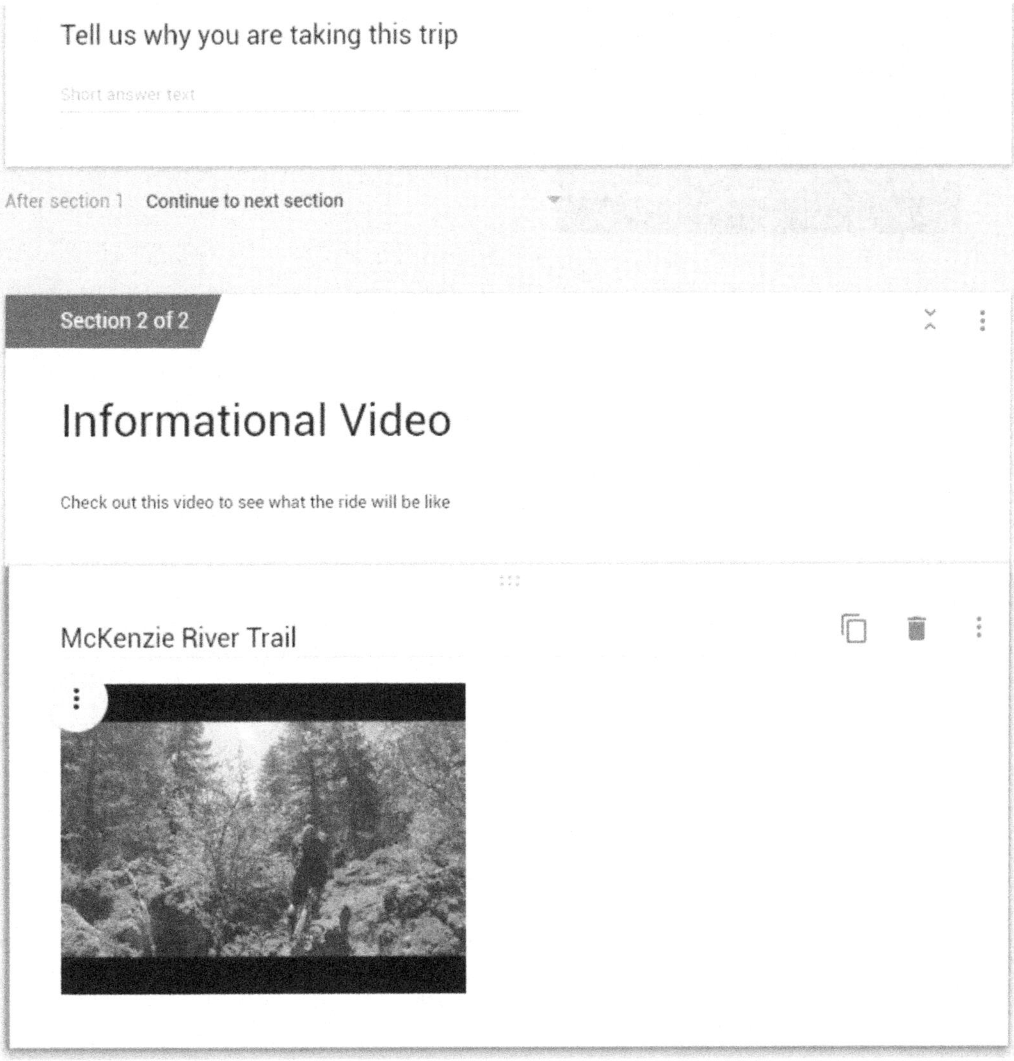

Figure 6.11

Then I will add a place for them to upload their completed forms for the trip by adding a new question and choosing *File upload* as the type. I chose to only allow documents or PDF files as the types of file they can upload.

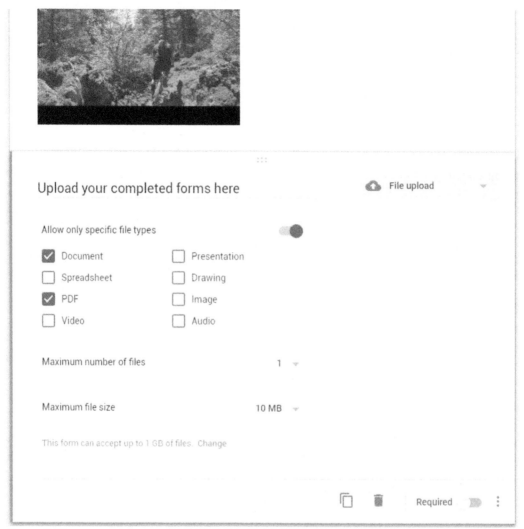

Figure 6.12

Finally, I will add another section and two questions giving them the option to choose two dates for the trip in July that work for them.

Chapter 6 – Google Forms

```
Maximum file size                      10 MB

This form can accept up to 1 GB of files.  Change


                                                        Required
```

After section 2   Continue to next section

```
Section 3 of 3

Pick 2 dates in July for this trip

Description (optional)


Date 1

Month, day, year


Date 2

Month, day, year
```

Figure 6.13

Customizing a Form

Before I send out my form to be filled out by the trip participants, I want to customize it a little bit first. If you take a look at figure 6.14 you will see the options that you have at the top right of your Forms window.

Figure 6.14

303

Chapter 6 – Google Forms

The first one that looks like a paint palette will let you change the theme color, background color font style, and add a header image. I changed the colors around as well as changed the font style. Then I added an image, but you will have to crop it to a rectangle size to fit as your form header.

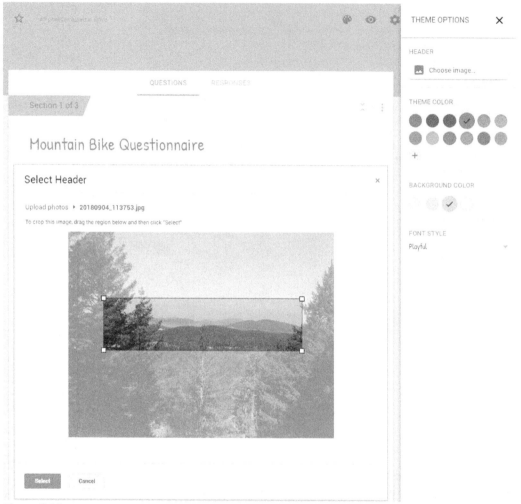

Figure 6.15

The next button on the top toolbar that looks like an eye will let you preview your form before sending it out. I added some more emojis to the first question and here is what my form looks like with its new colors and header image. Notice the red asterisk next to the *Do you have your own bike* question? That means that it's a question that is required to be answered.

Chapter 6 – Google Forms

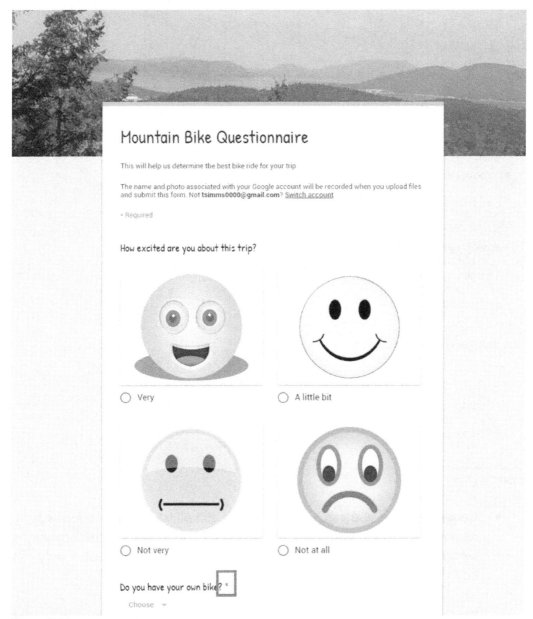

Figure 6.16

The gear icon at the top right will show you settings for the Forms app and has three categories.

305

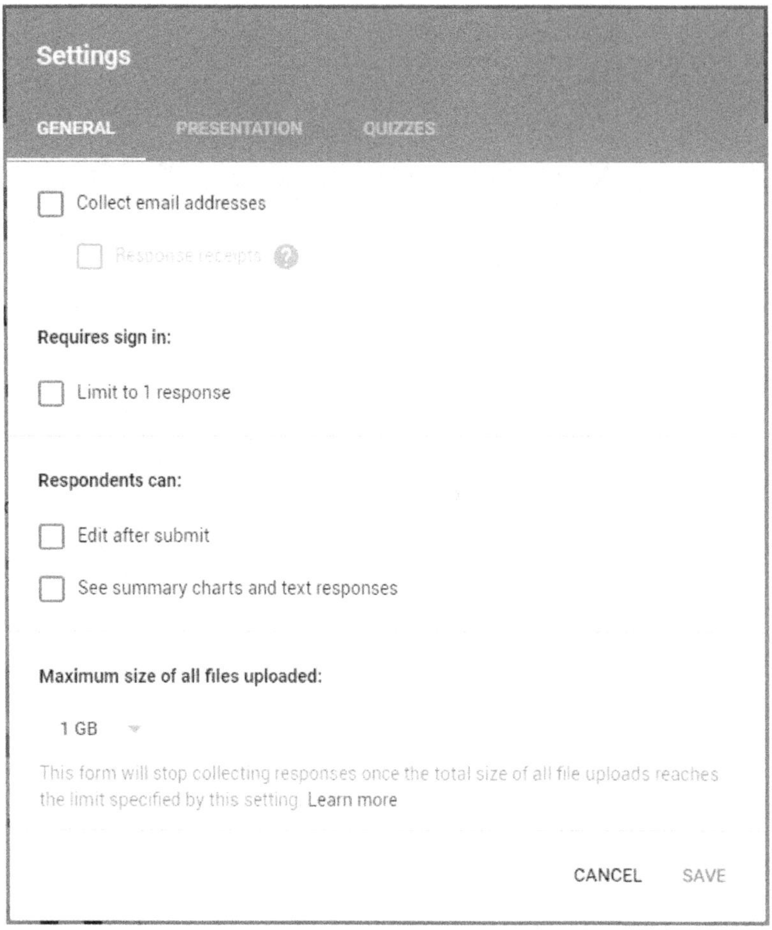

Chapter 6 – Google Forms

Figure 6.17

- **General** – Here you can do things such as collect email addresses from responders so you can use them later, and also change the answering settings such as how often they can respond to a question or if they can edit their responses.

- **Presentation** – Here you can do things such as shuffle the question order and have confirmation messages be sent out letting them know their answers have been recorded.

- **Quizzes** – If for any reason you want to turn your form into a test, you can do so from the *Quizzes* section and have it graded.

Chapter 6 – Google Forms

Sending Out a Form

Now it's time to send out the form to be filled out by the participants. You can do this by clicking on the Send button and entering in the email addresses of the people you want to send it to. You can also have the form included in the email by checking the *Include form in email* box, but I can't for mine because it has a question that requires a file upload.

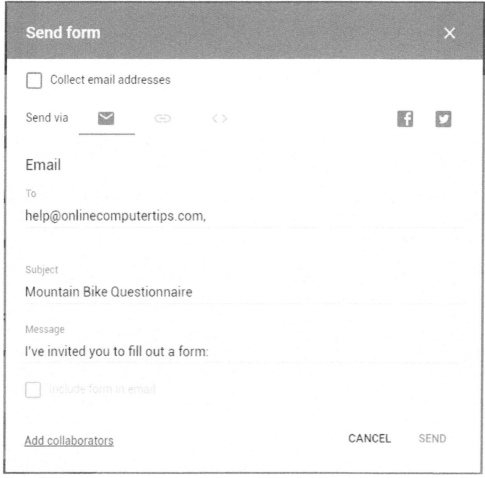

Figure 6.18

Clicking the paperclip icon will give you a URL link that you can copy and paste into an email manually if you would rather use your own email account to send the form.

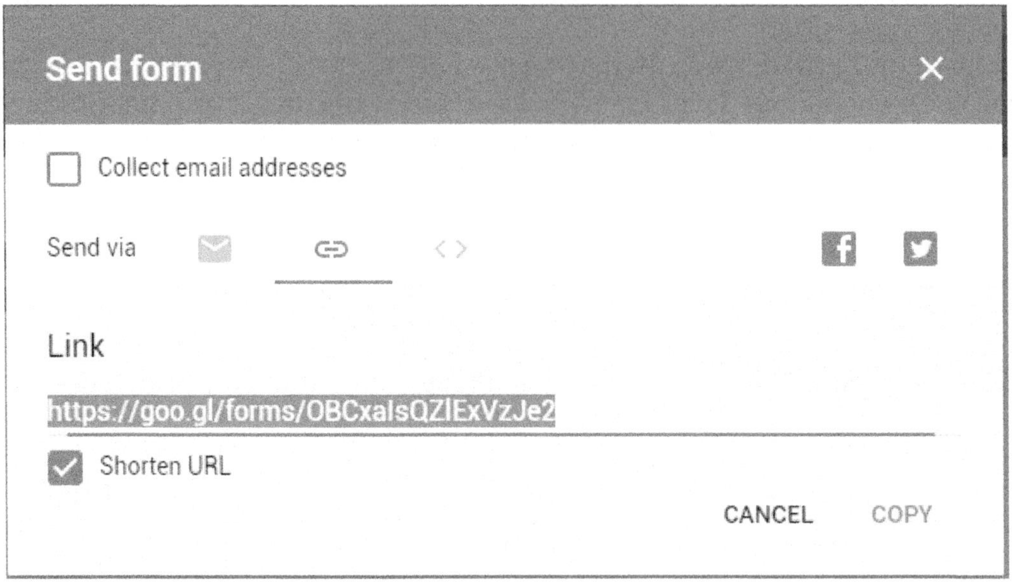

Chapter 6 – Google Forms

Figure 6.19

This is how the email will look when received on the other end. If I was able to use the *include form in email* option, the questions themselves would be in the email rather than just a button that says *Fill out form*.

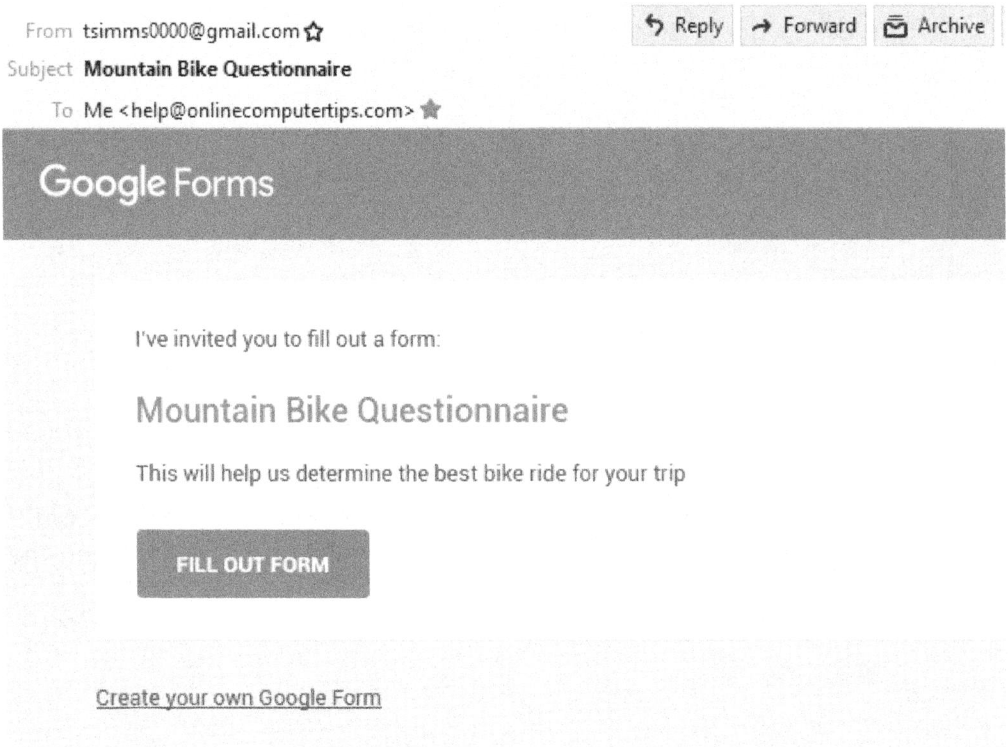

Figure 6.20

Chapter 6 – Google Forms

Viewing Responses

Now that my form has been sent out and my responses are coming in, I can see the results from the Responses section within Forms. I can view the responses as a summary like shown in figure 6.21, or as individual results as shown in figure 6.22.

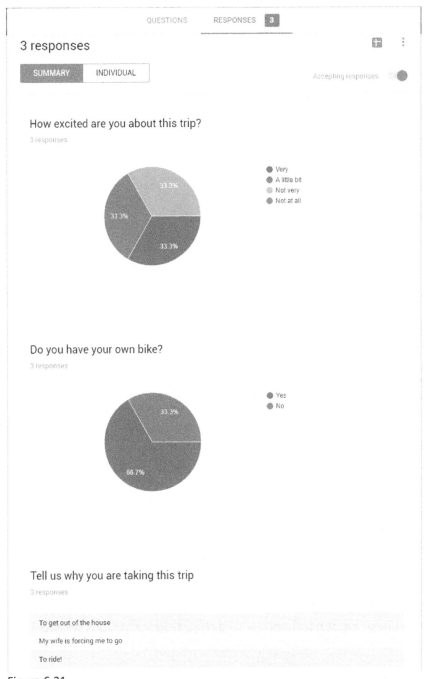

Figure 6.21

Chapter 6 – Google Forms

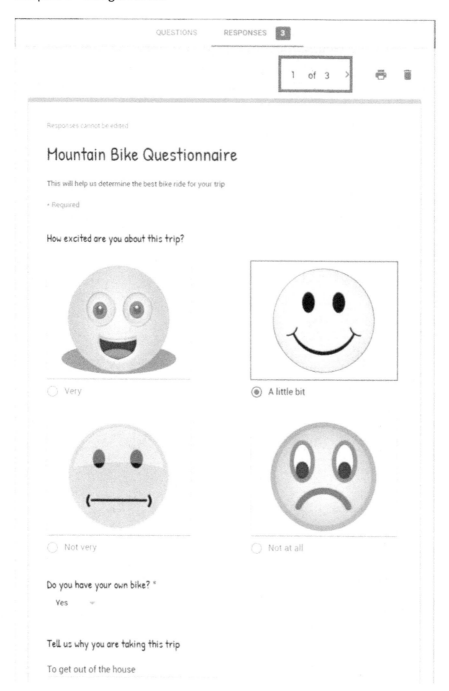

Figure 6.22

When you view the results in Summary mode, then you can click on the three vertical dots in the upper right hand corner to get additional options for working with your results.

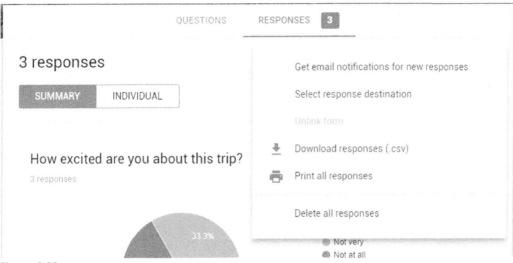

Figure 6.23

- **Get email notifications for new responses** – You can check this option if you would like to receive an email every time someone fills out your form.

- **Select response destination** – You can have your responses sent to a new or existing spreadsheet to be recorded so you can view them later.

Figure 6.24

- **Unlink form** – If you don't want any more responses to go to a spreadsheet, you can unlink your form here.

- **Download responses (.csv)** – Once your form is filled out, you can have Forms download all of the responses in a csv file that can be opened with Sheets, Excel, and even Notepad.

- **Print all responses** – This will print out all of your responses to your selected printer.

- **Delete all responses** – This will delete all of the responses that you have received so far.

Forms Options

There are a few more options I want to discuss in Forms that can be found by clicking the three vertical dots to the right of the Send button. I will be going over the ones that are not obvious as to what they do.

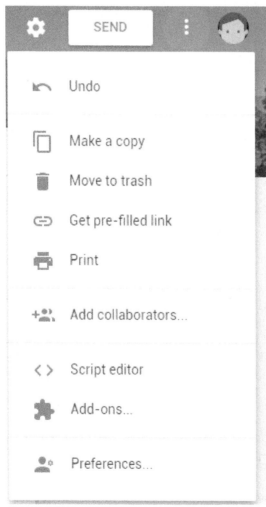

Figure 6.25

- **Make a copy** – It's easy to copy a Form if you like the way it's set up and want to make some changes to a copy rather than the original form. Once you click on *Make a copy*, all you need to do is name the form and decide where you want to save it in your Google Drive. You also have the option to share the form with the same people who you are sharing the original form with.

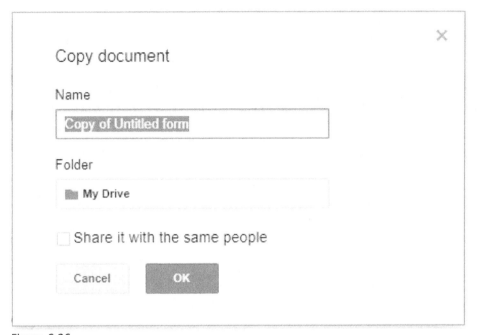

Figure 6.26

- **Add collaborators** – Just like with other Google apps, you have the option to give additional people access to your forms so they can work on them as well. You can invite them by having Forms send them an email, or you can send them a link to your form using your own email.

Chapter 6 – Google Forms

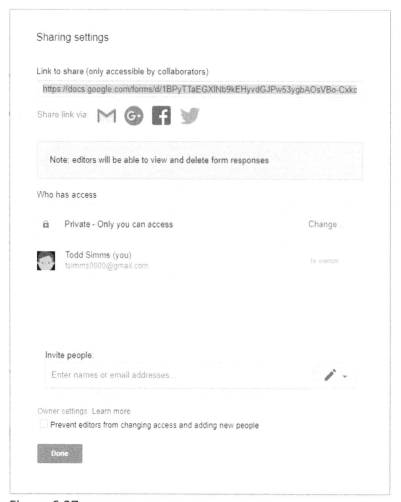

Figure 6.27

- **Add-ons** – Forms has many third party add-ons that you can download and install to improve the functionality of the app (figure 6.28).

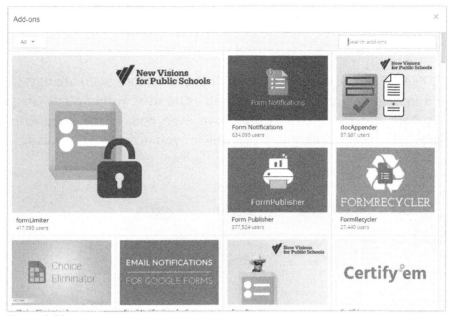
Figure 6.28

- **Preferences** – Forms only has a few settings in its preferences which apply to all forms that you create. You can apply settings to individual forms themselves while working in those forms. Figure 6.29 shows the settings you can apply to all forms if desired.

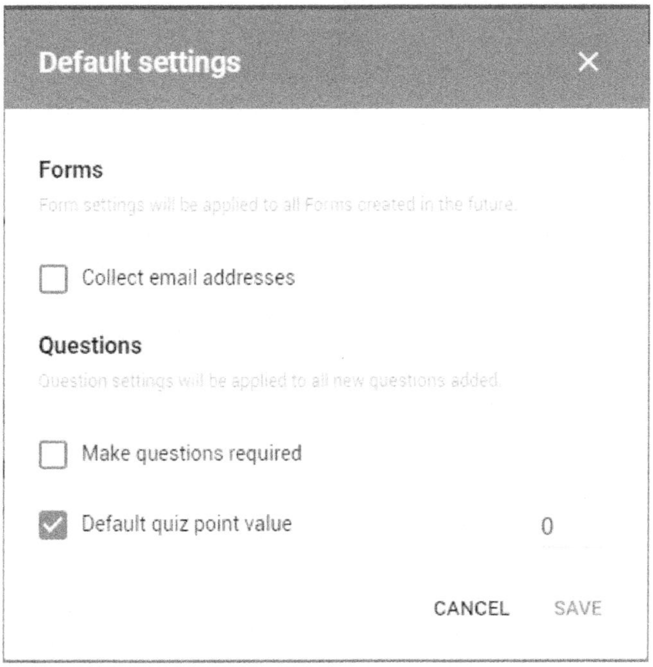

Figure 6.29

Chapter 7 – Google Keep

Google Keep is a basic yet powerful app that you can use to create notes that can be used for a variety of purposes, as well as be used within other Google Apps such as Docs and Sheets. You might have even noticed the Keep icon on the sidebar within these applications that will let you access your notes from those apps.

Figure 7.1

Keep Interface
The Google Keep interface is pretty basic, and there is not really much to it. There are no menu items like we saw in Doc, Sheets, and Slides. When you open Keep for the first time, you should see a screen similar to figure 7.2.

Chapter 7 – Google Keep

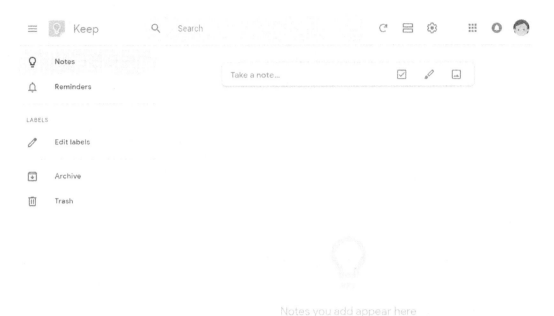

Figure 7.2

On the left side of the screen you have the *Notes* section, which will contain all of your notes. When you start to add labels to your notes you will have the ability to organize them more efficiently.

Under Notes is where your *Reminders* will be kept. If you need to be notified of something from your note, you can set reminders within the note and then these reminders will be listed here.

Once you start using labels with your notes they will be listed here, and you will be able to edit them from the *Edit labels* section. (I will get to this feature later on in the chapter.)

If you are a Gmail user, then you might already be using the *Archive* feature to put old emails that you don't need to refer to frequently in an archived location. You can do the same thing with your notes.

Trash is where you will find deleted notes. You can delete them forever from here or restore them if needed. Notes in the Trash are automatically deleted after seven days.

Chapter 7 – Google Keep

Taking Notes

To create a note, all you need to do is type in the box that says *Take a note,* or you can use one of the options within that text box to make a specific kind of note.

Figure 7.3

I will now briefly explain what each of these items does and then show you some examples:

- **New list** – A list is a note with checkboxes that you can mark as completed when you finish a task.

- **New note with drawing** – This will let you create a freehand drawing or use shapes to create a custom picture for your note.

- **New note with image** – This option inserts an image of your choosing on top of the note, and then you can enter related details underneath.

To create a simple note all you need to do is start typing in the box, and when you are done click on *Close*.

Figure 7.4

To create a list-type note simply enter each item on your list on a separate line and Keep will add checkboxes to your items.

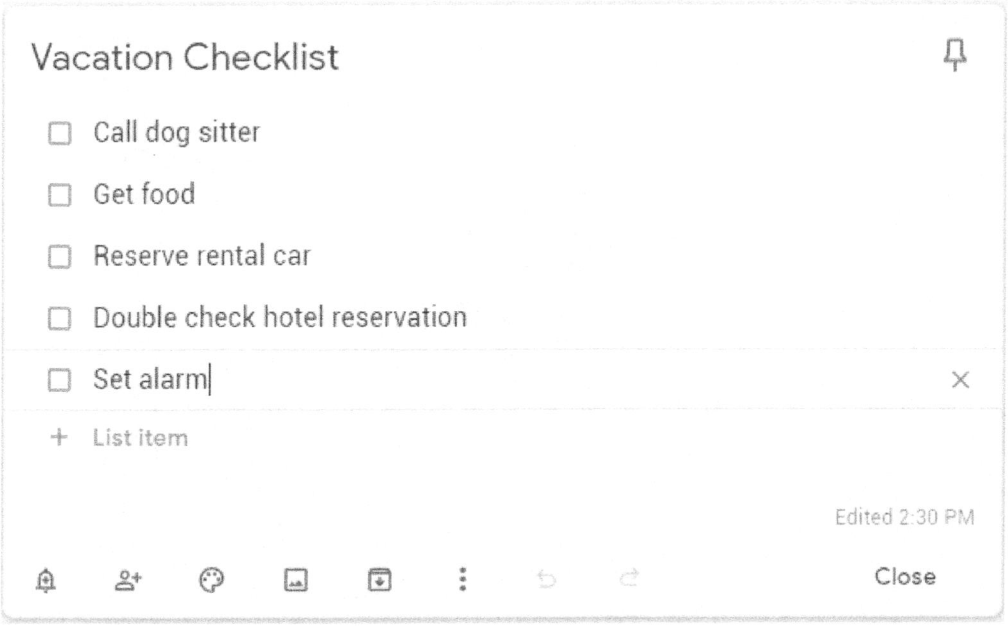

Chapter 7 – Google Keep

Figure 7.5

For a note with a drawing, all you need to do is draw whatever you want on your note and it will be displayed on top of your note. I wrote out the word *project* to show you what you can do with this feature later on in the chapter.

Figure 7.6

To create a note with an image, you will need to select a picture from your local device and Keep will add it to the top of your note.

Chapter 7 – Google Keep

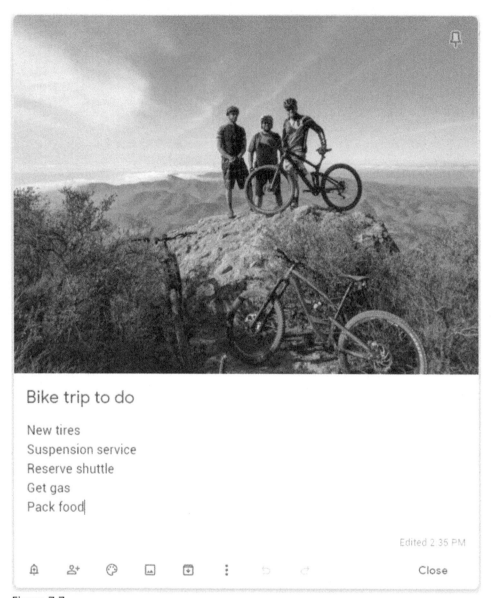

Figure 7.7

As you create new notes they will start to show up under the main Notes section (as seen in figure 7.8). You can edit any of your notes simply by clicking on them to open them up.

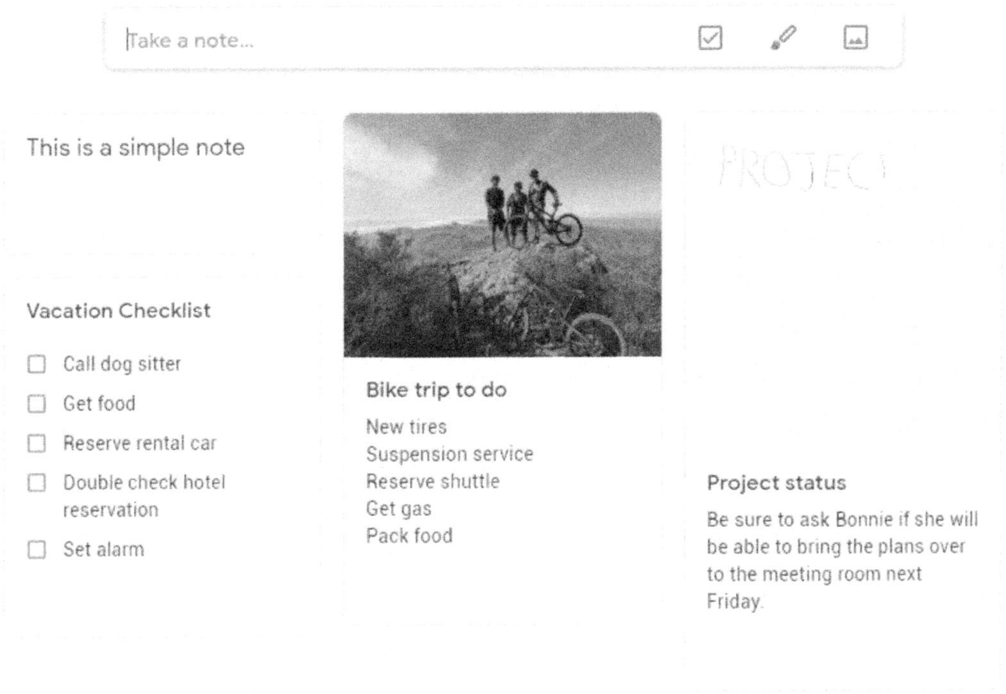

Chapter 7 – Google Keep

Figure 7.8

For the list-type notes, when you check the box next to an item, it will move it down to the *Completed items* area, showing that you are done with that task. If you change your mind, you can uncheck the box and it will move it back up to the non-completed list area.

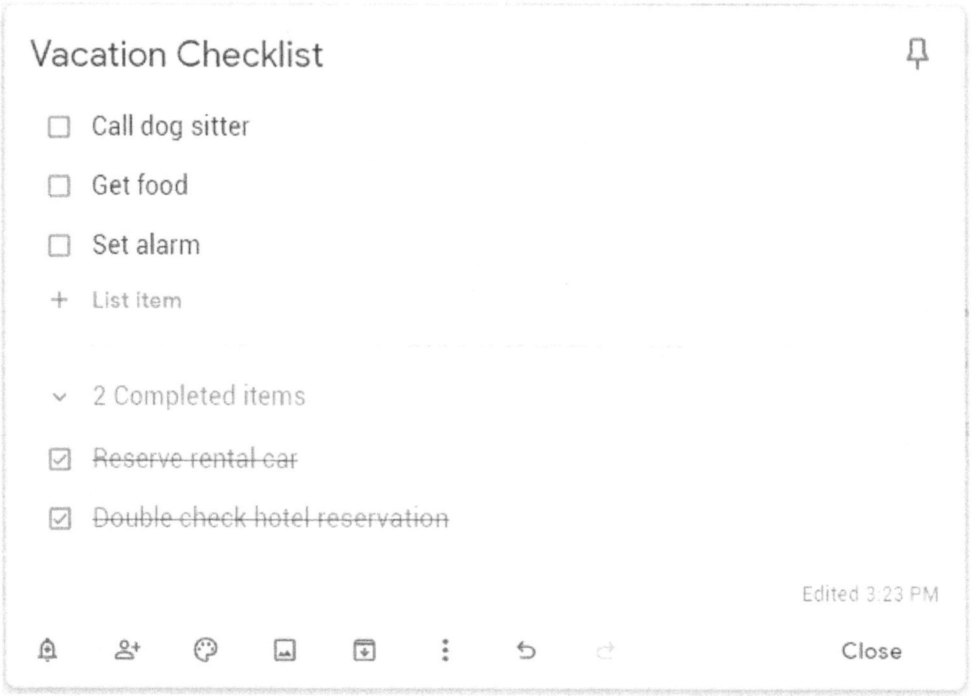

Chapter 7 – Google Keep

Figure 7.9

There are various icons on the bottom of each note that you can use to change the way your notes are configured.

Figure 7.10

The first one with the bell icon is for setting reminders, which I will be discussing later in the chapter. The second one with the silhouette and + sign is for sharing and collaboration, and I will have a section later in the chapter for that as well.

Next, we have the icon of the paint pallet, which can be used to change the color of your notes. If you get to the point where you have a lot of notes, you can use this to start color coding them to make them easier to keep track of.

The next icon is for adding an image to your note, which will make it look just like it does when you use the *New note with image* option.

Then we have the icon with the down arrow, which is used to archive that particular note. Then it can be found in the Archive section on the left hand of the screen if you need to go back to it. You can also unarchive it if needed.

322

Chapter 7 – Google Keep

There is a left pointing arrow and a right pointing arrow at the end of the icons, and those are to undo and redo the last action you performed.

In front of those arrows is an icon that is three vertical dots, and when you click on that, you will get some additional functions.

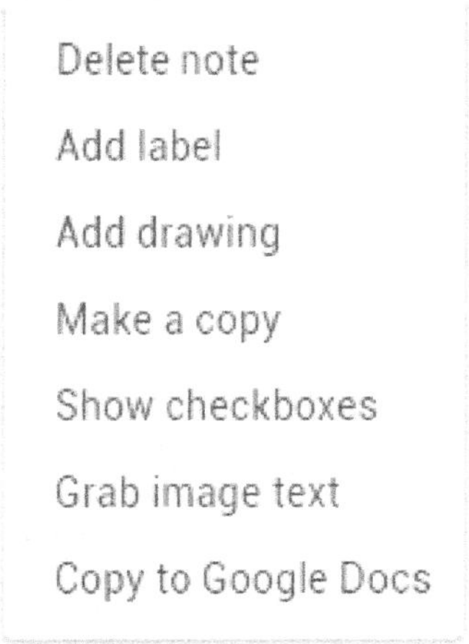

Delete note
Add label
Add drawing
Make a copy
Show checkboxes
Grab image text
Copy to Google Docs

Figure 7.11

Here is a quick summary of what each item does:

- **Delete note** – This should be pretty self-explanatory. When you delete a note, you can go to the Trash to recover it within seven days if needed.

- **Add label** – Labels are used to categorize your notes and make them easier to search for. When you add a label, then that particular label will show up in the Labels section within Keep. I will now add the label *Vacation* to my vacation and bike trip notes to show you how that works. Once you add a label to a note, that label becomes available as an item you can check when adding a new label to a different note so you don't have to retype it.

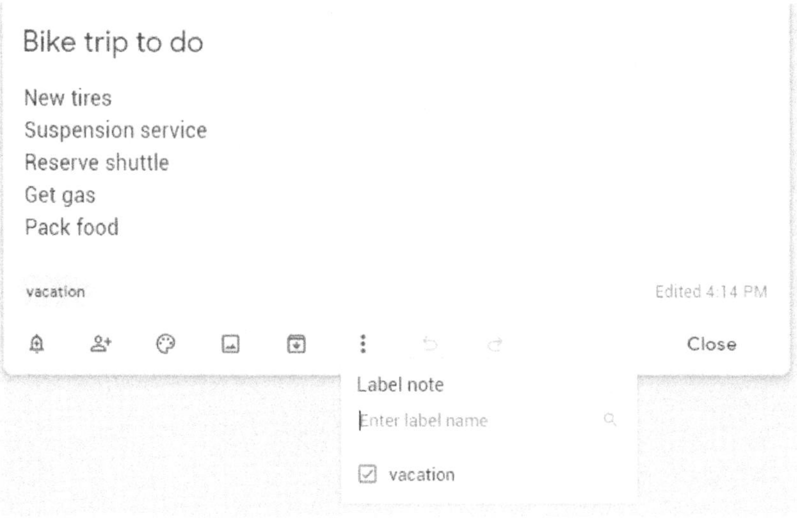

Chapter 7 – Google Keep

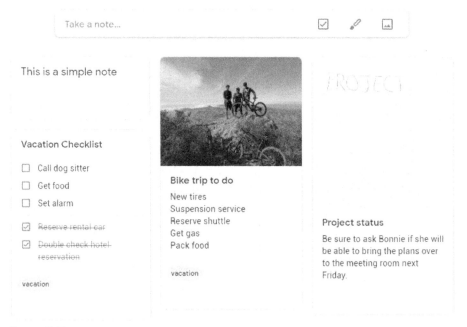

Figure 7.12

Now that I have added the vacation label to my Vacation Checklist and Bike trip to-do notes, you can see how they show up on each of the notes.

Figure 7.13

You can also see that I have a new label called *vacation* in my labels section within Keep.

Chapter 7 – Google Keep

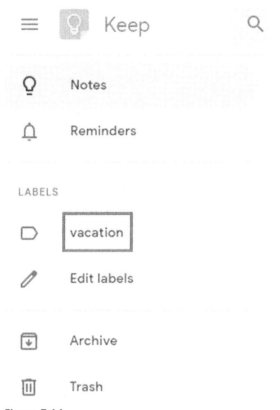

Figure 7.14

Add drawing – This choice allows you to add a drawing to an existing note.

Make a copy – If you have a note that you would like to make a copy of, then you can do that from here. Keep in mind that any sharing options you have for that note will not be copied over.

Show checkboxes – Basic notes that were not created as a list will not have checkboxes by default. You can use the *Show checkboxes* choice to have checkboxes placed next to the items on your list.

Grab image text – Here is where I wanted to show you why I wrote the word *project* in my drawing note. When you do this or have other images with words in them, Keep will try and read the text in the image and add it to the note. I chose the *Grab image text* option for my *project* note, and it was able to read the text from my drawing and add it to my note (figure 7.15).

Figure 7.15

- **Copy to Google Docs** – If you are a Google Docs user, you can have your note copied over to Docs and opened up in a new file just by clicking on *Copy to Google Docs*. When you do this, it will show the progress and then give you a link to open the document (figure 7.17).

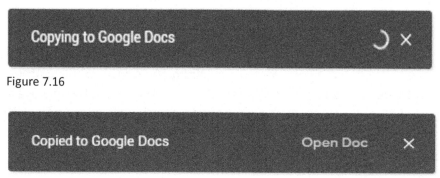

Figure 7.16

Figure 7.17

Figure 7.18 shows my bike trip note opened up in Google Docs.

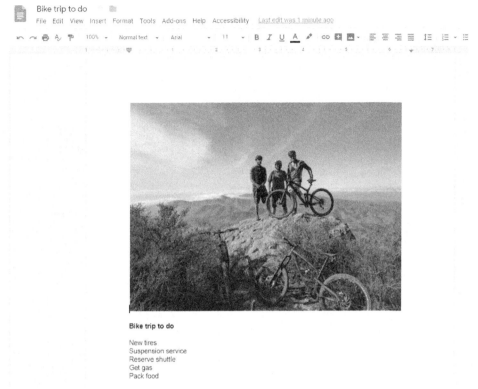

Figure 7.18

One thing I have mentioned before but will go over again is how other Google apps (like Docs) have a Keep button on the right sidebar, which will allow you easy access to your Keep notes (figure 7.19).

Chapter 7 – Google Keep

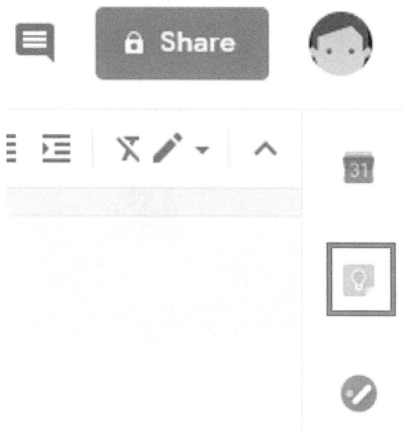

Figure 7.19

When you open Keep from Docs it will show you a list of your available notes that you can add to the current document or pin to the sidebar in Docs (figure 7.20). You can also perform actions such as archiving them, deleting them, or opening them in Keep. You also have the ability to create new notes right from Docs (as well as Sheets and Slides).

Chapter 7 – Google Keep

Figure 7.20

Chapter 7 – Google Keep

Setting Reminders

When you make notes it's very common to want to be reminded of the tasks within your notes. If you were to write them down on a sticky note, for example, then you would be on your own when it came time to remember to take action on your notes. Fortunately, that is not the case with Keep.

You can set a reminder on any note and it will be placed on your Google Calendar (discussed in Chapter 10). To do this, simply click on the bell icon on that note and choose when you want your reminder to take place. You can pick one of the default reminders such as Later today or Tomorrow, or you can select a date and time of your own by choosing *Pick date & time*.

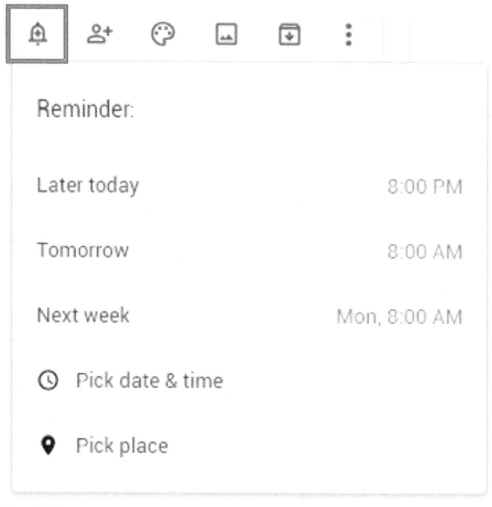

Figure 7.21

Chapter 7 – Google Keep

You also have the option to set up repeating reminders if you want to get reminded daily, weekly, monthly, yearly, and so on.

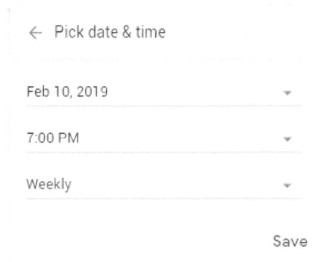

Figure 7.22

Once you set your reminder it will be shown on the note itself (in case you were wondering if you had set one or wanted to know the details about the reminder). You can also delete or edit the reminder from here if needed.

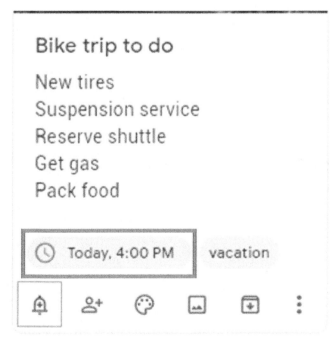

Figure 7.23

Chapter 7 – Google Keep

If you choose the *Pick a place* option (figure 7.24), Chrome will ask you if Keep can know your location to help you find the location you want to add to the reminder (figure 7.25).

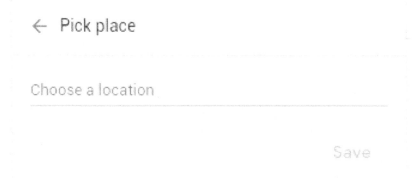

Figure 7.24

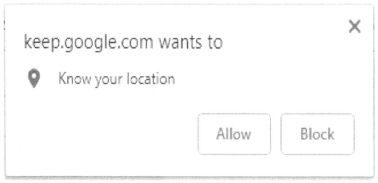

Figure 7.25

The location reminder will also show up in the note, just like the date and time reminder.

Once you set a reminder, you will see it in your Google Calendar, as seen in figure 7.26 on the 10th.

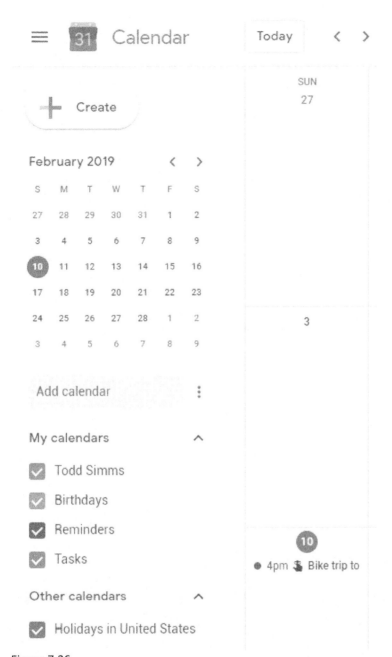

Figure 7.26

If you click on the reminder in your calendar it will bring up the details and allow you to do things such as edit, delete, or mark the note as done. You can also have your calendar open it up in Keep if desired.

Chapter 7 – Google Keep

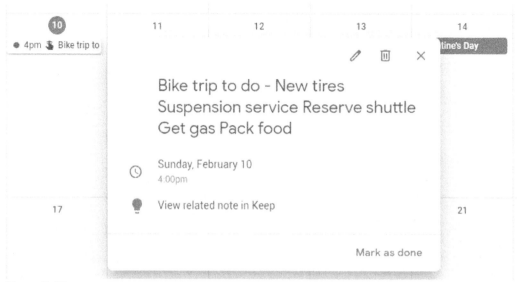

Figure 7.27

When the reminder time arrives, you will get a popup in your browser telling you about that note.

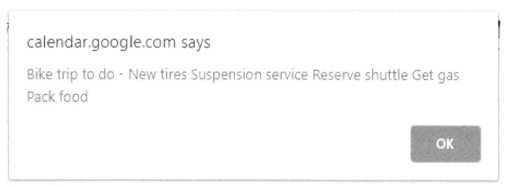

Figure 7.28

You may also get popups from your computer asking if you want to turn on Google Keep reminders, and it's up to you if you want to allow this or not.

Chapter 7 – Google Keep

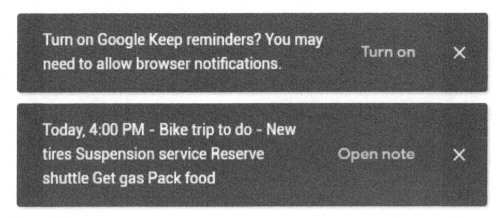

Figure 7.29

Searching for Notes
If you become a serious Keep user, then the amount of notes you create might start to get out of hand and become hard to find. Fortunately, there is a search feature within Keep that is there to help you out.

The search box is located at the top of the Keep window, and when you click on it you will see some options for what type of search you would like to perform. So, if you know you are searching for a particular drawing, you can click the drawing button in figure 7.30 to have Keep show you your drawings.

Chapter 7 – Google Keep

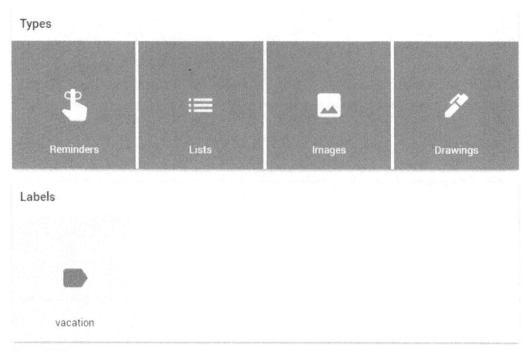

Figure 7.30

If you don't know what type of item you are searching for then you can type in a search term in the search box. If you take a look at figure 7.31, you can see that I typed in *dog sitter* in the search box, and notes brought up my note that had the search term in it.

Chapter 7 – Google Keep

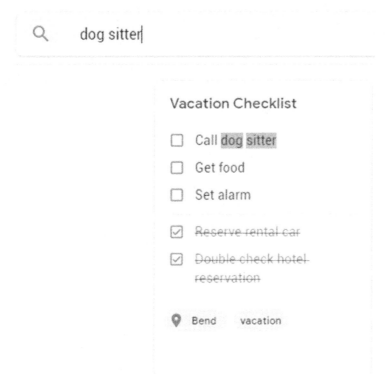

Figure 7.31

Settings
Keep is sort of limited on its configuration settings compared to some of the other apps that Google offers, but it still has a few things you can change or customize. If you click on the gear icon at the top right of the window, you will have a few choices to help you make the most out of Keep.

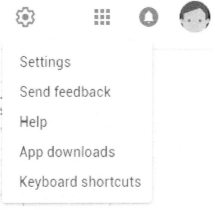

Figure 7.32

Chapter 7 – Google Keep

The actual *Settings* area itself doesn't offer too much configuration, but you might want to take a look at it and see if there are some things that you might benefit from if you change them.

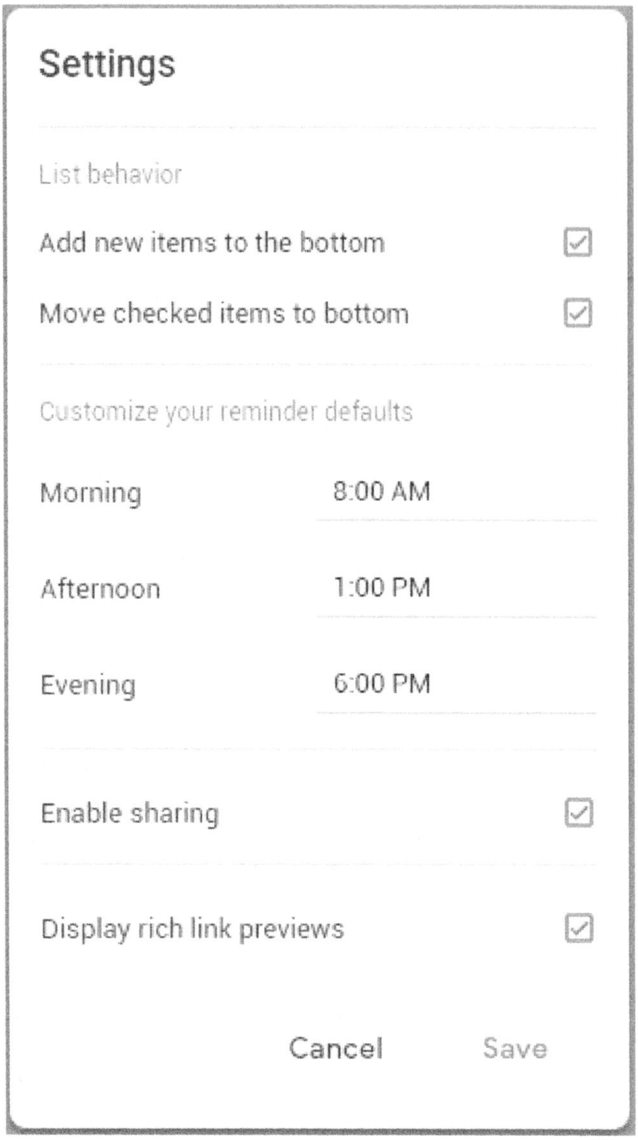

Figure 7.33

For example, if you don't like to have your new list items or checked items added to the bottom of the list, you can change that here. You can also change the Keep reminder defaults if that is something you would like to use but don't like its suggested times.

Chapter 7 – Google Keep

Just like with other Google Apps, Keep has a lot of keyboard shortcuts that you can use to speed things up when using the app. I would take a look at these and see what's available, because if you don't know about the keyboard shortcuts you will most likely never use them.

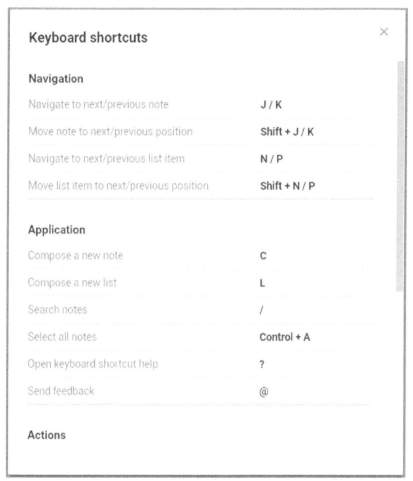

Figure 7.34

If you plan on using Keep on a regular basis (or any of the Google Apps, for that matter) I really recommend that you learn some of the more common keyboard shortcuts. Once you have these down, you don't even have to think about them, and will be using them instinctively.

339

Sharing Notes

Keep allows for collaboration or sharing of notes with other users in case you need to share the information about those notes. When you click on the Collaborator icon in a note, it will bring up a dialog box asking you who you would like to share that note with.

Figure 7.35

Once you have shared your note with someone else, there will be a new icon on that note telling you that it has been shared (figure 7.36). If you don't want to share the note anymore, simply click on that icon and then click the X by that user's name or email address.

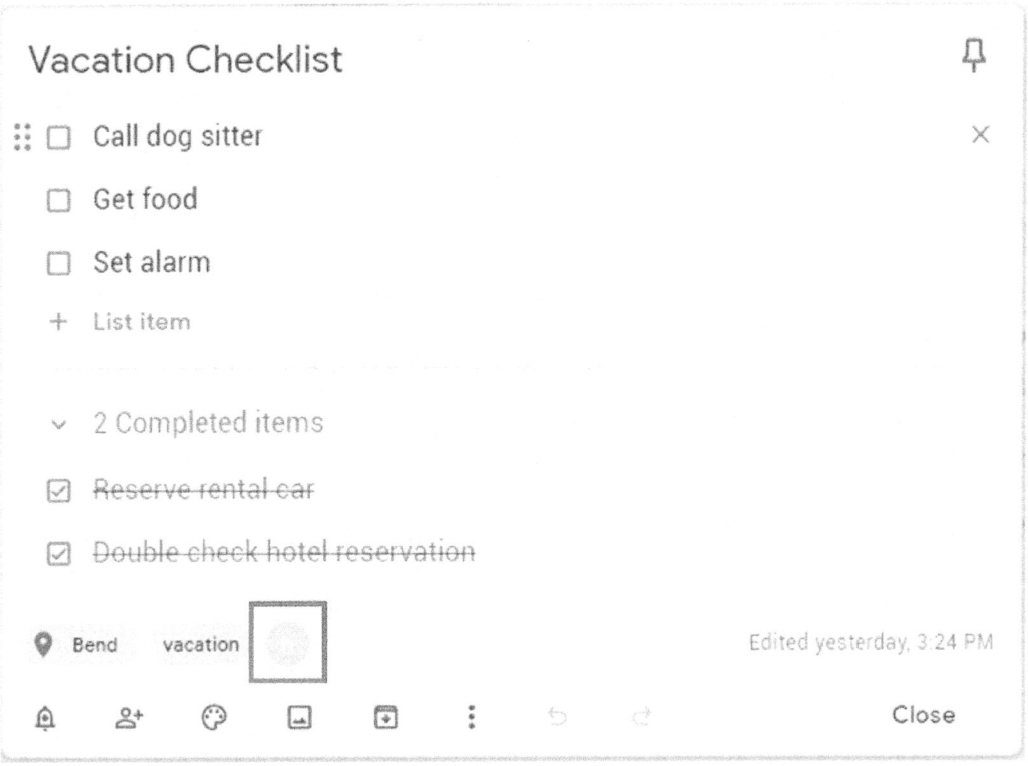

Vacation Checklist
Call dog sitter
Get food
Set alarm
List item
2 Completed items
Reserve rental car
Double check hotel reservation
Bend
vacation
Edited yesterday, 3:24 PM
Close

Figure 7.36

When you share a note, the person you shared it with will get an email similar to figure 7.37.

Todd shared a note with you - Project status
Todd Simms
to me
Todd (tsimms0000@gmail.com) shared a note with you.
Project status
Open in Keep
Google Keep: Save your thoughts, wherever you are.

Figure 7.37

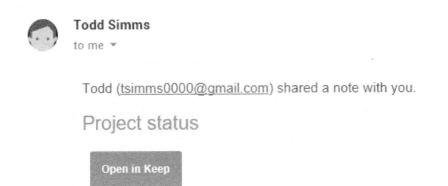

Chapter 7 – Google Keep

Google Keep Chrome Extension
If you are using the Google Chrome web browser, then you might have heard of Chrome extensions that you can download and install into your browser. These extensions offer additional functionality for a variety of things, such as having the ability to keep all of your passwords stored in one place or blocking pop-up ads and so on.

Google offers an extension for Chrome called the Google Keep Chrome Extension that is free to download and install. FYI, you need to be careful when installing Chrome extensions because you never know what can be in them, even though Google tries their best to block ones that might be malicious. However, the Keep extension is made by Google, so you should be just fine installing it.

Once you install the extension and sign in (if needed), you can go to other websites and do things such as save images, websites, text, and so on to your Keep notes just by right clicking on the item and choosing *Save to keep*.

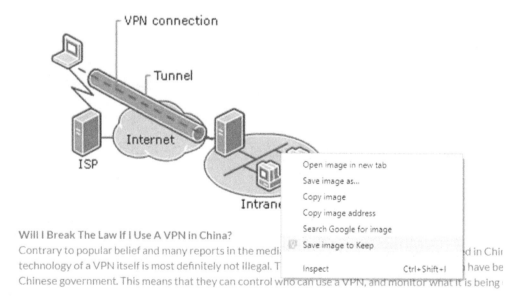

Figure 7.38

Chapter 7 – Google Keep

Figure 7.39

Then when you go back to Keep, you will see the note that has been created using the Chrome extension.

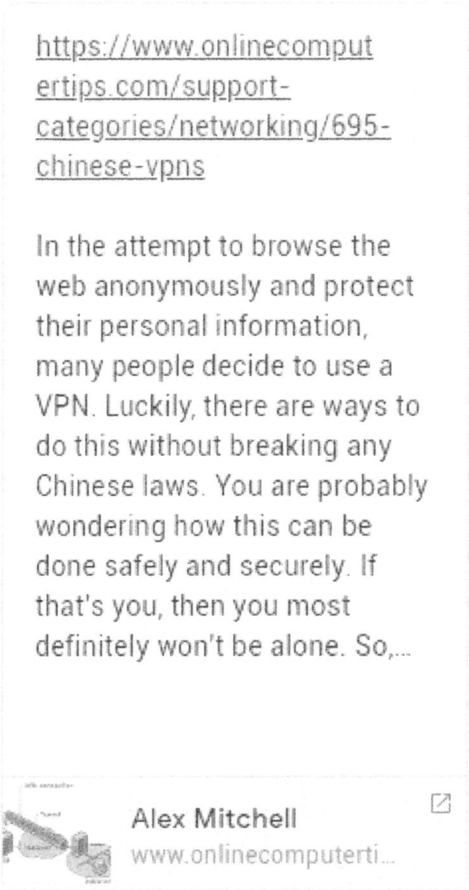

Figure 7.40

Chapter 7 – Google Keep

To get the Keep Chrome extension, just go to the Chrome Web Store and do a search for Google Keep. Then when you find it, click on the Add to Chrome button. (Just make sure you are using the Chrome web browser when doing this.)
https://chrome.google.com/webstore/category/extensions

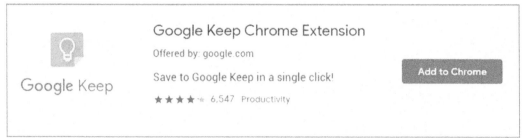

Figure 7.41

 Of course, Google wants you to use their Chrome web browser, just like Microsoft wants you to use their Edge web browser (Internet Explorer replacement). To try and force you to do so, they will make the Google Apps work better in Chrome then any of the other browsers.

Chapter 8 – Google Photos

Now that everyone has a smartphone, photographs are a way of life, and we now feel the need to take pictures of anything and everything and send them to everyone we know (whether they want them or not!).

With all of our devices being connected to each other, we like to be able to access all of our information from any one of them at any time. That is what is so great about Google Apps, because it allows you to do so with just one account. When you use Google Photos, you will be able to access all of your pictures from anywhere you are that you can sign in with your Google account. Plus, you can do the same with videos if you like.

Photos Interface
The Google Photos interface is pretty simple and easy to figure out once you've used it for a little while. It will organize your photos by date and group them so they are in chronological order. If you want to have specific types of pictures grouped together, then you can create albums to accomplish that. There is also an option to create a photo book that you can send to another person for them to view.

When you first open Photos, you might get prompted to install the desktop uploader if you are on your PC to assist you with uploading pictures from your computer to your Photos account. (I will have a section on this later in the chapter.)

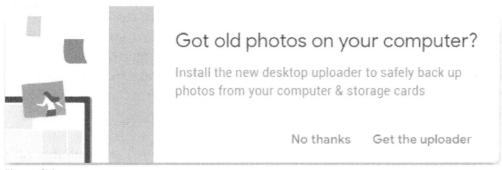
Figure 8.1

If you don't have any pictures in your account, then you will be prompted to add some. You might be tempted to start dragging and dropping pictures into your

Chapter 8 – Google Photos

Photos account randomly, but you might want to think about how you want to organize them so it doesn't end up being a mess of photos and videos.

Figure 8.2

I mentioned how Photos will arrange your pictures in chronological order. Whether or not this works correctly will depend on how your device labels pictures and how you are using Photos. Most modern smartphones and even cameras will tag photographs with the current date and time, and even the location it was taken at based on the location of your phone at the time the picture was taken.

Some devices (such as the Google branded smartphones) will automatically upload your pictures to "the cloud" as you take them, which will also help with organizing them by date. If your device is not tagging pictures with the date and location information, then go into its settings and see if it has been disabled.

Chapter 8 – Google Photos

If you do have some pictures in your Photos account, which you might not have realized you did, they will be displayed when you log in. As you can see in figure 8.3, you have a menu section on the left which can be hidden if you don't want to see it. It has various areas such as albums and photo books where you can go to create albums and so on. I will be going over each of these sections in this chapter.

Also, notice at the bottom of this menu that it shows you how much space you are using out of your total space. In my case, I am using 2.8 GB (gigabytes) out of 15. Keep in mind that higher resolution pictures will be larger in size and take up more of your available space. With today's high resolution cameras in our phones, these image file sizes are much larger than just a few years ago. Also keep in mind that video files will take up much more space than photographs.

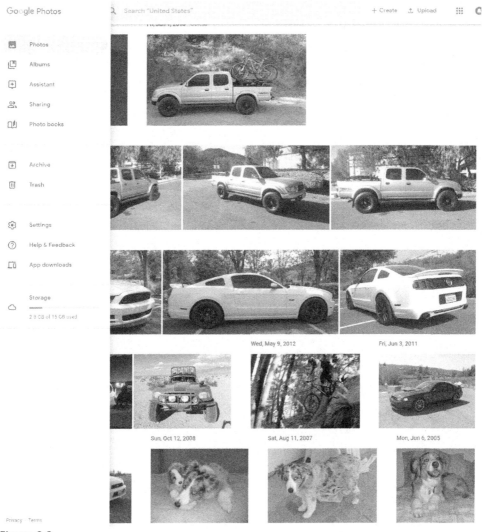

Figure 8.3

Chapter 8 – Google Photos

Adding Photos

There are a couple of ways you can add pictures to your Photos account. One way is to click on the *Upload* button at the top of the page and then browse for the files you want to add.

Figure 8.4

Another way is to just drag and drop pictures from your computer right into the Photos browser window.

 File management skills are very important when using computers and even other devices, because if you don't know where your files are located or how to find them, things will be much more difficult to figure out.

You can also click on the *Create* button and start with a new album, photo book, or one of the other options to start organizing your photos and videos as you upload them.

Chapter 8 – Google Photos

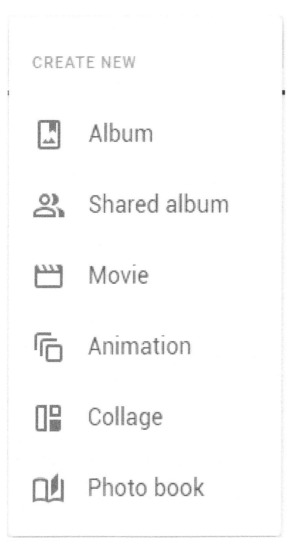

Figure 8.5

You have a couple of choices when you upload pictures to your Photos account. If you choose to let Google decide the quality of your pictures, then it won't count against your storage limit. But if you want to keep your pictures at a really high resolution, then it will count against your total available space (which is fine unless you are getting *low* on space).

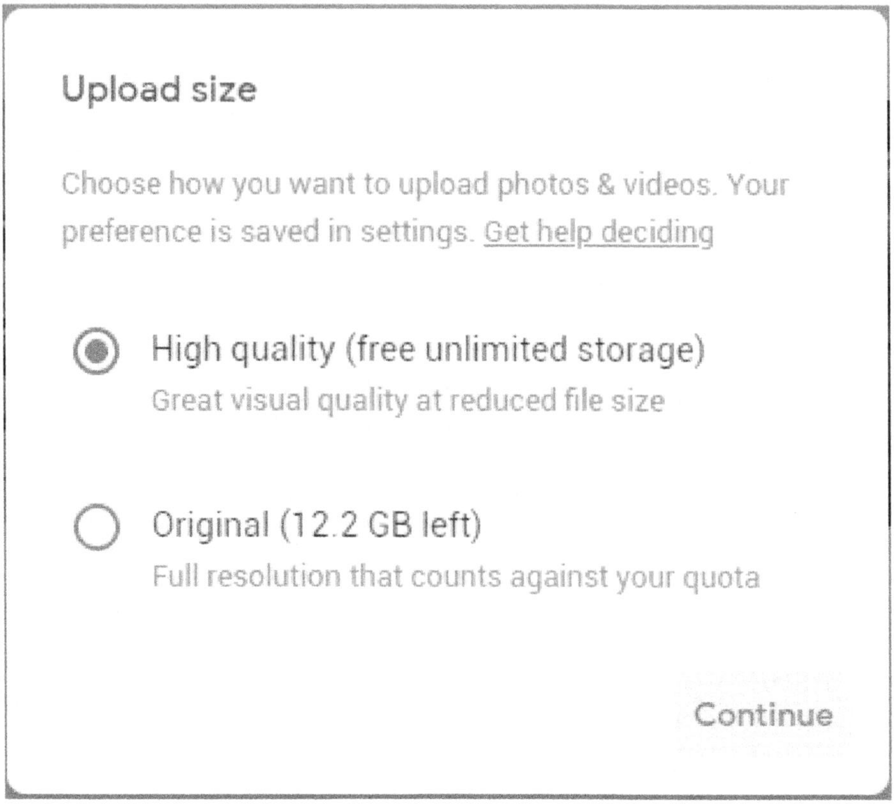

Chapter 8 – Google Photos

> **Upload size**
>
> Choose how you want to upload photos & videos. Your preference is saved in settings. Get help deciding
>
> ● High quality (free unlimited storage)
>   Great visual quality at reduced file size
>
> ○ Original (12.2 GB left)
>   Full resolution that counts against your quota
>
>   Continue

Figure 8.6

After the picture is uploaded, Photos will give you an option to add it to an album or to a shared album, which is nice if you are organizing your pictures as you are uploading them. If you don't want to add it to an album, then simply click on the X (figure 8.7).

Figure 8.7

After your image is uploaded, it will be marked with the date and location if the picture itself has been tagged. This will happen with uploaded videos as well (figure 8.8).

Figure 8.8

Desktop Uploader\Backup and Sync
I mentioned the Desktop Uploader at the beginning of this chapter, and since I am on the subject of uploading photos and videos, I figured now would be a good time to go over the Desktop Uploader itself. Google calls this add-on software *Backup and Sync*, and most likely will stick with that name, so I will refer to the software as Backup and Sync from now on.

This software is available for Windows and Mac computers, as well as Android and iPhone devices. When you go to the download page on your computer, you will see the options for all of these devices.

Chapter 8 – Google Photos

Back up a lifetime of photos

Backup and Sync
Automatically back up photos from your Mac or PC, connected cameras and SD cards

For mobile devices
Get the Google Photos app to back up and view photos on your Android and iOS devices

Figure 8.9

Once the Backup and Sync program is installed it will immediately synchronize certain files and folders with your Google Drive online. If you click on the cloud icon in the system tray (for Windows) you will be able to see the progress (figure 8.10).

Chapter 8 – Google Photos

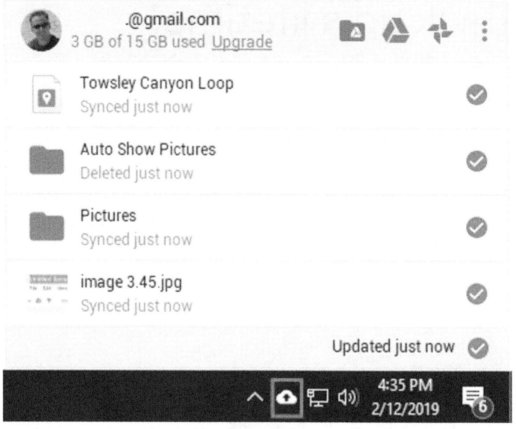

Figure 8.10

There are four icons at the top of this status box that you can click on to view your files and change your settings.

Figure 8.11

- **Open Google Drive folder** – This will open the local Google Drive folder on your computer (assuming you have your Google Drive set up).

- **Visit Google Drive on the web** – This will open Google Drive online so you can see what files of yours are stored there.

- **Visit Google Photos on the web** – This will open Google Photos like we have been working with so far.

- **Settings** – There are several settings here, such as being able to pause the synchronization and the ability to add a new Google account to sync with.

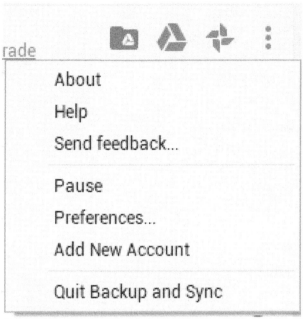

Figure 8.12

The main option you will be using here is for the *Preferences*. There are three sections of preferences that you can adjust. The first one lets you choose which local folders will be synced and how you want your photos to be treated when uploaded to your account (figure 8.13).

The second one is similar, and allows you to change which folders on your Google Drive will be synced with your local device.

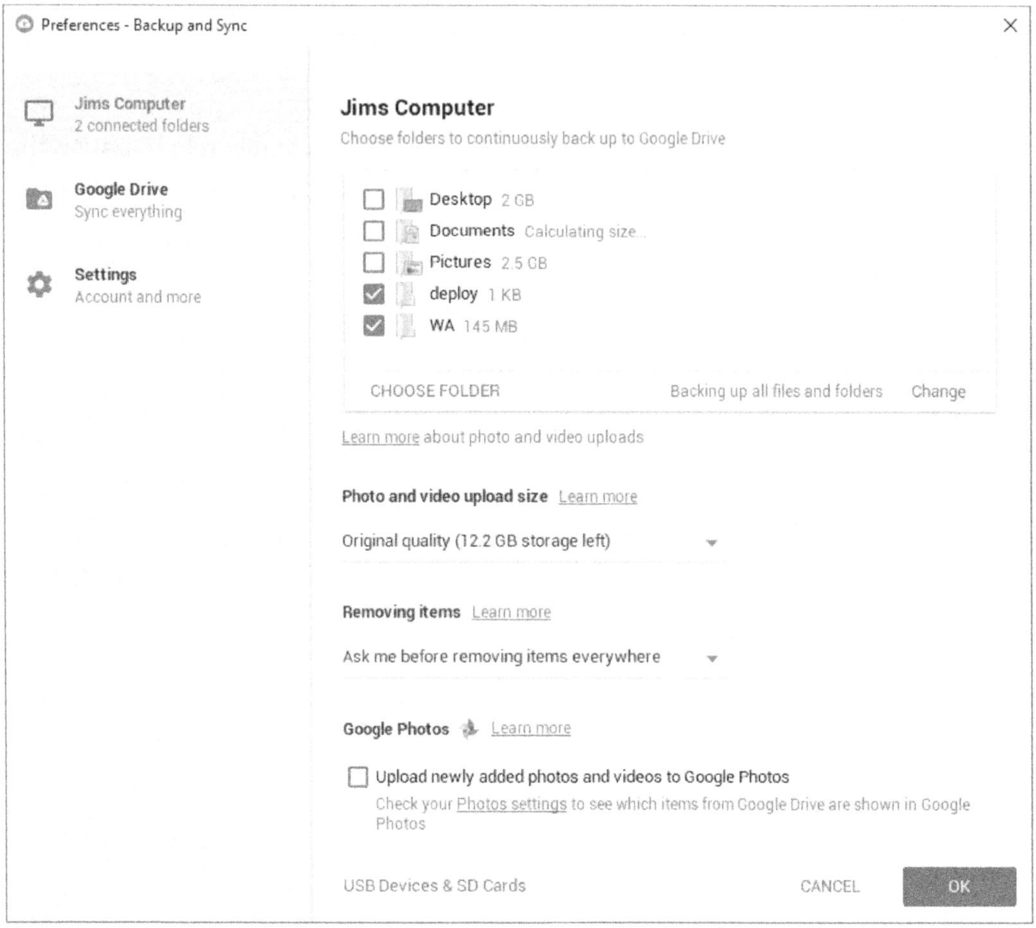

Chapter 8 – Google Photos

Figure 8.13

The last option for Settings is used to manage things such as whether or not Backup and Sync will run when you turn on your computer, and will also give you a place to upgrade your storage (for a price) if you need more space. If you would like to know the storage pricing as of the writing of this book, then check out the *Google One Plans and Features* section in Chapter 2.

Chapter 8 – Google Photos

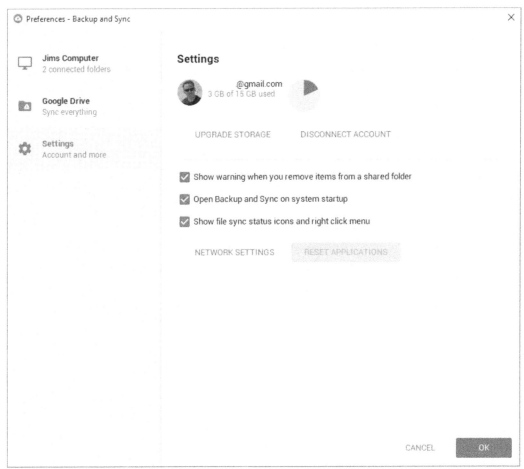

Figure 8.14

So, if you decide to use Backup and Sync, then every time you add new photos or videos to your computer they will be uploaded to your Photos account (assuming you have configured the Backup and Sync software with the right settings and folders). As you can see in figure 8.13, the default settings for me do not include syncing the *Pictures* folder.

Creating Albums

Albums are used to organize your photos and videos, just like you would with a physical photo album for your "old school" printed pictures. Photos will create some albums of its own when you have a bunch of uncategorized pictures uploaded, as you can see in figure 8.15.

Chapter 8 – Google Photos

Figure 8.15

To create a new album, simply click on the *Create album* button to begin the process.

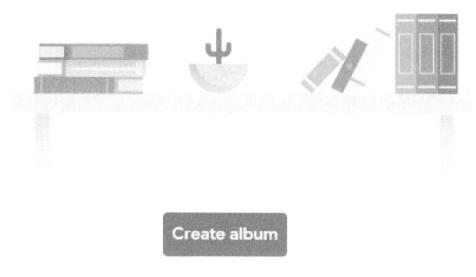
Figure 8.16

You will then be prompted to add a title to the album and then some photos. You can choose from your pictures that you have already uploaded, or you can click on *Select from computer* to upload new ones to your new album. There is also an option to search for photos if you have a lot and it's hard to find what you're looking for (figure 8.17). When you're finished, then click on the *Done* button and your new album will be ready to view (figure 8.18).

Figure 8.17

358

Chapter 8 – Google Photos

Figure 8.18

You will be prompted to share your new album with family and friends if you choose to do so, but this step is optional.

There will be three buttons at the top right of your album that you can use to perform various functions.

Figure 8.19

- **Add photos** – If you would like to add more pictures to this album, you can do so by clicking the *Add photos* button.

- **Share** – This option will allow you to share the album with people in your contacts or others by adding their email address. There is also an option to share your album on Facebook and Twitter if you have one of those social media accounts. Finally, you can create a link that you can copy and paste into an email and send off to someone. Then the person you

Chapter 8 – Google Photos

shared the link with will be able to see the pictures and videos within your album, but not any of your other pictures or videos.

- **More options** – Clicking the three vertical dots will open the *More options* choices.

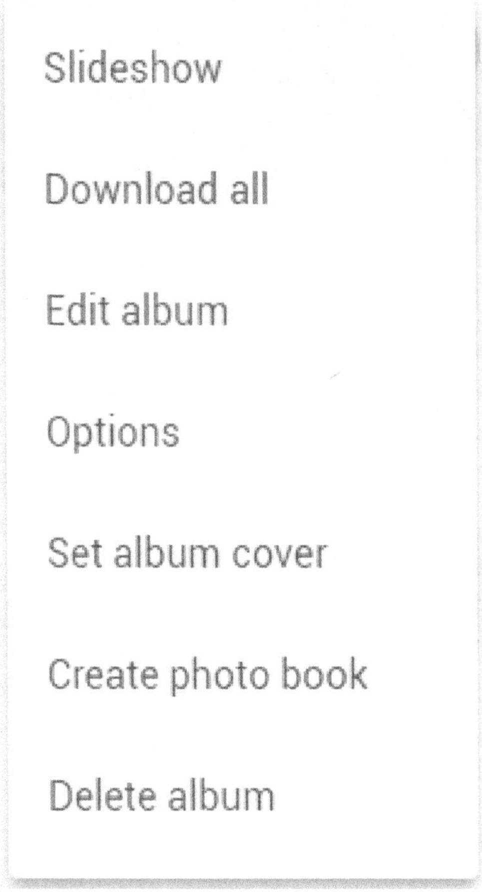

> Slideshow
>
> Download all
>
> Edit album
>
> Options
>
> Set album cover
>
> Create photo book
>
> Delete album

Figure 8.20

Here you have many choices in changing how your album looks, plus some other options.

- *Slideshow* – This will run a full screen slideshow presentation of all the pictures within the album.

- *Download all* – Choosing *Download all* will let you download all of the pictures in the album to your local device.

- *Edit album* – If you want to rename your album or change the orders of the pictures, then you can do so from here.

- *Options* – This will let you turn the sharing of the album with anyone who has the shared link on or off.

- *Set album cover* – If you want to choose a different default photo for the album cover, then you can do so from here.

- *Create photo book* – Here you can create a photo book, which I will be discussing later in this chapter.

- *Delete album* – Finally, if you do not want the album anymore, you can delete it here. It will not delete the actual pictures, but only the album.

Photo Assistant
The Photo Assistant is a feature that offers you suggestions regarding things such as adding photos to an existing album or moving older photos to your archive. It's not a very helpful feature, in my option, and you may not find yourself using it too often.

One interesting thing it will do is "stylize" a selected photo and send it to you to view, and then from there you can do things such as save it to your photos or share it with others. By *stylize,* I mean it will enhance the way it looks with colors or effects to make it stand out more.

The Photo Assistant will behave differently on your computer compared to your mobile device. For example, it might let you know that your phone is getting low on internal storage space or that your battery is getting low.

The Assistant uses what Google calls "cards" to show you suggestions or the results of its stylized photographs. From there you can do things like get information on a card or delete it if it's not needed. Figure 8.21 shows an example of a stylized photo card with the option to save or share it with others. The more photos and videos you add to your account, the more cards that will be created.

Chapter 8 – Google Photos

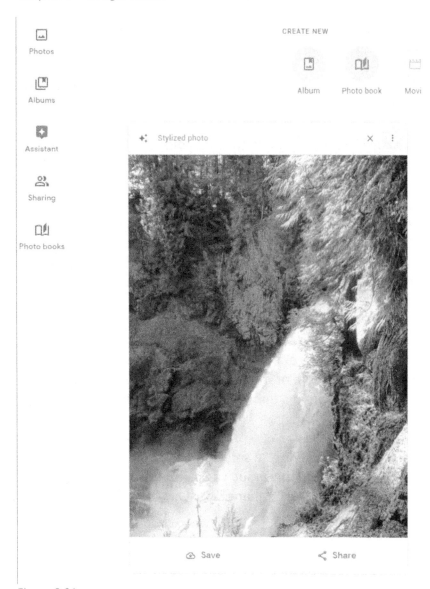

Figure 8.21

To dismiss the card you can click on the X at the top right corner. To delete the card, click on the three vertical dots and choose *Delete permanently*. It's possible to disable the Photo Assistant altogether from the Photos settings, which I will go over later in the chapter.

Photo Books
Photo Books is a service from Google where you can choose pictures from your storage images and have custom photo books printed out and sent to you. These are not free, of course, and start at $9.99 and go up depending on how many

pictures you use, the number of pages, and if you want hardcover or softcover. Think of them as Albums that you can have printed out in a custom book format.

Figure 8.22

When you go to *Photo book* in Google Photos, you will see some suggestions as to what kind of books you can create, and Photos will try and select pictures from your collection to match that category.

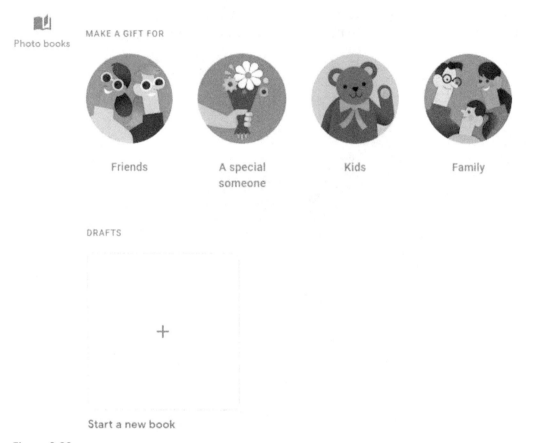

Figure 8.23

If you see the message shown in figure 8.24, that means that you don't have face grouping enabled in your settings (settings will be discussed later). Face grouping is used by Photos to "tag" faces so it can help to organize the people in your photos.

Figure 8.24

Chapter 8 – Google Photos

Even if you turn it on, you might get a message like the one in figure 8.25 telling you that you don't have enough face groups to choose from.

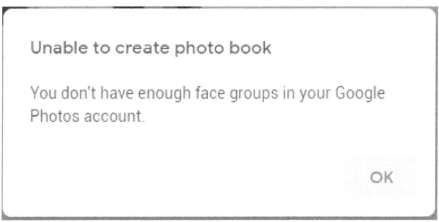

Figure 8.25

This just means that you didn't tag any people in your photos when you uploaded them, but you can do that after the fact if you wish. That way when you search for someone it will bring up the results based on who or what or where you are searching for. For example, if I type in "dog" in the search box, here is what Photos finds.

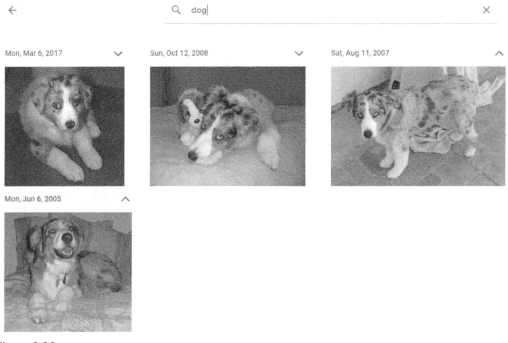

Figure 8.26

Chapter 8 – Google Photos

I didn't tag these pictures with the word "dog", but Photos was smart enough to know that the object in the pictures is a dog.

Getting back to Photo Books, once you start a new one you can choose any pictures from your account. Then when you are done you can organize them the way you like by dragging them around your screen. The first picture will be the title image, and you can add some text for the title as well. If you take a look at figure 8.27, you will see that there are a couple of pictures (of the dog) that have exclamation points on them. This is telling me that the images are low resolution and might not print out that well.

Figure 8.27

When you are satisfied with your image selection and layout, you can choose the Checkout button and Photos will give you the cost of your picture book based on how many images you have and what type of book you want to have created.

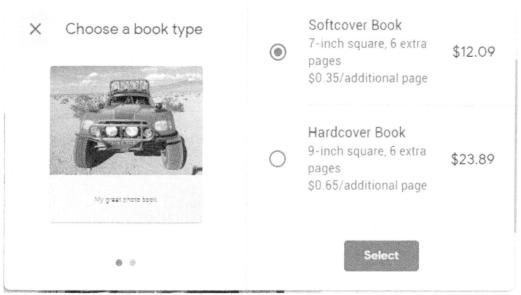

Figure 8.28

Then you can go through the checkout process, make your payment, and wait for your photo book to arrive.

If you want to save it to edit or purchase later, you can save it as a draft and it will then show up under the *Drafts* section of Photo Books (figure 8.29).

Chapter 8 – Google Photos

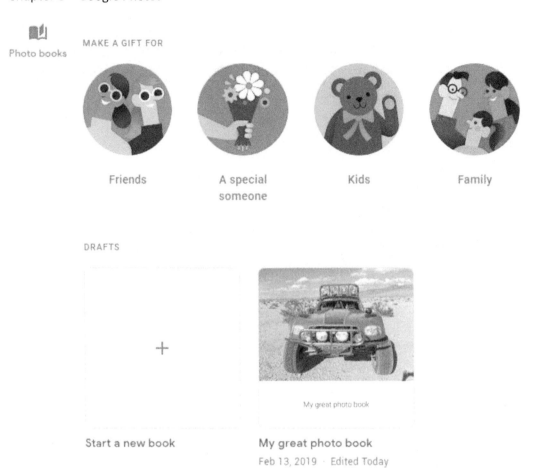

Figure 8.29

<u>Sharing</u>

Just like with all the other apps, sharing is a big part of the Google experience, and that is no different for Photos. Plus, I'm sure you know how much people love to share their photos anyway.

When you go to the Sharing section in Photos it will show you your shared photos and videos (if you have any). It will also show you any albums that have been shared with you by other people.

Chapter 8 – Google Photos

Figure 8.30

If you want to get rid of albums that have been shared with you then you can click on the three vertical dots on the album image and choose *Leave album*. There is also an option to block the user who is sharing photos with you as well as report abuse in case you end up with a photo stalker!

For any albums that you created, you will have the option to delete them, which will remove photos added by the other user(s) and prevent them from accessing your photos and videos that you have shared.

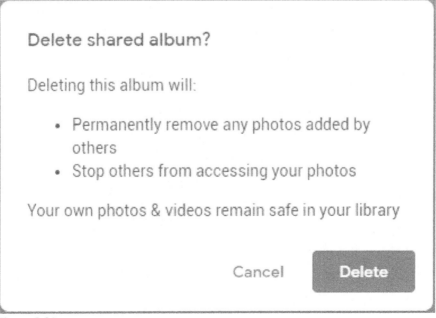

Figure 8.31

369

Chapter 8 – Google Photos

To create a shared album simply click on *Start a new share* (as seen in figure 8.30). Then you will need to give the album a title and choose which photos and\or videos you want to be included in this album. Once you have made your selections click on the *Done* button. Then you can review your album and will have the option to click on *Share* to start the sharing process. If you don't want to share it right away, you can always perform this step later.

Figure 8.32

When you click on *Share* it will bring up your Google contacts (discussed in Chapter 11) for you to choose from, and you can start typing in a name and it will auto populate the rest of it for you. If the name is not in your contacts, then you can just type in the email address of the person you want to share with. When you are done, simply click on the send arrow and that's it!

Figure 8.33

Chapter 8 – Google Photos

Afterward, you will see all the people that you have shared the album with and be able to add additional people by clicking the + button.

Jun 6, 2005–Mar 6, 2017

Figure 8.34

When you go back to the main sharing area you will now see your new shared album, along with any other shared albums you might have.

Figure 8.35

When the person you shared the album with logs into their Google Photos account, they will then see the album you have shared with them (figure 8.36).

Chapter 8 – Google Photos

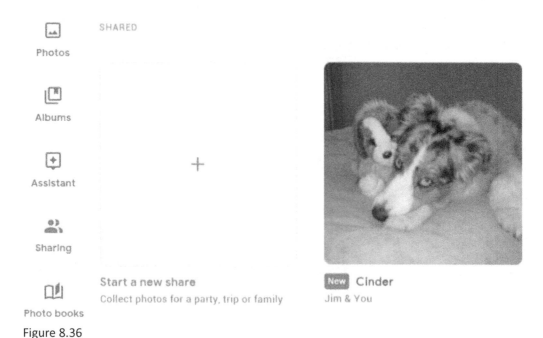

Figure 8.36

You can also share individual pictures or videos with people by selecting them from your photos and then clicking on the share button at the top right of the screen. Then you will share them the same way you share an album, and they will see the specific shared picture within their *Sharing* section alongside any shared albums.

Figure 8.37

Settings

Google Photos has a Settings area where you can go and adjust various settings to make Photos work the way you want it to work. (Or at least *more* like you want it to work.) The Settings section is located on the main menu on the left of the Photos interface. As you can see in figure 8.38, there are a variety of things you can change.

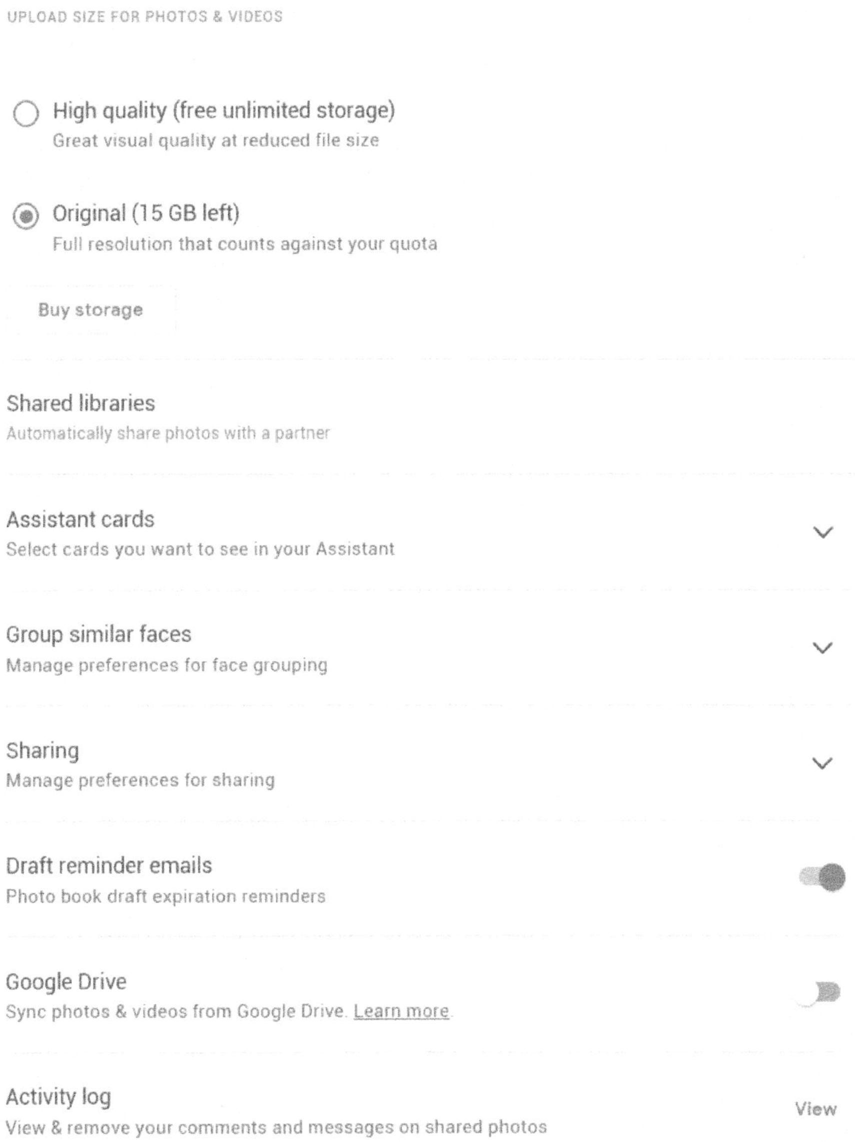

Chapter 8 – Google Photos

UPLOAD SIZE FOR PHOTOS & VIDEOS

○ **High quality (free unlimited storage)**
Great visual quality at reduced file size

⦿ **Original (15 GB left)**
Full resolution that counts against your quota

Buy storage

Shared libraries
Automatically share photos with a partner

Assistant cards   ⌄
Select cards you want to see in your Assistant

Group similar faces   ⌄
Manage preferences for face grouping

Sharing   ⌄
Manage preferences for sharing

Draft reminder emails
Photo book draft expiration reminders

Google Drive
Sync photos & videos from Google Drive. Learn more.

Activity log   View
View & remove your comments and messages on shared photos

Figure 8.38

I have gone over some of these already, but I now would like to get into a little more detail about what these options do.

- **Upload size for photos and videos** – I had mentioned earlier in the chapter how you can have unlimited photo storage space if you let Google decide how large your image files are, but if you wanted to keep them at their original (and most likely higher) resolution, then it will count against your storage space.

I also mentioned how there is an option to buy additional storage space, but if you are running low and want to try to recover some space without deleting any files, then you can try the *Recover storage* option. This will compress your files and convert your high resolution photos to a lower resolution, so if that's not a big deal to you, then you can give it a shot. It will tell you at the top how much space you will recover by doing so. As you can see in figure 8.39, I will recover 15.6 MB (megabytes) if I were to do this.

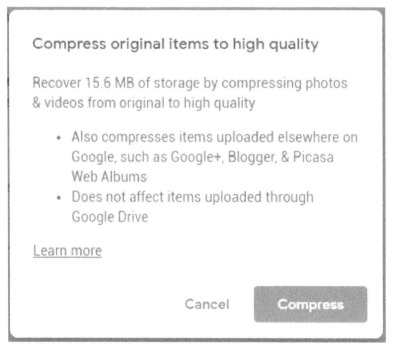

Figure 8.39

- **Shared libraries** – This option lets you automatically share your photos (and videos) with people of your choosing every time you add more to your Photos library. You can set up this sharing by clicking on *Shared libraries*.

- **Assistant cards** – If you don't think you will have any use for the *Assistant card* feature of Photos, then you can turn off specific parts or the entire thing from here.

- **Group similar faces** – I mentioned how Photos can group faces to make it easier to search for a specific person or make an album containing photos from specific people. If you want to use this feature, then you need to make sure that it is enabled from here.

- **Sharing** – The *Sharing* options allows you to do things such as enable sharing suggestion notifications and remove location tags from your shared items in case you don't want others seeing that information.

- **Draft reminder emails** – If you have started working on a Google Photo Book and left it in draft status without finishing it, then Google will send you reminders that you still have a work in progress unless you turn this option off (which I would!).

- **Google Drive** – If you are using Google Drive for online storage, then you can have Photos automatically synchronize your pictures and videos right to your Drive if this option is turned on. Just keep in mind that you will need to keep an eye on storage space if you are the type that likes to take a lot of pictures.

- **Activity log** – When you share photos or albums, others can comment on them and send you messages about them. If you click on *View* in this setting, you can see those comments and messages all in one place.

Mobile Devices

Using Google Photos on a mobile device such as your smartphone or tablet will work a little differently than it does on your desktop computer. Since you will be taking your pictures from your smartphone, Photos will group these pictures in with your other Photos pictures as well, and you won't see them on your computer unless you have the synchronization turned on.

If you don't have Google Photos installed on your phone, then you can get it from the App Store (iPhone) or Play Store (Android). If you have an Android device, then there is a good chance it came preinstalled since Google owns Android.

The mobile version of Photos has a very similar interface to the desktop version (figure 8.40). It will have most of the same menu items as the desktop version and function basically the same. One mobile specific feature is called *PhotoScan,* which is a separate app you can install to scan a paper picture into your phone or tablet using its built-in camera. Then you can place them in Photos with all the rest of your pictures.

Chapter 8 – Google Photos

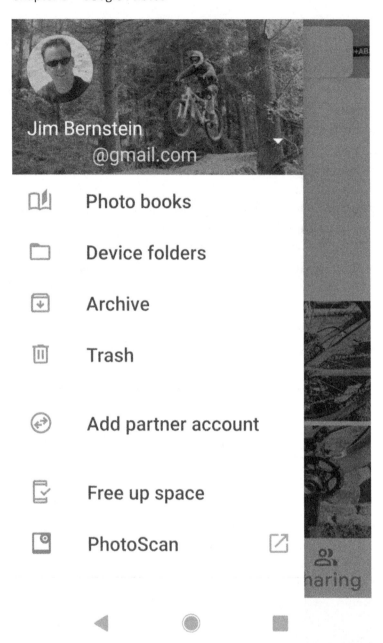

Figure 8.40

There are additional options on the app (just like the desktop version) that you can get to by tapping on the three vertical dots by the search box (on Android devices at least) and they will allow you to do things like change the layout or make albums and photo books.

Chapter 8 – Google Photos

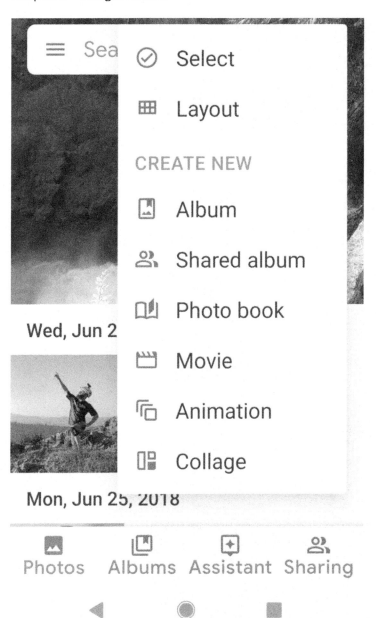

Figure 8.41

The *Movie* option is kind of fun because you can select a group of pictures and have the app put them into a slideshow type movie with music that you can then save and share. The *Animation* option works the same way, but is not as fancy.

I really like the Collage option because it's an easy way to make nice looking collages that you can create for a group of related images and then save and share.

Chapter 8 – Google Photos

Figure 8.42

If you plan on using Photos for your main picture and video storage, you should definitely check out the app since it will allow you to manage your pictures and videos from anywhere you have an Internet connection.

Chapter 9 – Gmail

Email has been around for many years now, and is a such a big part of our lives that we would be lost without it. (Thank goodness we would still have text messaging as a backup!) We use email for work, school, and our personal lives and it's always been a useful tool when it comes to fast communication between each other.

Google has their own email service that they call Gmail (guess what the G stands for), and it has been around since 2004 and has millions of people using it—mostly because it's popular, widely supported, and free. Gmail hasn't changed too much throughout the years, but there have been new features added, and, of course, there is the integration factor with the other Google apps and services.

There is actually quite a lot to Gmail, and you can actually find entire books on the subject. But for this chapter I will just be going over the basics to get you going in being proficient in using Gmail.

Gmail Interface
Most email applications have the same look to them, where you have your inbox and other folders on the left hand side, and then your listing of emails on the right hand side. Gmail works the same way, but the folders you will have on the left will vary from account to account as you create custom folders to help sort your email.

As you can see in figure 9.1, there are various folders on the left hand side such as Inbox, Sent, Drafts, and so on. There are also several Categories which I will discuss later in this chapter. Clicking on *More* will expand this list and show additional folders and options.

On the right of figure 9.1 are the email messages themselves in the *Inbox,* and they are sorted by date by default. You can click a column header to change the sort order to something else (like who the sender is, etc.). The Inbox is where new mail shows up and stays until you delete it or move it to a different folder. The first column shows who the email is from and the next column shows the subject.

Chapter 9 – Gmail

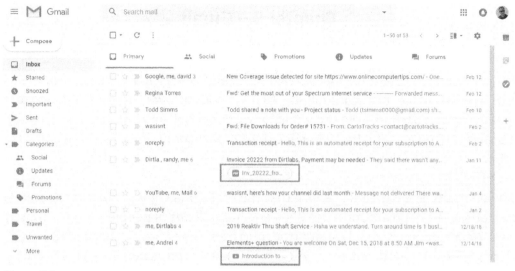

Figure 9.1

If you click on the down arrow next to *Inbox*, you can choose from a variety of *Inbox Types* which will sort your email differently.

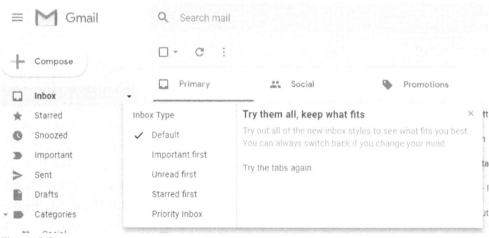

Figure 9.2

On the top right it shows the number of emails in the inbox, which in my example is fifty-three. Google gives you plenty of room for email storage, so you most likely will never run out of space unless you are an email maniac who gets a lot of emails with attachments and keeps every email you ever get!

Speaking of attachments, they will show up under the email that contains the attachments. In figure 9.1 the attachments are highlighted with a box around them so you can see what I am referring to.

Chapter 9 – Gmail

By default, Gmail will just show you your listing of emails with no previews, and you will have to click on one to have it open for viewing. You have the option to have your messages displayed with a vertical or horizontal split if you want to see previews of the email without having to open them. You can do this by clicking the down arrow next to the *Toggle split pane mode* button at the right side of the toolbar.

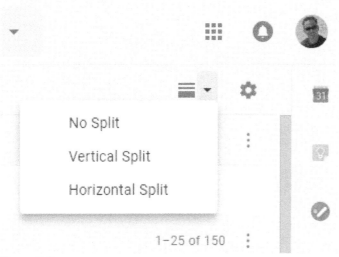

Figure 9.3

Figure 9.4 shows what the messages will look like with the *Horizontal Split* option turned on. In this example, the email from Todd Simms is highlighted, and then the email itself is displayed in the preview window at the bottom of the screen.

Chapter 9 – Gmail

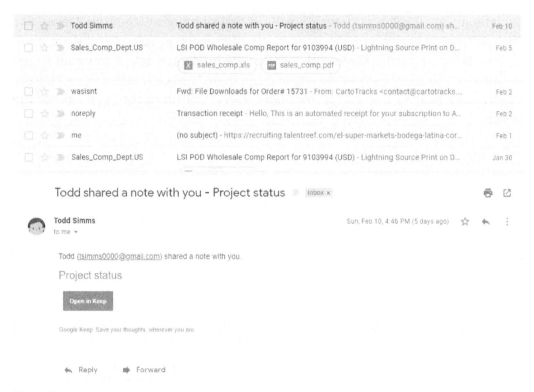

Figure 9.4

Figure 9.5 shows how it would look using the *Vertical Split* option.

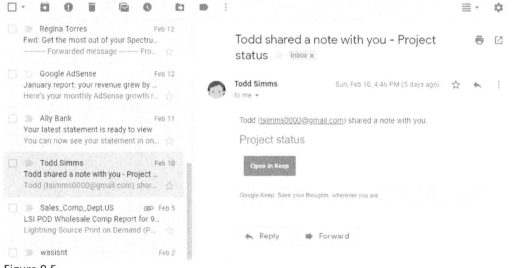

Figure 9.5

At the left side of the toolbar you will find a box that can be used to select different types of email. This makes it easier than manually selecting a bunch of emails one

Chapter 9 – Gmail

at a time. The ↻ symbol is used to refresh the folder you are in, so if you want to have Gmail check for new messages immediately, then simply click on this icon.

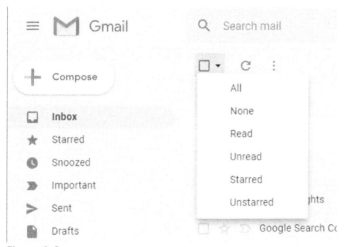

Figure 9.6

 Pressing the F5 key on your keyboard will also refresh you email, and also works to refresh any web page that you are on. (This is assuming you are running Microsoft Windows. You can try Command-R for a Mac.)

When you have an email (or emails) checked, then this toolbar will change to what you see in figure 9.7, and give you many more options to choose from to manage those selected messages.

Figure 9.7

Chapter 9 – Gmail

Here is what each one of these tools will do to the selected emails:

1. This can be used to select either all of the messages, or to deselect the messages.

2. This is used to archive email, which will send it to the All Mail folder and remove it from your inbox to keep it less cluttered.

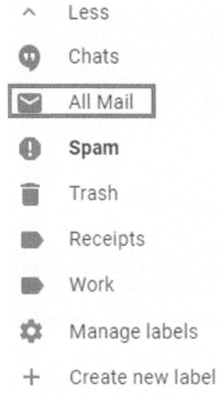
Figure 9.8

3. If a particular email is junk and you want to mark it as such, then you can use this *Report spam* button.

4. Like most apps, when you see a trash can, that means delete. Gmail is no different!

5. When you read an email it will go from a bolded type to un-bolded, showing it has been read. If you want to mark a read email as unread, then this is where you can do it.

Chapter 9 – Gmail

6. The *Snooze* option will make the selected email pop back up at the top of your inbox at a date and time of your choosing. These emails can be seen in the Snoozed folder on the left hand side of the Gmail window if you need to view them before they "wake up". You can also "unsnooze" them from here if needed.

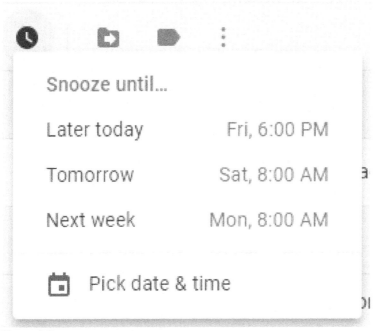

Figure 9.9

7. If you need to move an email to a different folder, then you would use the *Move to* option and then choose a destination from your existing folders.

8. Labels are used to label an email with a specific type of category so you can easily find them in your inbox. You can also find them in the labels section in your folders. You can choose from one of the default labels or create your own.

Chapter 9 – Gmail

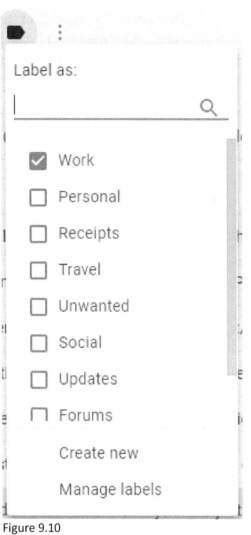
Figure 9.10

Figure 9.11

Figure 9.12

Chapter 9 – Gmail

9. The three vertical dots contain even more choices that you can apply to your emails.

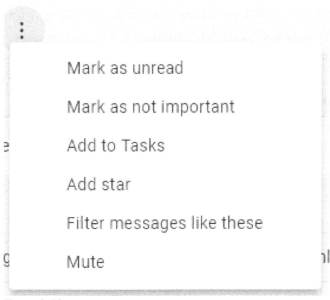

Figure 9.13

- **Mark as unread** – If you want to mark an email as read without having to open it, then you can use the *Mark as unread* option.

- **Mark as not important** – By default, each email will have a gold arrow in front of it, but if you choose to mark it as not important, it will remove that gold arrow in favor of a clear one. This can easily be reversed by going back and choosing *Mark as important*.

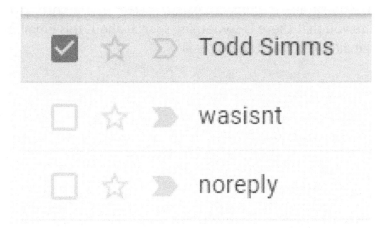

Figure 9.14

- **Add to Tasks** – You can add emails to your Tasks or things to-do list so you remember to work on them later to complete that task. Once you add an email to your tasks, you can get to them by clicking the *Tasks* button on the right side of your email. Notice how there is also the Keep icon as well, which allows you easy access to your notes.

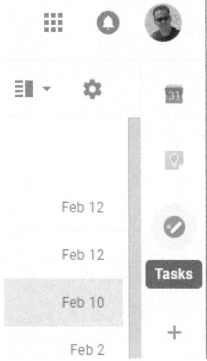
Figure 9.15

- **Add star** – Adding a star simply makes the clear star a solid gold color, indicating to you that there is something special about this email. You can sort your email by starred items as well.

Figure 9.16

- **Filter messages like these** – If you want to find all the emails that match a criteria of a specific email, then you can use the *Filter messages like these* to do so. Once you choose this option, you can filter your messages on a variety of things (as shown in figure 9.17).

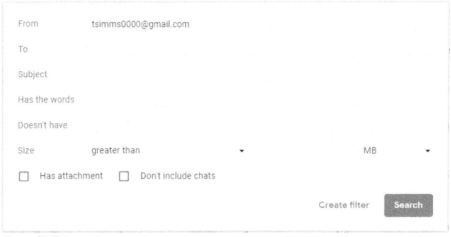

Figure 9.17

In my example I just left the default filter, which was to filter by the *tsimms0000@gmail.com* email address, and here are the results.

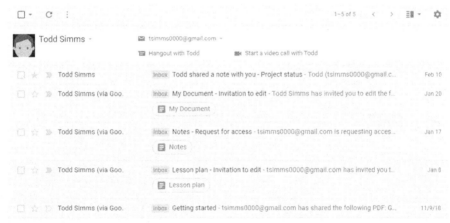

Figure 9.18

- **Mute** – This option allows you to mute a conversation, and you won't see any further messages from that conversation in your inbox. Any additional emails that come in for that conversation will be automatically archived.

Chapter 9 – Gmail

One last thing I want to go over in this section is the search feature in Gmail at the top of the app. It's very similar to the *Filter messages like these* option, which I just discussed (figure 9.17), but it starts with a blank slate for you to enter your search criteria in. You don't need to use the form to do searches, but can just start typing in things such as an email address or something from the subject or body of an email to start seeing results.

You can either choose from one of the suggested results (like shown in figure 9.19), or press Enter on your keyboard to see all of the results (as shown in figure 9.20).

Figure 9.19

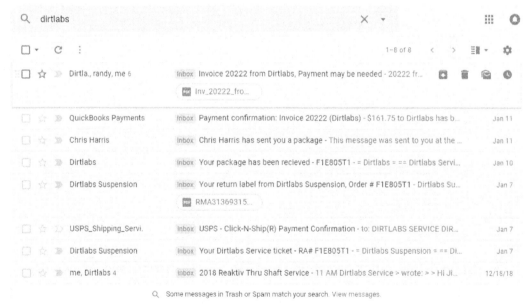

Figure 9.20

390

Chapter 9 – Gmail

Categories

If you are like most people, then you get a lot of emails, and sometimes it's difficult to keep them organized and find the ones that are the most important to you. This is where Categories come into play, and some people like them while others don't really care for them.

Categories are tabs you can have display in your Inbox to help you organize your incoming emails automatically, and this is where the potential problem lies. Since Gmail doesn't know what emails you want in what category, it tries to figure it out on its own and categorizes them for you, and it's not always right, even though it does do a pretty good job. Gmail has its default categories such as Primary, Social, Promotions, Updates, and Forums. If you are using the Default Inbox view, then these categories will be displayed as tabs above your messages.

Figure 9.21

If not, then you will still see them on the left with your folders and labels. You don't have to show all of the categories, and you can select which ones you want to have displayed from the Gmail settings (which I will go over later in this chapter).

Here is what types of email Gmail will place in each category:

- **Primary** – General email conversations\messages that don't fit into other tabs.

- **Social** – Messages from social networks like Facebook and Instagram as well as online dating services and other related websites.

- **Promotions** – Special deals, offers, and other marketing emails.

- **Updates** – Messages that might include purchase or trip confirmations, bills, invoices, and statements.

- **Forums** – Emails from online forums, discussion boards, and other mailing lists.

Some categories will get more use than others depending on what type of email you usually get. For example, I get a lot of email in the Update category compared to the other ones.

Categories can be a little confusing, and can cause you to miss emails if you don't think to check your category tabs when checking your email. If you don't want to use Categories, you can disable them in the settings by unchecking the ones you don't want to show or changing your Inbox style from Default to one of the others. (I have never been a fan of Categories, and like to see all of my email in one place.)

Sending and Receiving Emails
Now comes the time in this chapter where we will send and receive some emails so you can see how it all works. This process is not very difficult, but if you are new to Gmail (or even email itself), then it will definitely help make things easier.

Sending Email
You might have noticed the big button at the top left of the Gmail window that says *Compose*. This is the button you will click on to send out an email to another person or even multiple people. When you click on *Compose*, a box will open up in the lower left corner, allowing you to enter the information for your email (figure 9.22).

The process is pretty simple, and all you need to do is type in the email address or addresses in the *To* box. Just be sure to type it correctly and use the @ symbol and no spaces. It should be in the format *name@company.com,* and of course you will change the name and company.com to whatever email address domain they use. If you have any contacts setup, then Gmail will load the matching ones as you type.

Clicking on the word *To* itself will bring up your contacts if you have any. (Contacts will be discussed in Chapter 11.) Also, make a note of the CC and Bcc in the upper right hand corner of figure 9.22. They are used if you want to add additional email addresses so they can be sent to other people who are not considered the main recipient. Cc stands for Carbon Copy, and Bcc stands for Blind Carbon Copy. When you use the Bcc field, then the email addresses entered in there will not be seen by other people who get the same email.

Chapter 9 – Gmail

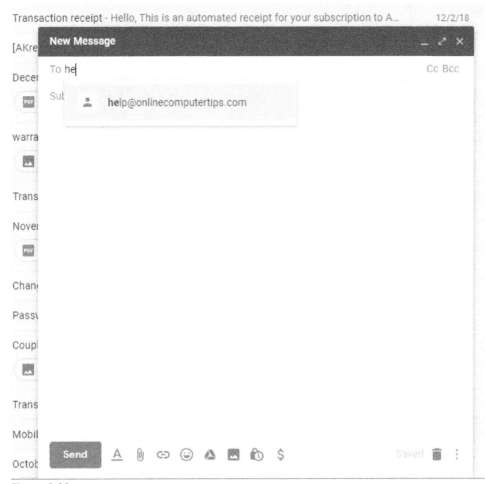

Figure 9.22

Then you will need to enter a *Subject* for the email on the *Subject* line, and then the text for the email itself in the main box. Figure 9.23 shows a typical standard format email ready to send out.

Chapter 9 – Gmail

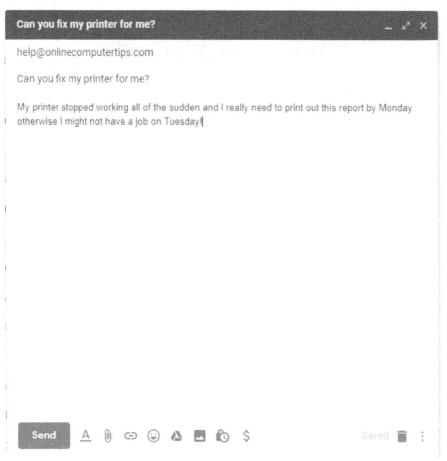

Figure 9.23

Of course, you don't need to send out typical standard (and boring) emails, and have many options to spruce them up a little. Figure 9.24 shows all the available tools we can use to edit and configure an email.

Figure 9.24

Of course, you don't *need* to use any of these additional features, but it's good to know what each one does.

1. This one will obviously send the email, so make sure it's ready to go before clicking it!

2. Clicking on the underlined A icon will open up the formatting options, where you can do things such as change the font, font color, bold the text, add bulleted lists, and so on.

Figure 9.25

3. The paperclip icon is used to add attachments to your email. You can add more than one if you like, but just be aware of file size limitations when including attachments in emails. As you add attachments, they will be shown at the bottom of the email along with their file size. Clicking on the X next to an attachment will remove it from the email, but not from your computer or device.

Figure 9.26

4. If you want to insert a link to a website or an email address that someone can click on to compose a new email you can do that from the link icon.

5. The smiley face icon can be used to add an emoji to your message (if you are into that sort of thing!).

6. This next icon will let you place a file from your Google Drive into your email. It will display a little differently than an attachment from your computer (since it's not actually including the file, but rather a link to the file in your drive). In figure 9.30, the Google Drive attachment is called *Consulting proposal*.

7. Next, we have the *Insert Photo* option that will let you insert a picture into the body of your email from your Google Drive, local computer, or from a website. You can insert the photo in-line with the text of your email, or as an attachment. I will insert a waterfall picture in-line with the text in my email (figure 9.30).

8. *Confidential mode* can be used to protect sensitive information within an email. You can use this mode to set an expiration date for messages or revoke access at any time. The people who receive these confidential messages won't be able to forward, copy, print, or download the email.

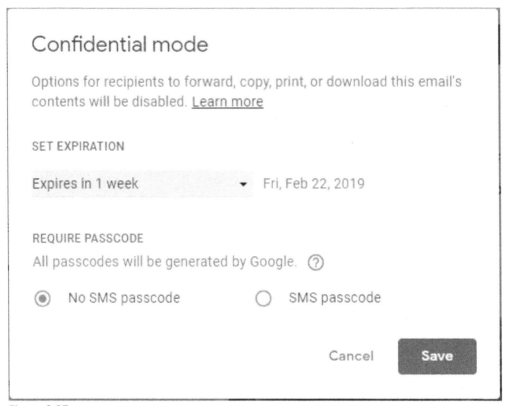

Figure 9.27

9. The dollar sign icon is used to send money or request money via Google Pay. This is similar to PayPal, and you will need to set up a payment account with a debit card before using this service.

Chapter 9 – Gmail

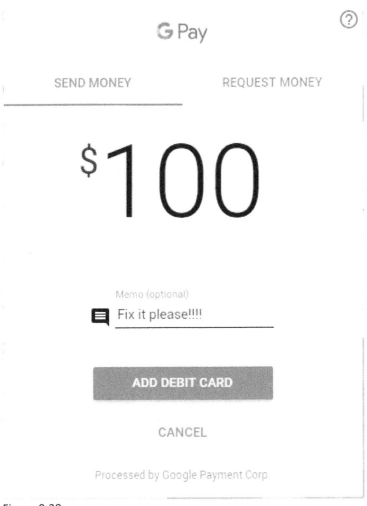

Figure 9.28

10. Once again, the trash can icon is used to delete the email before sending it.

11. The three vertical dots have additional options such as making the email full screen if needed, adding a label to the email, use plain text mode (no formatting), print (discussed later), and run a spell check. *Smart Compose feedback* is used to offer suggestions as you type to help you compose your emails faster.

Chapter 9 – Gmail

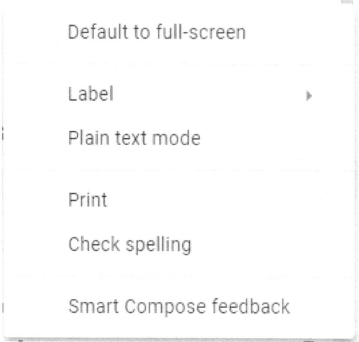

Figure 9.29

As you can see in figure 9.30, I finally have my email ready to go, and will now click on send. Then we can see how it looks on the receiver's end.

Chapter 9 – Gmail

Figure 9.30

If you get a message like the one in figure 9.31, it means that something from your Google Drive does not have the appropriate sharing setup. In my case, it's the *Consulting proposal* file from my Drive. To get around this, I will use the option to *Turn link sharing on,* but you may need to choose a different option based on your needs.

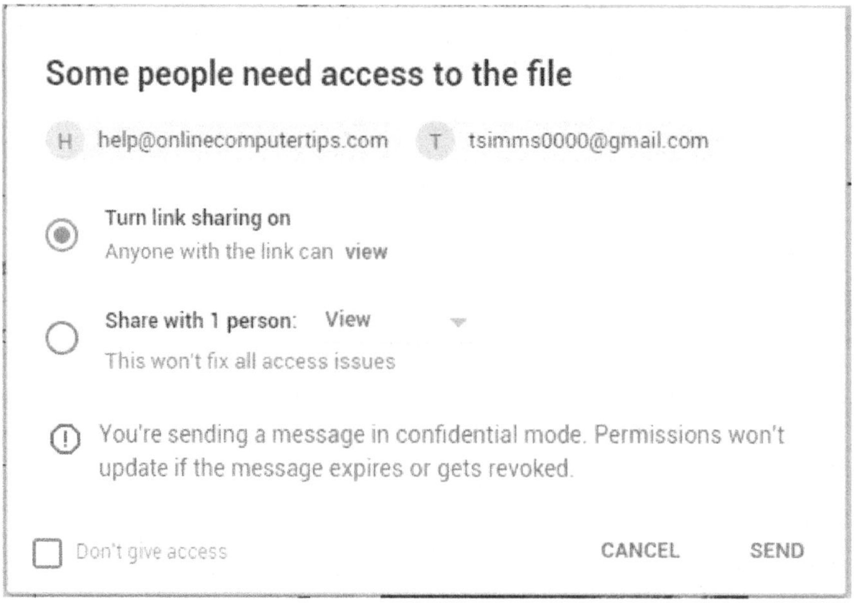

Chapter 9 – Gmail

Some people need access to the file

H help@onlinecomputertips.com   T tsimms0000@gmail.com

⦿ Turn link sharing on
  Anyone with the link can view

○ Share with 1 person: View ▾
  This won't fix all access issues

⚠ You're sending a message in confidential mode. Permissions won't update if the message expires or gets revoked.

☐ Don't give access   CANCEL   SEND

Figure 9.31

Now that my email has been sent, let's look at how it will appear in a couple of different situations. When sent to a non-Gmail email account the email will look similar to figure 9.32. Then the recipient would have to click on the *View the email* link to actually see the email, and would get a warning like shown in figure 9.33 since they are not a Gmail user.

Chapter 9 – Gmail

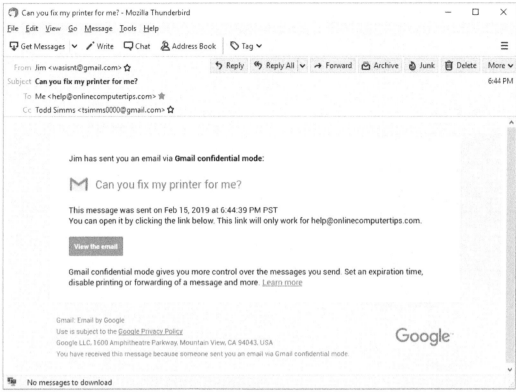

Figure 9.32

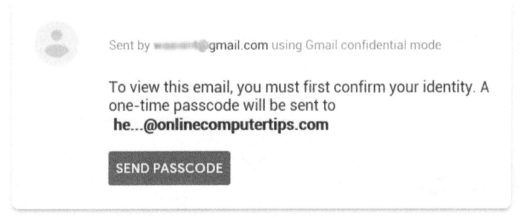

Figure 9.33

Chapter 9 – Gmail

If the recipient is a Gmail user, then they will be able to see the email just fine.

Figure 9.34

 **Tip** If you are not attaching shared Google Drive files or using confidentiality mode, then non-Gmail users should see the emails you sent to them just fine.

Receiving Email
Now that you know how to format and send an email, I want to discuss what you can do with emails that you *receive*. Figure 9.35 shows a typical email as seen in Gmail. I have labeled the subject, sender, body (email content), attachment, Gmail folder location, and date received sections of the email itself. Plus, you have the

Chapter 9 – Gmail

icons for archive, report spam, send to trash, and so on, on the top that we saw in the inbox earlier in this chapter.

Figure 9.35

As you can see, you get a lot of information within the email telling you pretty much anything you want to know. But if you want to know even more detailed information about the sender, you can click on the down arrow next to your name under the sender's email address. In this example, I will click the down arrow next to the words *to me*. This type of information would be useful for tracking sender information or email troubleshooting.

Chapter 9 – Gmail

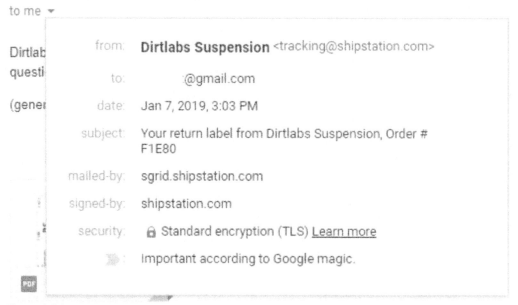

Figure 9.36

To reply to or forward an email, you can simply click the *Reply* or *Forward* button at the bottom of the email. Then you can type in who you want to forward it to, or for a reply type in the text you want to send back to the sender (figure 9.37). Notice at the bottom of figure 9.37 that is says *saved* by the trash can icon. That means Gmail has saved this email in the Drafts folder in case I want to go back and finish and send it later rather than right away. Clicking the trash can icon will delete the email without sending it. Clicking the ellipsis above the formatting toolbar will show the original email below your reply (as seen in figure 9.38).

Figure 9.37

404

Chapter 9 – Gmail

Figure 9.38

If there is more than one person included on the email, then you will have a *Reply all* option, which will send your reply to everyone else who got the email. If you just want to send your reply to the sender then you would simply click on *Reply*.

Figure 9.39

Gmail includes other actions that you can take on your email, and to see these you will need to go to the three vertical dots next to the star and forward arrow to the right of the date of the email (figure 9.40).

Chapter 9 – Gmail

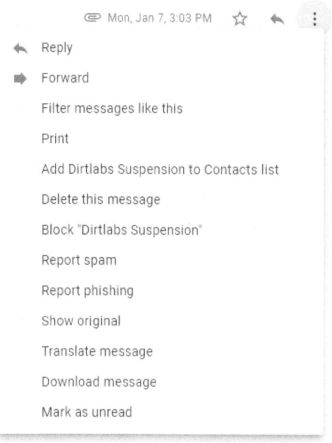

Figure 9.40

Here is what each one of these options does:

- **Reply** – This will allow you to reply to the email the same way clicking on the *Reply* button does.

- **Forward** – This will allow you to forward the email the same way clicking on the *Forward* button does.

- **Filter messages like this** – If you want to find all the emails that match a criteria similar to this email, then you can use the *Filter messages like this* to do so.

- **Print** – This will let you print out your email. (I will be going over printing later in this chapter.)

Chapter 9 – Gmail

- **Add "sender" to Contacts list** – This option will add the email address and whatever additional information is available for the sender of the email to your contact list.

- **Delete this message** – Choosing this option will add the sender of the email to your Google Contacts (which will be discussed in Chapter 11).

- **Block "sender"** – This option will block the sender on your end so you won't get any emails from them anymore. (However, it won't prevent them from sending you emails from *their* end.)

- **Report spam** – If the email is junk and not something you want to see in your inbox, then you can mark it as spam and it will be put in your *Spam* folder. Any similar emails you receive in the future will be automatically placed in your spam folder.

- **Report phishing** – Phishing scams are when someone tries to "lure" you into giving them your personal information (like passwords or bank account information). You can use this option to report these types of scams to Google. (I'm not sure if it will really do much good or not though.)

- **Show original** – This is mainly used for troubleshooting email by showing you the path the message took from the sender to you. (You will most likely never use this unless requested by some sort of tech support.)

- **Translate message** – If you receive an email in another language, then Gmail can use Google's Translate software to translate it into your own language so you can read it.

- **Download message** – Gmail give you the option to download the email into a .eml file, which you can then send to other people or use as a backup by storing it on your computer or other location.

- **Mark as unread** – This will mark a read email as unread and make it bold again.

Chapter 9 – Gmail

Printing Emails

Although printing emails is not as common as printing documents, there will be a time when you need to do so. Printing emails from your Gmail account is not difficult, and works in a similar fashion to the other Google Apps.

You can start your print job by clicking on *Print* from the three vertical dot menu I just discussed, or you can click on the printer icon at the top right of the email. Then you will be shown a preview of what your print job is going to look like with your printing options on the left side of the preview.

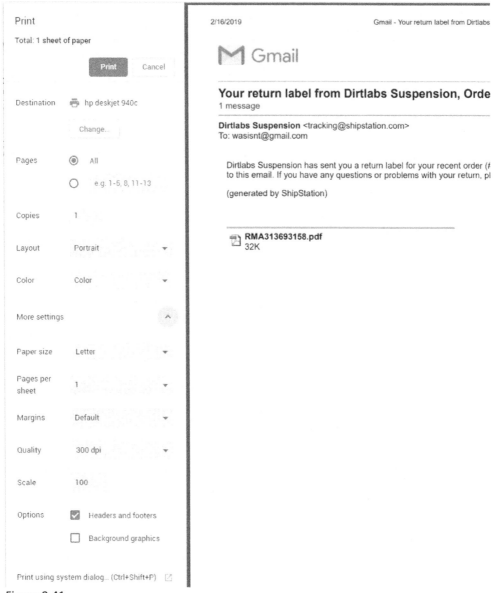

Figure 9.41

From here you have the option to select which printer you want to use (if you have more than one installed on your computer). You can also choose which pages you want to print if you don't want to print them all. You have the option of printing a series of pages or selected pages. Here are some examples:

- If you enter **3** it will print only page 3.

- If you enter **1-5** it will print pages 1, 2, 3, 4, & 5.

- If you enter **2,4,7** it will print those three pages.

- If you enter **1-5, 2,4,7** it will print pages 1 through 5 and then pages 2,4, and 7.

Copies determines how many copies of all the pages you decided to print will actually print out.

Layout determines whether your printout will be in portrait (wide) or landscape (tall) format.

Color lets you choose to print your email with or without the colors. If you want to save on ink and don't need the colors, then you can choose *Black and white*.

Paper size is used to choose the size of the paper that you have in your printer. If you have multiple paper trays with different sizes, then you can change the size here. (Just make sure it's printing using the tray with the size you want.)

Pages per sheet will let you print more than one page on a single piece of paper. Just keep in mind that the email pages will appear smaller when printed because they will need to fit on the page. Figure 9.42 shows an example of a two page email getting printed on one sheet of paper.

Chapter 9 – Gmail

Figure 9.42

Margins can be changed to allow you to fit more of a page on a sheet of paper. You can use one of the default sizes, or you can choose your own custom margins.

Quality is not something you usually need to worry about when printing emails, even if they have images, because the quality of the images in emails are usually on the lower side to begin with. The default 300 dpi setting should be fine for most, if not all, of your printing needs.

Scale is used to determine how the email fits on the page. Usually you will do 100% so it takes up as much of the page as possible, but if you want to shrink it down or blow it up, then you can enter in a lower or higher number.

Headers and footers show additional information at the top and bottom of the email, such as the date and subject on the top and website URLs on the bottom. When printing an email uncheck and check the box to see exactly what it does.

The *Background graphics* checkbox is used to print or hide images behind text in the background of your email. It is off by default because it saves on ink and makes the email easier to read without an image in the background.

Chapter 9 – Gmail

Print using system dialog will let you use the print interface from your operating system rather than from Gmail. In my case I am using Windows, so figure 9.43 shows what my printer system dialog box looks like.

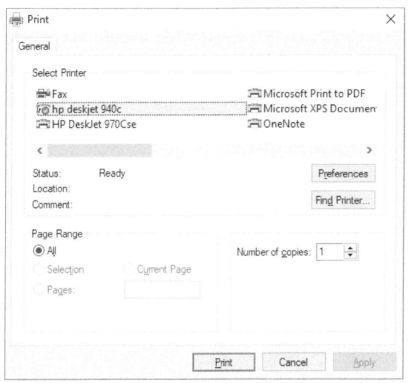

Figure 9.43

Managing Your Email
Email management is an important thing to practice to avoid things getting out of hand, resulting in you having to spend way too much time doing things such as looking for messages and making sure you have read and replied to important emails. If you get a lot of email on a regular basis, things can get out of hand quickly!

One of the best ways to manage your email is to create labels (or "folders", as they are also referred to) so you can keep things organized, which will allow you to find what you are looking for without too much work. As I mentioned before, all new email will show up in your Inbox, and it's up to you to do something with it after that. You can create rules\filters in Gmail to have it organize things for you, but it's not quite as easy as it is for say Microsoft Outlook, and is beyond the scope of this book. But if you feel like trying it, then you can do a little research and see if you can get it to work.

Chapter 9 – Gmail

As you go through your Inbox you can get an idea of what types of labels or categories you might need to help you to organize your emails. Then, to create a new label, all you need to do is go to the gear icon at the top right of the Window and choose *Settings*. Then go to the Labels tab and click on *Create new label* in the Labels section. You can also click on *Create new label* at the bottom of your existing labels on the left hand side of the screen. When using the first method, you can see your existing labels and make changes if needed.

Figure 9.44

Then you will enter a name for your label and decide if you want to nest that label under an existing label, which is like making it a subfolder of another folder. I am going to name my label *Simpson Project*, nest it under my existing Work label, and then click on *Create*.

412

Chapter 9 – Gmail

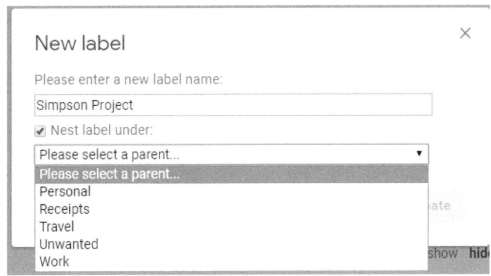

Figure 9.45

Now you can see in figure 9.46 that I have a *Simpson Project* label under my *Work* label.

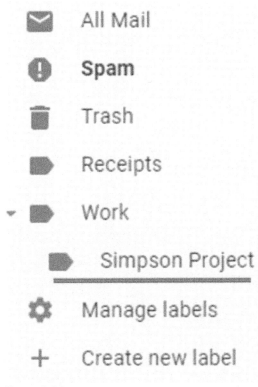

Figure 9.46

Chapter 9 – Gmail

Now that I have my new label, I will want to move the appropriate emails into that "folder" so I can start my organization process. To do this, I can simply drag the emails I want to move to the new label (figure 9.47), or check the box next to the email itself and use the *Move to* button, then choose my new label from there (figure 9.48).

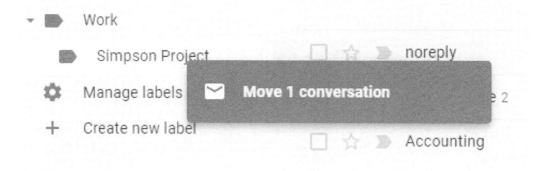

Figure 9.47

Chapter 9 – Gmail

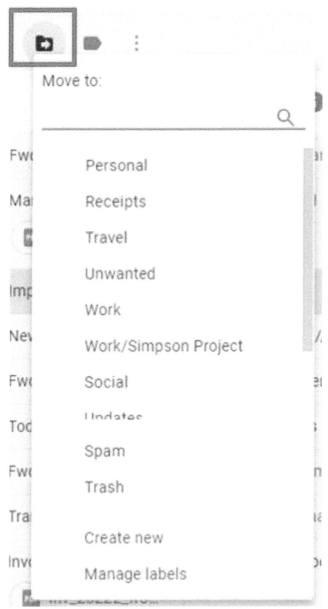

Figure 9.48

You can have emails assigned to more than one label if you need them organized in more than one location. To apply another label to an email, you will need to select that email and then go to the labels icon on the toolbar, then choose what labels you want applied to that email (figure 9.49).

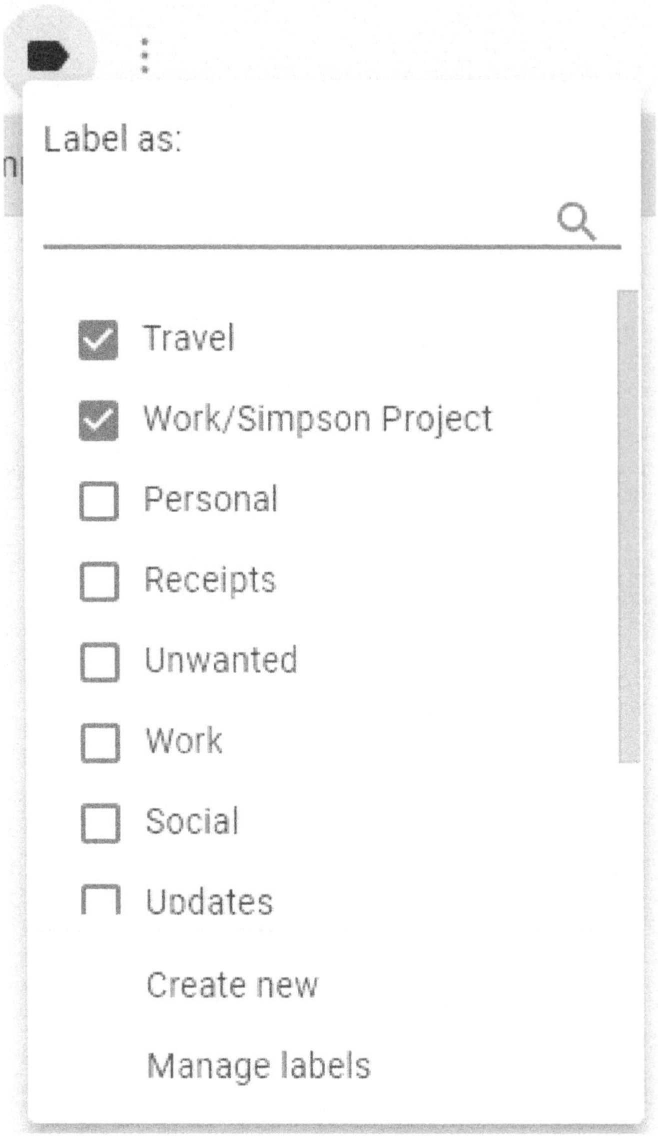

Chapter 9 – Gmail

Label as:

☑ Travel
☑ Work/Simpson Project
☐ Personal
☐ Receipts
☐ Unwanted
☐ Work
☐ Social
☐ Updates

Create new

Manage labels

Figure 9.49

Then when you open that email it will show the labels that have been assigned to it, plus it will appear within the corresponding labels folders.

Chapter 9 – Gmail

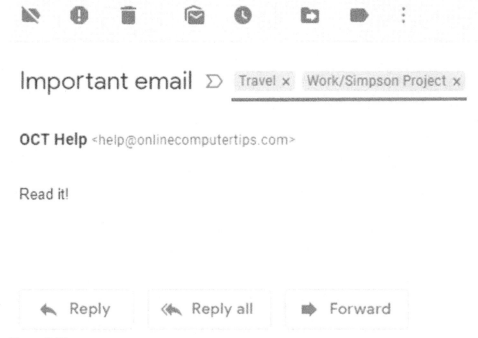

Figure 9.50

After you get your labels created you can click on the three vertical dots next to one of them and further customize it, such as changing the color or even adding an additional sub-label (figure 9.51).

Chapter 9 – Gmail

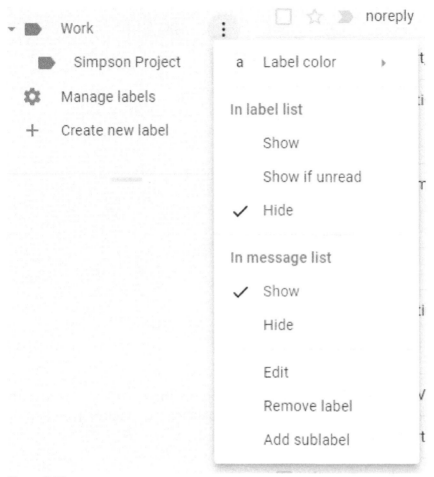

Figure 9.51

The *In label list* option will determine whether or not your label will be shown in the main label list above more\less, or below in the section that is hidden unless you click on more. Figure 9.52 shows how the Work folder is shown when the *Hide* option is selected, while figure 9.53 shows how it is shown with the *Show* option selected. The *Show if unread* option will have that label show on top *only* if there are unread messages within it.

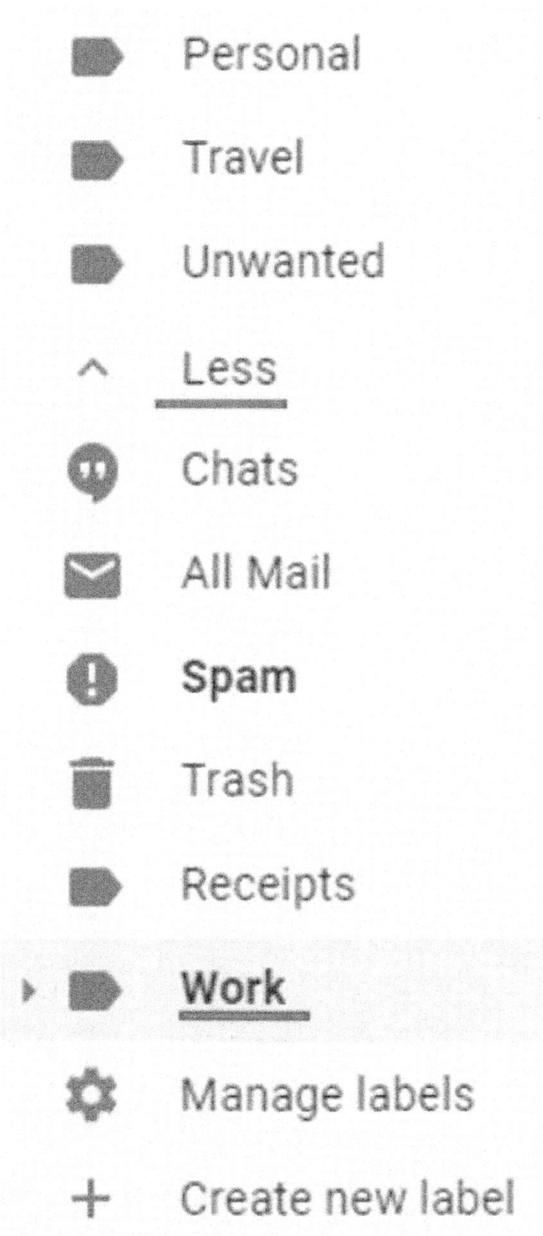

Chapter 9 – Gmail

- Personal
- Travel
- Unwanted
- ^ Less
- Chats
- All Mail
- **Spam**
- Trash
- Receipts
- **Work**
- Manage labels
- Create new label

Figure 9.52

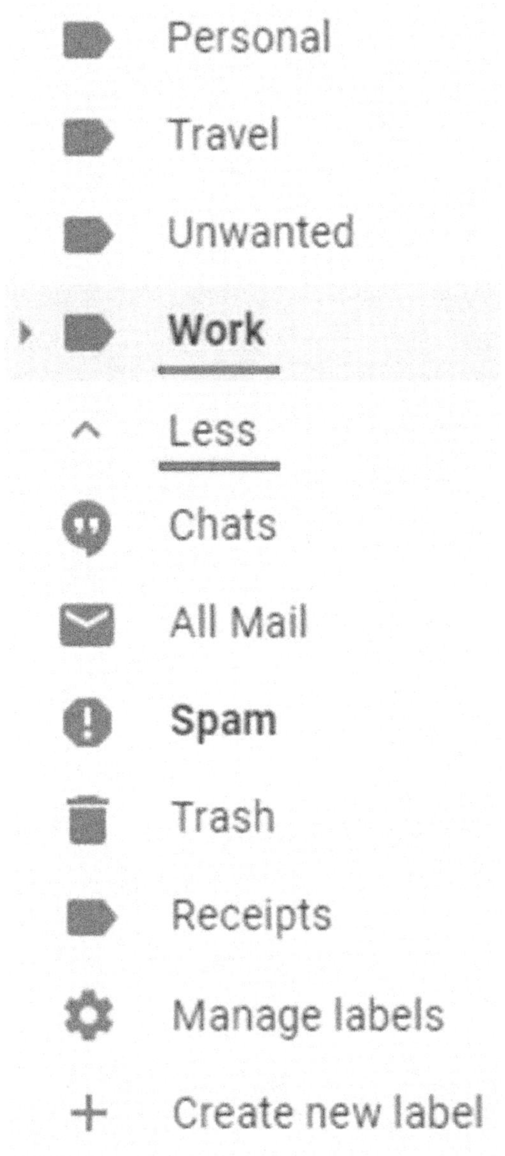

Chapter 9 – Gmail

- Personal
- Travel
- Unwanted
- **Work**
- Less
- Chats
- All Mail
- **Spam**
- Trash
- Receipts
- Manage labels
- Create new label

Figure 9.53

The *In message list* option will hide that label on your messages in the main message list. If you take a look at figure 9.54 you will see that I have labeled the email with the *Personal* label, and it shows up when looking at my message list. If I were to hide the *Personal* label in the message view, it would not show as seen in figure 9.55.

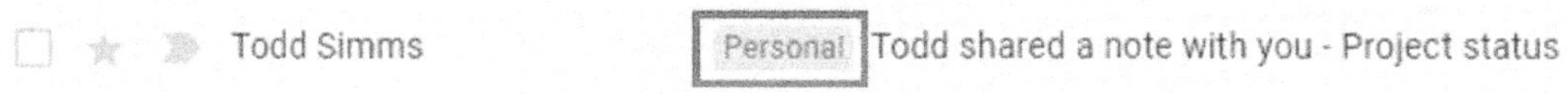

Todd Simms — Personal — Todd shared a note with you - Project status

Figure 9.54

420

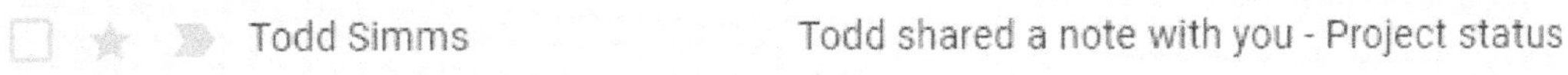

Todd Simms
Todd shared a note with you - Project status

Figure 9.55

Even if the label is hidden in the message list view, it will still show up when you open the message itself.

Todd shared a note with you - Project status
Inbox x
Personal x
Todd Simms
to me
Feb 10, 201
Todd (tsimms0000@gmail.com) shared a note with you.

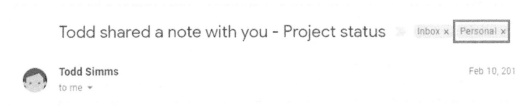

Figure 9.56

The *Edit* option will allow you to change the label name and its location, like if you want to make it a sub label of another one, for example. The *Remove label* option will remove that label from your list and any emails that it appears on. Finally, the *Add sublabel* option will allow you to create a sublabel for the current label you are on.

Managing Spam

Junk mail is a way of life, and no matter how hard you try, you will always get some in your inbox. Some people will get way more than others. It's always a good idea to watch out where you enter your email address because many places will then sell your email address to other people so it can be used to send you junk you most likely don't want.

Gmail does a pretty good job of filtering spam messages on its own, but it's a good idea to check your Spam folder to make sure that it didn't mislabel an email as spam when it shouldn't be. Figure 9.57 shows an example of my Spam folder, and you can see that these messages are most likely something I don't want in my Inbox. There is a link at the top of the page that says *Delete all spam messages now,* which will empty out the folder to help keep things clean.

Chapter 9 – Gmail

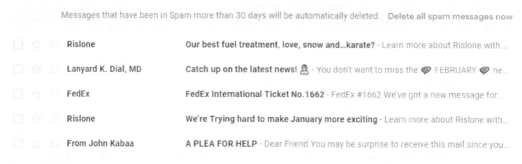

Figure 9.57

If I were to open one of the Spam messages (which I would avoid doing, for the most part) it could have a message that looks like figure 9.58. You can see there is a button named *Report as not spam* if you don't want messages from this sender automatically put in your Spam folder. Also, notice how there is a Spam label at the top of the message.

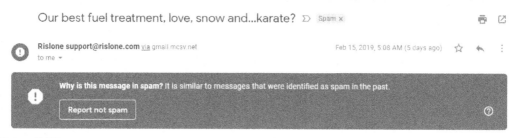

Figure 9.58

You can mark emails in your Inbox as spam if Gmail happens to miss them so they will be marked as spam next time one comes in. If you have the email open, you can mark it as spam by clicking the three vertical dots at the top right and choosing *Report spam*. If you don't want to risk opening it, then just simply put a checkmark in the box next to the email, click on the *Report spam* button in the toolbar (it's shaped like a stop sign), and the email will be marked as spam and sent to your Spam folder.

Account Settings
The last thing I want to discuss in this chapter is the Gmail settings, and there are a lot of them! I will not go over each and every one, but rather the ones that I think will be more common to adjust and most beneficial to the average Gmail user.

You can get to the Gmail settings by clicking on the gear icon at the upper right side of the window and then clicking on *Settings*. As you can see from figure 9.59,

Chapter 9 – Gmail

there are many tabs or categories for different settings, and each tab has multiple settings underneath it.

Settings

General Labels Inbox Accounts and Import Filters and Blocked Addresses Forwarding and POP/IMAP Add-ons Chat Advanced Offline Themes

Figure 9.59

I will now go over the more important Gmail settings from each section rather than bore you to death with a bunch of information you will never use! Plus, you can browse through all of these settings yourself and see what they do.

General – These basic settings change the way Gmail looks for the most part. Here are some of the more useful settings:

- **Images** – Having this on or off will allow you to decide if you want images that are embedded (not attachments) into the body of the email to be displayed or not.

- **Smart Compose** – This will give you suggestions for what to say while you are typing, kind of like your smartphone does.

- **Conversation View** – This setting is one you should try out to see which way you like, because it makes a big difference when reading emails with multiple back and forth replies. One thing I never liked about Gmail was how these types of emails were hard to sort out because they got too jumbled up when they got too big.

    By default, Conversation view is enabled so all of the replies will be shown in one entry for the entire conversation. If you look at figure 9.60 you will see there is an ongoing conversation between me and OCT with six messages between us.

Chapter 9 – Gmail

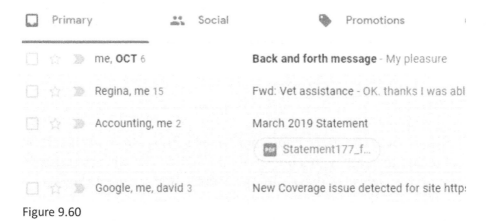

Figure 9.60

Then when I open that email it will show all of the back and forth replies in one place (figure 9.61), which is fine until you start getting into really long conversations, and then things can get a little jumbled.

- **Smart Reply** – Works like Smart Compose, but this time with replies.

- **Desktop notifications** – This will allow Gmail to use popup notifications on your computer when a new email comes in. You can also set it to only notify you when important emails arrive so you are not bothered by all your incoming email.

- **Picture** – If you want to have your picture show up in your emails, then you can choose this option. Keep in mind that it will not show up for everyone that you send email to, and mostly to other Gmail users.

- **Signature** – Signatures are used to display information about yourself (such as your title and phone number) at the bottom of the email messages that you send. You can configure one here and have Gmail add it to outgoing emails as you create them.

- **Vacation responder** – This is used to send an automatic reply to any email you get when you are out of town so you don't have to do it while on vacation etc. You will type in a default message, and Gmail will reply with that message to your incoming emails.

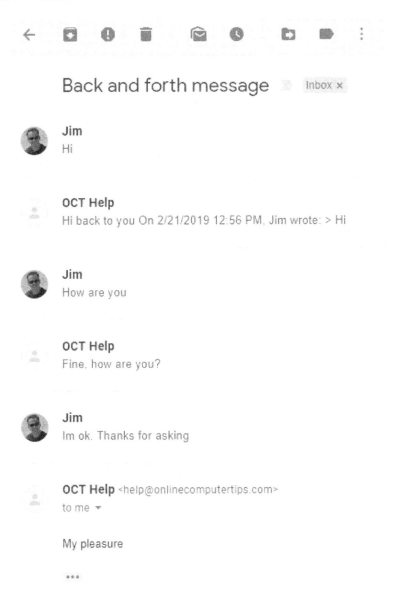

Figure 9.61

When I turn Conversation view off, then each email that was addressed to you will be shown separately in your inbox. Notice how there are three emails for this conversation, meaning I have received three and sent three to make a total of six from figure 9.61.

Chapter 9 – Gmail

Figure 9.62

Labels – I have gone over labels in detail but if you want to customize your labels such as showing, hiding or removing them then you can do so from here (figure 9.63).

Chapter 9 – Gmail

Settings

General **Labels** Inbox Accounts and Import Filters and Blocked Addresses Forwarding and POP/IMAP Add-ons Chat
Advanced Offline Themes

System labels	Show in label list		
Inbox			
Starred	**show** hide		
Snoozed	**show** hide		
Important	**show** hide		
Chats	show **hide**		
Sent	**show** hide		
Drafts	**show** hide show if unread		
All Mail	show **hide**		
Spam	show **hide** show if unread		
Trash	show **hide**		

Categories	Show in label list	Show in message list	
Categories	**show** hide		
Social	**show** hide	show **hide**	
Updates	**show** hide	show **hide**	
Forums	**show** hide	show **hide**	
Promotions	**show** hide	show **hide**	

Labels	Show in label list	Show in message list	Actions
Create new label			
Personal 1 conversation	**show** hide show if unread	**show** hide	remove edit
Receipts 0 conversations	show **hide** show if unread	**show** hide	remove edit
Travel 0 conversations	**show** hide show if unread	**show** hide	remove edit
Unwanted 0 conversations	**show** hide show if unread	**show** hide	remove edit
Work 0 conversations	**show** hide show if unread	**show** hide	remove edit
Simpson Project 1 conversation		**show** hide	remove edit

Note: Removing a label will not remove the messages with that label.

Figure 9.63

Inbox – These settings only apply to your Inbox, and you can do things such as hide any categories you don't want shown and also change settings for Importance markers, which are used to mark emails as important. If you have created any

427

Chapter 9 – Gmail

filters (email rules) for your mail, then you have the option to have Gmail ignore those filters for important email.

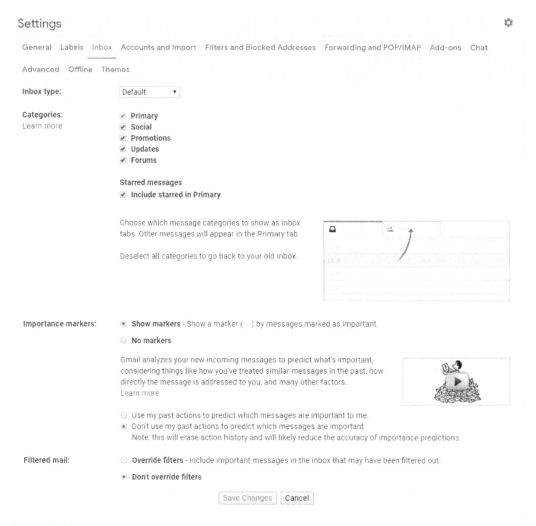

Figure 9.64

Accounts and Import – This is where you can make changes to your account such as changing your password and setting up recovery options. Recovery options include giving Google your phone number or an alternate email address to be used in case you get locked out of your Gmail account.

You can also import email and contacts from your old email account so you don't have to start over or forward anything to your Gmail account. (This won't work with *all* email accounts, so I can't say if you will really be able to use this or not.)

Chapter 9 – Gmail

This area will also show you your available storage for email and give you a link to purchase more space if needed. Always try to delete any email you don't need or empty your trash and spam to free up space first.

Filters and Blocked Addresses – I mentioned filters earlier in this chapter where you can set up a rule to take action on an email based on certain criteria. Here you can see your applied filters and create new ones as needed. You can also see any email addresses that you have blocked in the past and unblock them if needed.

Forwarding and POP/IMAP – Gmail will let you forward your incoming emails to another account, so if you want to have a secondary place to get your email or have them forwarded to another person, you can do so from here. If you want to use another email client such as Microsoft Outlook, then you can adjust how that works from this section as well.

Add-ons – Just like with many of the other Google Apps, you can install add-ons into Gmail to add features and additional functionality to how it works.

Chat – Chat is used to have conversations with other users by using an online messaging format rather than email. Think of it as texting on your computer.

Advanced – You most likely won't find yourself changing any options here, but these settings allow you to finetune how Gmail works. (Most of the options are disabled by default.)

Offline – Gmail has a feature that will let you do things such as read, respond, and search your email even without an Internet connection. If you respond to an email or compose a new one, then it will automatically be sent once you have your Internet connection back.

Themes – If you want to change the plain and boring look of Gmail, then you can apply a custom theme to your account to spice things up a bit with some images and color.

Chapter 10 – Google Calendar

One important tool everyone needs to keep their lives in order is a good calendar. Sure you can have the type that's on your wall that you write your appointments down on with a pen, but that doesn't do you any good when you're not at home (unless you feel like taking it along with you!).

Thankfully, you can use the Google Calendar to have a place where you can put all of your important meetings and appointments so you have access to them anywhere that you can sign in to your Google account from. Once you create a Google account, you will automatically have a Google Calendar to go along with it.

Calendar Interface
The Gmail Calendar is very similar to other calendar apps out there, but, then again, there's only so many ways you can make a calendar look! Once you open your calendar you should first decide how you would like it to be displayed. If you click on the dropdown box at the upper right, you will be able to see your available options such as show the entire month, week, day, and so on. Figure 10.1 shows the calendar in the month view.

Chapter 10 – Google Calendar

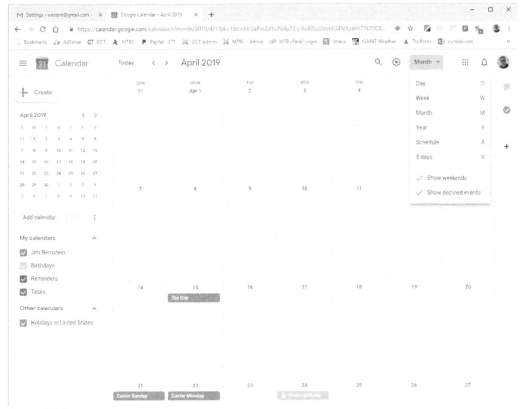

Figure 10.1

If you look at the left hand side of the calendar in figure 10.1, you will see that there is a smaller month view, which will always be there no matter what main view you are using. This way if you need to get to a specific date that is not shown in your view, you can click on that day and go right to it.

Under that is the categories that will be shown on your calendar. You can turn these on and off by unchecking the box next to them. For example, if you didn't want birthdays to show on your calendar, you can just uncheck the box next to *Birthdays* and they will be hidden.

Clicking on the three vertical arrows next to a category will bring up some options for that category (figure 10.2). If you click on *Display this only*, then all the other categories will become unchecked and hidden. You can also choose to hide that category from your list or change its color. I will be going over Settings later in this chapter, so I won't worry about that for now.

Chapter 10 – Google Calendar

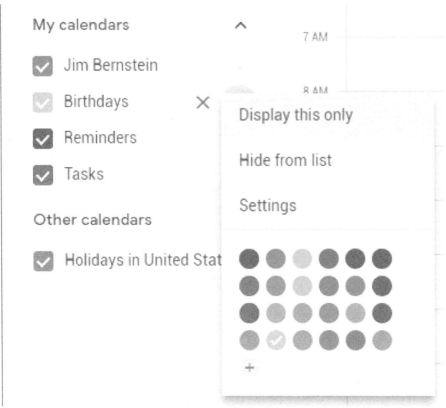

Figure 10.2

I wanted to point out a few things at the top of the calendar that you should be aware of. Clicking on the three horizontal lines will hide and unhide the left side navigation options, which include the mini calendar and the categories. Clicking the *Today* button will bring you to the current date, allowing you to see what's going on today. The left and right arrows will change the displayed date on the calendar by week in week view, month in month view, and so on.

Figure 10.3

Clicking on the magnifying glass will allow you to search your calendar for certain things based on specific criteria. Or you can just type in a word and see what the search finds for you.

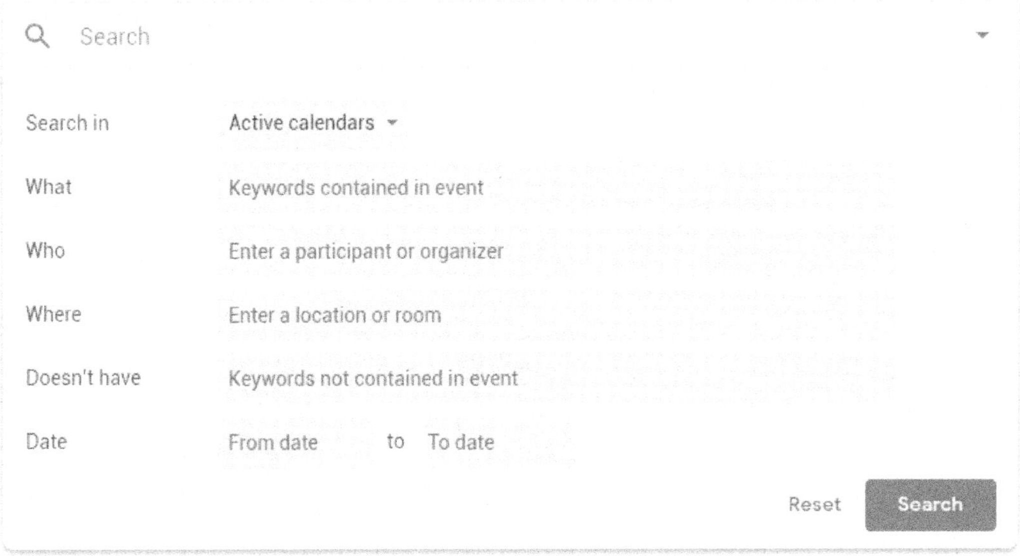

Chapter 10 – Google Calendar

Figure 10.4

Adding Events
One of the main reasons people use calendars is to keep track of important appointments or events. These types of events can be work meetings, doctors' appointments, and so on. Google calendar allows you to add these events to your calendar so you can check on them from anywhere you can connect to your calendar.

There are a couple of ways to add events to your calendar. One way is to click on the *Create* button at the upper left of the window. When you click the Create button, Google Calendar will use the current date to create the event on. If you want to create an event on a different date, then all you need to do is click on that date itself and Calendar will bring up a new event box. Then you can choose to add an event, reminder, or task. I will be going over reminders and tasks later in this chapter, so for now we will stick with events.

Chapter 10 – Google Calendar

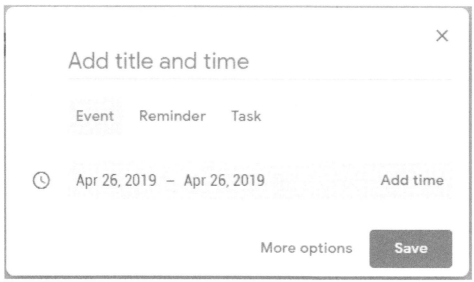

Figure 10.5

Then you can simply enter the title and time for the event, click on Save, and you are done.

Clicking on the *More options* button will bring you to a different screen with some advanced options (figure 10.6).

 Double clicking on a date will bring you right to the *More options* settings so you don't have to click on the *More options* button. A saved step is a saved step!

When creating an event from the advanced options, you have much more control over how your event will be created. You can enter in additional information such as the event's location and if you will be using any conferencing apps such as Google Hangouts.

Chapter 10 – Google Calendar

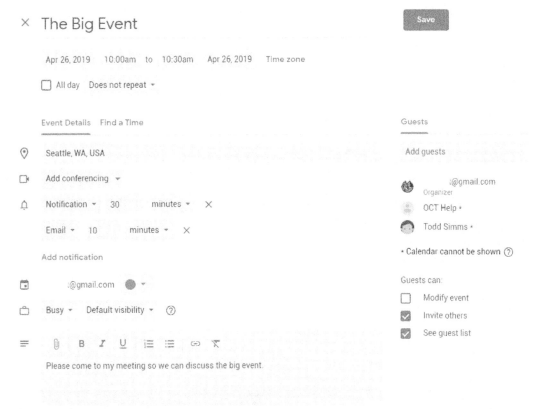

Figure 10.6

There is also the option to add guests to the meeting, which will send them an email inviting them to attend if you choose that option. Below the Guests section there are options as to what the guests can do, such as modify the event, invite other people, or see the guest list.

Under *Notification,* you can enter how soon before the event you want to be notified so you don't forget to attend. You can use either a popup notification, email notification, or both. Then you can have your calendar show you as busy if you are sharing it with anyone else.

When you click on *Save* it will ask you if you would like to send the invite email to the guests that you listed in the event.

Chapter 10 – Google Calendar

> Would you like to send invitation emails to Google Calendar guests?
>
> ⓘ   Cancel changes   Don't send   Send

Figure 10.7

When the guests receive the email, they will be able to act on it by accepting or declining it, or replying with a maybe. Figure 10.8 shows how a non-Gmail user would see the email, while figure 10.9 shows how a person with a Gmail account would see the email. Notice how they both have the option to accept etc.

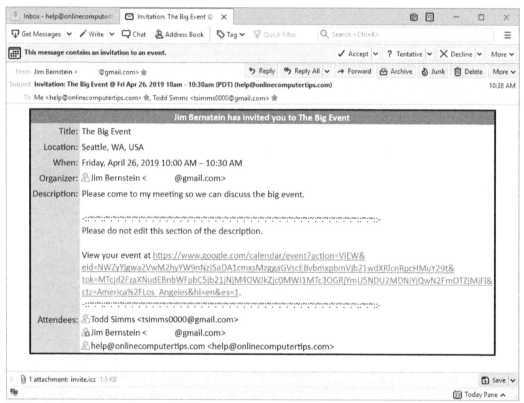

Figure 10.8

Chapter 10 – Google Calendar

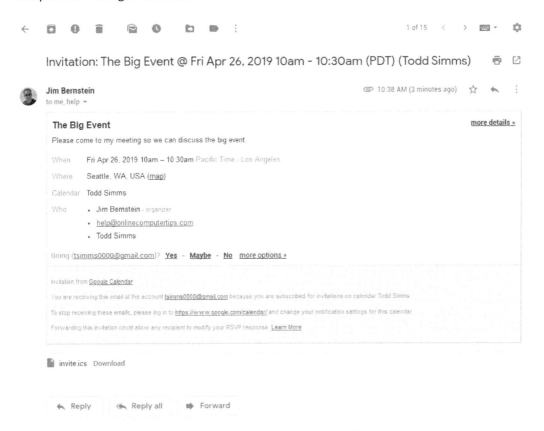

Figure 10.9

When A Google user accepts the invitation, it will be automatically added to their Google Calendar. Then they can click on the event itself to see the details.

Chapter 10 – Google Calendar

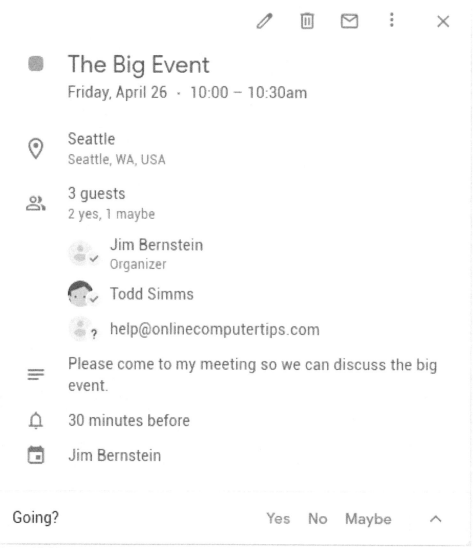

Figure 10.10

When a non-Google user clicks the link to view the event, they will be taken to a page similar to figure 10.11, where they can see information about the event and who has agreed to attend. They can also make their decision as to whether or not they are going, and add notes if they choose. To add it to their calendar, they can download the invite.ics file attachment as seen at the bottom of figure 10.8, and use it to add the event to their own calendar (such as one used with Microsoft Outlook, etc.).

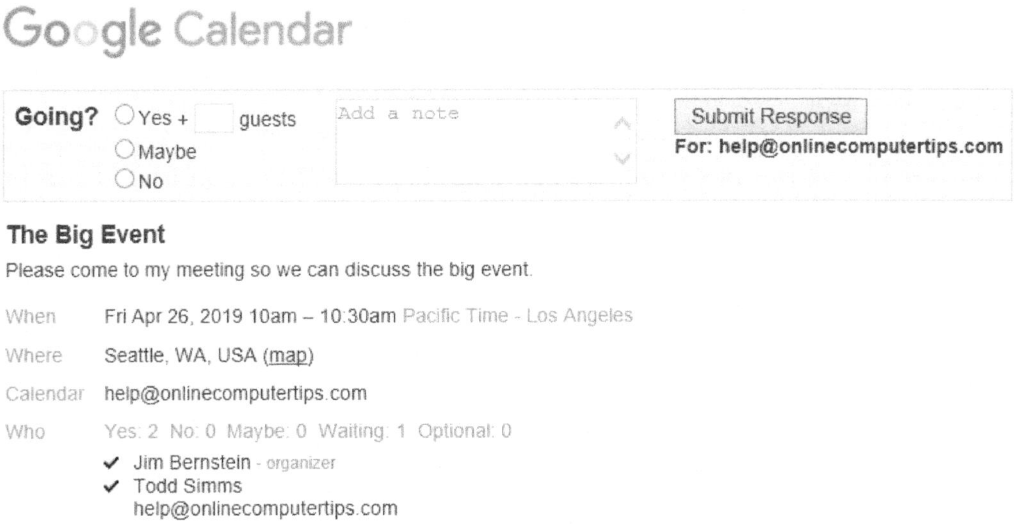

Chapter 10 – Google Calendar

Google Calendar

Going? ○ Yes + ☐ guests Add a note   Submit Response
○ Maybe   For: help@onlinecomputertips.com
○ No

The Big Event
Please come to my meeting so we can discuss the big event.

When   Fri Apr 26, 2019 10am – 10:30am Pacific Time - Los Angeles
Where   Seattle, WA, USA (map)
Calendar help@onlinecomputertips.com
Who   Yes: 2 No: 0 Maybe: 0 Waiting: 1 Optional: 0
          ✓ Jim Bernstein - organizer
          ✓ Todd Simms
             help@onlinecomputertips.com

Figure 10.11

When you click on the event in your calendar, there are a few options to choose from at the upper right side of the popup window.

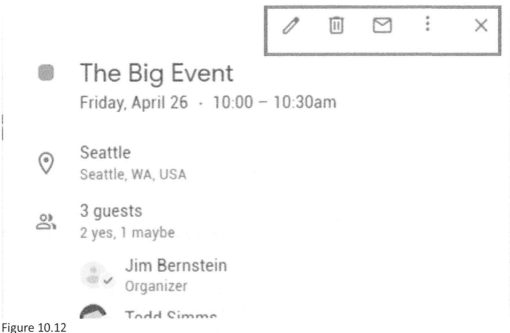

Figure 10.12

- **Edit** – This will bring you back to the screen shown in figure 10.5, allowing you to change any of the event settings.

439

- **Delete** – This will allow you to delete the meeting, which will remove it from other people's calendars (assuming they are using a Google Calendar).

- **Email** – If you need to send some additional information to your event guests, you can use the Email option to do so.

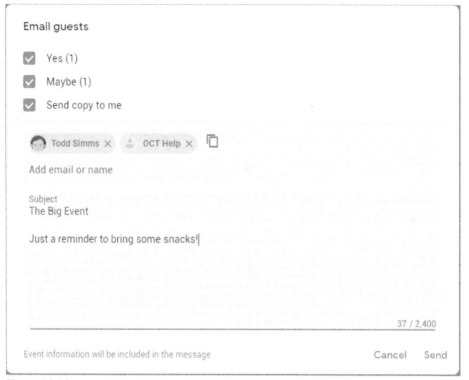

Figure 10.13

- **Options** – The three vertical dots gives you some additional options to choose from.

    o *Print* – If you want to print out a copy of the event details, you can do so from here.

    o *Duplicate* – The *Duplicate* option will make an exact copy of the event that you can use on a different date or time so you don't have to recreate it from scratch.

    o *Publish* event – If you want to add the event to your website, you can use the *Publish* option to get the HTML code needed to do so.

Chapter 3 – Google Docs

> Or you can just get a link to the event that you can send out to other people who are not guests.

Figure 10.14

- o *Change owner* – If you decide that you don't want to be in charge of the event and would rather give the responsibility to someone else, then you can change the event's owner.

Reminders
Reminders can be used in place of Events for simple things such as making sure you pick up some milk on your way home from work or to turn in your timesheet before going home for the day. Then, when the date and time of the reminder occurs, you will be notified from your calendar of that reminder.

You set up Reminders the same way you do for Events, by clicking on the day you want to set the reminder for, but this time you'll click on the word *Reminder* on the window that pops up.

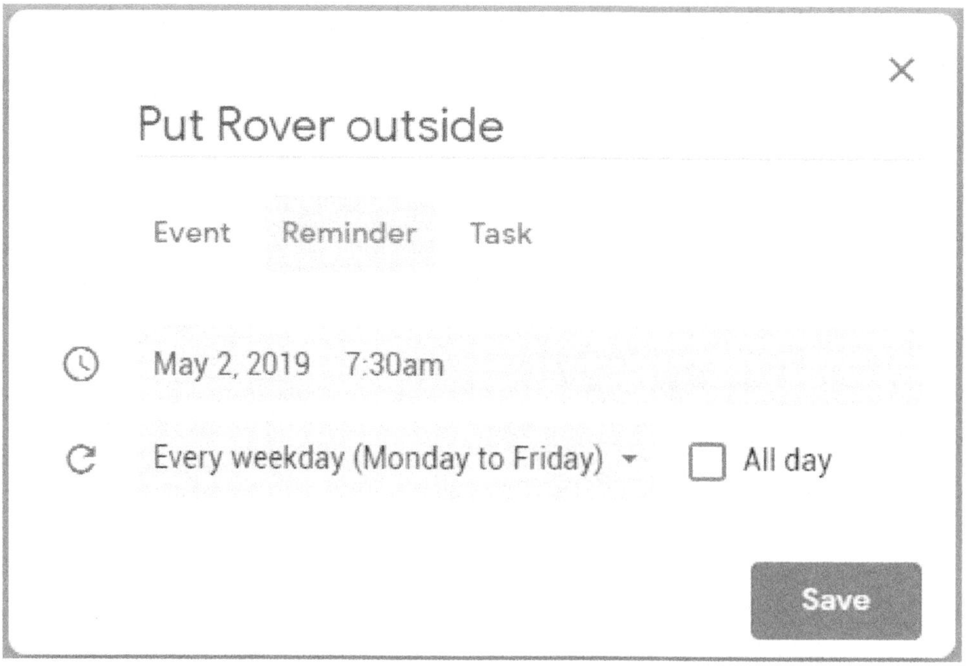

Chapter 10 – Google Calendar

> **Put Rover outside**
>
> Event   Reminder   Task
>
> 🕐   May 2, 2019   7:30am
>
> ↻   Every weekday (Monday to Friday) ▼   ☐ All day
>
> **Save**

Figure 10.15

From here you can click on the date or time and change it to whatever settings you need to set the reminder for. Then you can have it be a one-time reminder or set it to repeat daily, weekly, monthly, and so on if needed.

I chose to set a reminder to put the dog out at 7:30 every weekday morning starting on May 2nd so I will get reminded to do so before going to work. Now when I look at my calendar, I can see that the reminder is listed on every weekday and not on the weekends (figure 10.16).

Chapter 10 – Google Calendar

Figure 10.16

If I need to edit the reminder for a specific day, all I need to do is click on the reminder for that day and choose the edit pencil icon. Then it will ask me if I want this change to apply to just the one day, or all of the days that I set the reminder for.

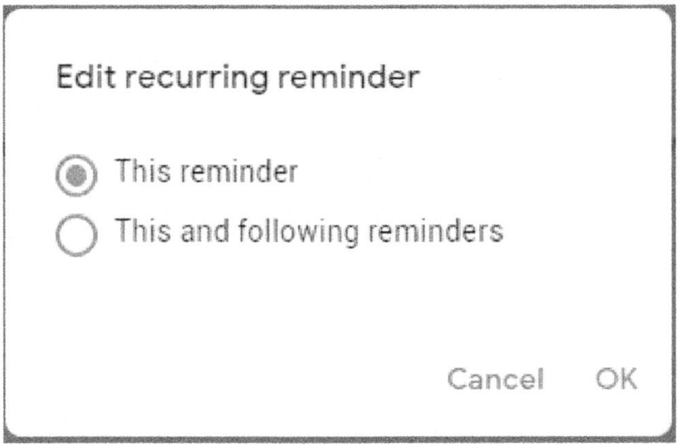

Figure 10.17

To delete a reminder simply click on the trash can icon. You will have the same choice to delete it just for the one day, or to delete all of the reminders.

If you want to delete all of the reminders, be sure to open the first one, otherwise it will only delete the reminders that occur after the date you've deleted.

Tasks

Tasks are used to assign yourself... well, *tasks* that you can mark complete when completed. Think of them as a to-do checklist that you would normally write down on a notepad, but now you can check your tasks from anywhere you can access your Google account. You can even have multiple task lists, so if you want to have one for work and then a separate one for home, you can do that.

To create a task, you will simply click on the date you want to apply that task to (just like you did with Events and Reminders), but this time click on the word *Tasks*. Then you will enter the details of the tasks and choose which task list you want to place it on if you have more than one.

Chapter 10 – Google Calendar

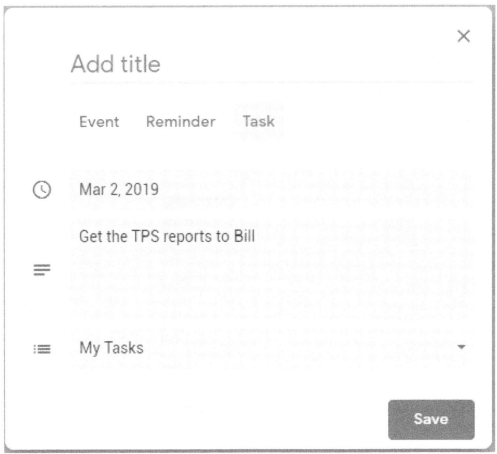

Figure 10.18

Then when you go back to your calendar (or other Google App) and click on the Tasks button, on the right hand side of the screen you will be shown your tasks.

Chapter 10 – Google Calendar

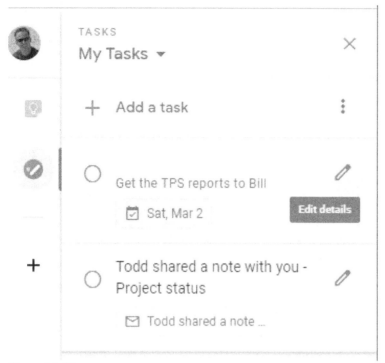

Figure 10.19

From here you can also add additional tasks, switch to a different task list, or even create a new one.

Clicking on the pencil icon will let you edit the task if needed, and you can do things such as give it a title, change the date, add a subtask, delete the task, assign it to a different task list, and even change the contents of the task itself.

Clicking the circle to the left of the task will mark it as complete and then remove it from your task list and move it down to the bottom under *Completed*. Then the task will show up on your calendar for that day and be marked as completed.

Adding Additional Calendars
If you are a super busy person with a lot going on, having one calendar might not be enough, or your one calendar might start getting out of hand. Fortunately, Google lets you create additional calendars to help you stay organized.

To add an additional calendar simply click on the three vertical dots next to *Add calendar* below the mini month view calendar at the left of the screen.

Chapter 10 – Google Calendar

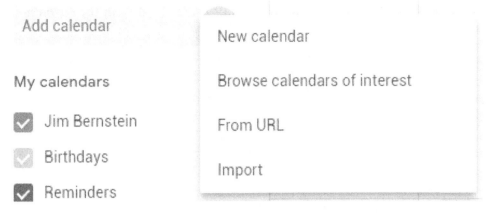

Figure 10.20

You will be presented with four options to choose from:

- **New calendar** – Here you can create another calendar and name it whatever you please.

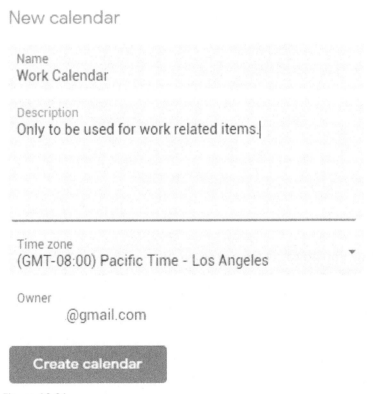

Figure 10.21

447

Chapter 10 – Google Calendar

Then it will show up under your calendar list, and you can turn it on and off as needed.

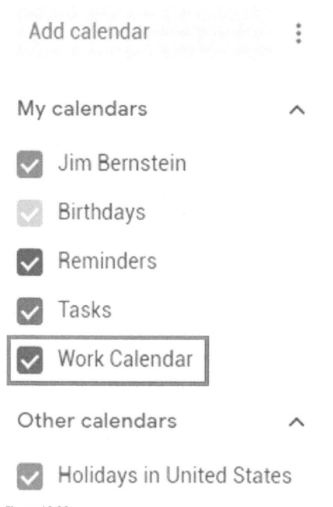

Figure 10.22

Then, when you go to create a new event, reminder, or task, you will have the option of selecting your new calendar to place that item on. Events from your new calendar will show up in the same color as the one assigned to that calendar (which you can change if desired).

Chapter 10 – Google Calendar

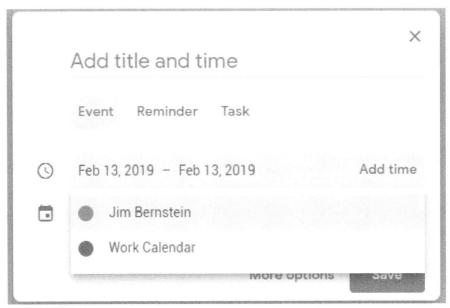

Figure 10.23

- **Browse calendars of interest** – Google has a selection of preconfigured calendars that you can browse and then add to your list of calendars if you find one or more of them useful (figure 10.24).

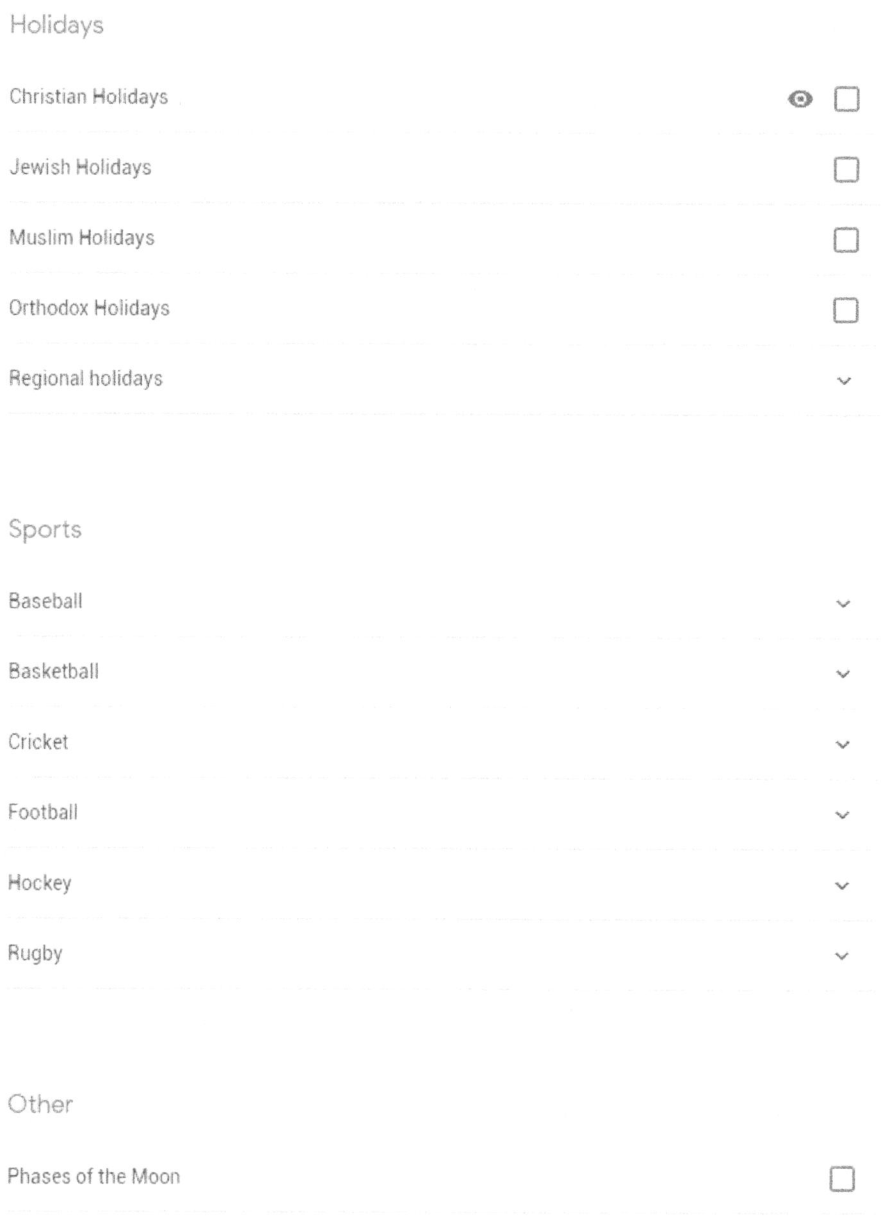

Chapter 10 – Google Calendar

Holidays

Christian Holidays

Jewish Holidays

Muslim Holidays

Orthodox Holidays

Regional holidays

Sports

Baseball

Basketball

Cricket

Football

Hockey

Rugby

Other

Phases of the Moon

Figure 10.24

- **From URL** – If someone has a published calendar that they want to share with you, then you can import it into your calendar by using the From URL link. All you need to do is copy the URL (address) of the calendar and paste it into the box.

- **Import** – If you have a calendar file from a supported calendar application, then you can import it into your own calendar by uploading the calendar file from your computer.

Chapter 10 – Google Calendar

One last thing I want to mention before moving to the next section is the *Trash* setting within your calendars. If you delete an event, it will be moved to your trash, and you can see deleted events by going to the gear icon and then clicking on *Trash*.

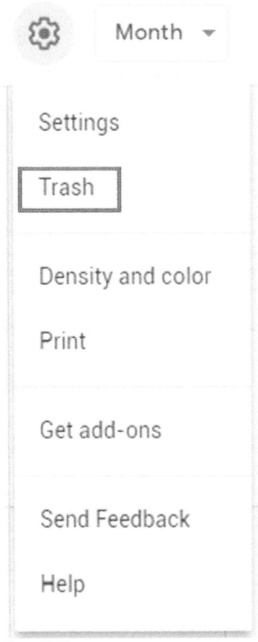

Figure 10.25

Chapter 10 – Google Calendar

Then you will see your calendars and be able to see deleted events from each one. Keep in mind that these deleted events will only be kept for *30 days,* and then they will be automatically deleted. To restore an event, all you need to do is check the box next to it and click on the restore arrow to have it put back to its original location.

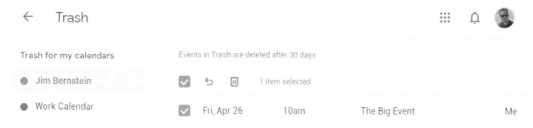

Figure 10.26

Settings

Google Calendar has its own settings that you can change just like the other Google Apps. To get to these settings, click on the gear icon, and then click on *Settings* (figure 10.25). There are several categories to choose from, and I will go over the important settings from each one:

General Settings – Here you will find settings that affect the overall functionality of your calendar.

- **Language and region** – Allows you to change your default language as well as country and date\time format.

- **Time zone** – Here you can change your time zone settings so all of your events etc. are displayed correctly.

- **World clock** – If you would like to use the World clock, you can enable it here.

- **Event settings** – This is where you can change the default settings for new events, such as the default duration, guest permissions, and alerts.

- **View options** – Here is where you can enable or disable view options such as show weekends and show declined events and also change the start day of the week along with other options.

- **Events from Gmail** – By default, events from your Gmail messages will automatically be added to your calendar when you accept them. If you don't want this to happen, then you can disable it here.

- **Keyboard shortcuts** – Keyboard shortcuts are enabled by default, but you can disable them if you do not want to use them or if they are interfering with some other keyboard shortcuts you use.

Add Calendar Settings – These are not really settings that you can change, but it is another way to add a new calendar such as a calendar of interest or from a URL (which I already discussed earlier in this chapter).

Import & Export – Here you can import a calendar from another Google Calendar or other calendar application (which I have mentioned already in this chapter). You can also export any one of your own calendars to a file so you can give it to someone else to import into their account.

Calendar Specific Settings – For each calendar that you have in your account, you can change the settings to customize it to your needs. Here are the choices you have for changing your calendar specific settings:

- **Calendar settings** – Here you can change the name of the calendar along with its description. You can also change its time zone and also export it if needed.

- **Access permissions** – If you are sharing your calendar with others (or the public in general), then you can determine if you want it to show all event details or only your free or busy time. You can also get a sharable link from this section that you can send to others via email.

- **Share with specific people** – Here is where you can share your calendar with specific people. Just click on the *Add people* button and type in the email addresses of those you want to share it with.

- **Event notifications** – Changing the settings here will change the default types of notifications and their notification times that are set up when you create a new event.

- **All-day event notifications** – This will do the same thing as the Event notification settings, but for all day events.

- **General notifications** – If you want to change the default notification type from email to none for notifications such as new events, changed events, canceled events, event responses, and so on, you can do that here.

- **Integrate calendar** – I mentioned that you have the ability to get HTML code to integrate your calendar into your website, and can also have a URL to give out to others so that they can access your public calendar. Here is another place where you can get that information and even customize it if desired. It's more of an advanced setting, so don't worry if it doesn't make any sense when you look at it.

- **Remove calendar** – This will remove the specified calendar from your Google Calendar list, and will also delete any events associated with it.

Chapter 11 – Contacts

For the final chapter on our journey through Google Apps, I will be discussing Google Contacts and how to make the most out of them. Contacts are a pretty basic topic, so this chapter will not be too involved, but there are still some things to look out for with your contacts so you can make sure you are using them correctly.

I want to begin by saying if you are an Android smartphone user, then your phone contacts will automatically be integrated with your Google account since Google created the Android operating system. This makes things nice when you get a new phone, because once you sign in the first time, all of the contacts from your Google account will be there waiting for you.

You can edit your contacts from your smartphone or from your computer. For this chapter, I will be working off my computer and looking at my contacts via the Google Chrome web browser.

Contacts Interface

When you first open your contacts you will see them listed in alphabetical order (like shown in figure 11.1). Of course, yours won't have all the email addresses and phone numbers wiped out!

Chapter 11 – Contacts

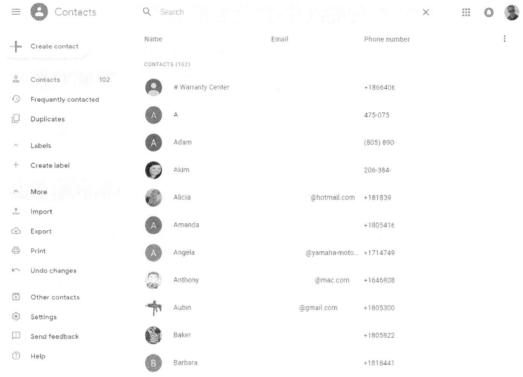

Figure 11.1

If you don't want them to be displayed in alphabetical order, you can click on the three vertical dots to the very right of phone number and then click on *Change column order* (figure 11.2). Then you can choose to sort your columns by name, email, phone number, job title, and labels by simply dragging and dropping the categories in the order you want, and then clicking on *Done*.

Chapter 11 – Contacts

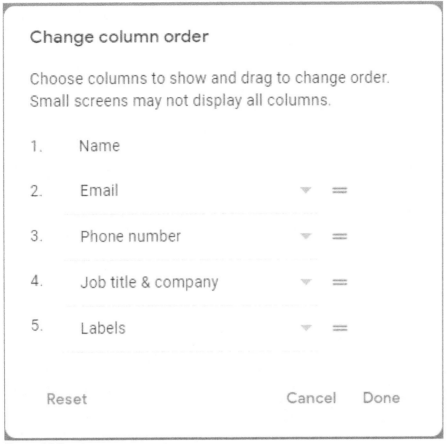

Figure 11.2

Google remembers who you contact the most (yes, it's scary), and will display those people in the *Frequently contacted* section on the left hand side of the window. So, if you have a lot of contacts that you access frequently and don't want to have to do a lot of scrolling or searching for them, you can see if they show up here.

When you open up a contact, it will display any information that you have entered for that person plus any additional information that Google might have on them (such as a YouTube channel or business information). Then you can do things like click on their email address to open up a new email to that person. If you have a Google Voice account setup, then you can click on their phone number to start a phone, video, or message conversation using Google Hangouts.

Chapter 11 – Contacts

Figure 11.3

To edit the contact's information, you will click on the pencil icon and then you will be able to change, remove, or add information to that contact.

If you click on the *More fields* link at the bottom of the settings, you will get a lot more additional fields that you can fill in to store extra information about that person (figure 11.4).

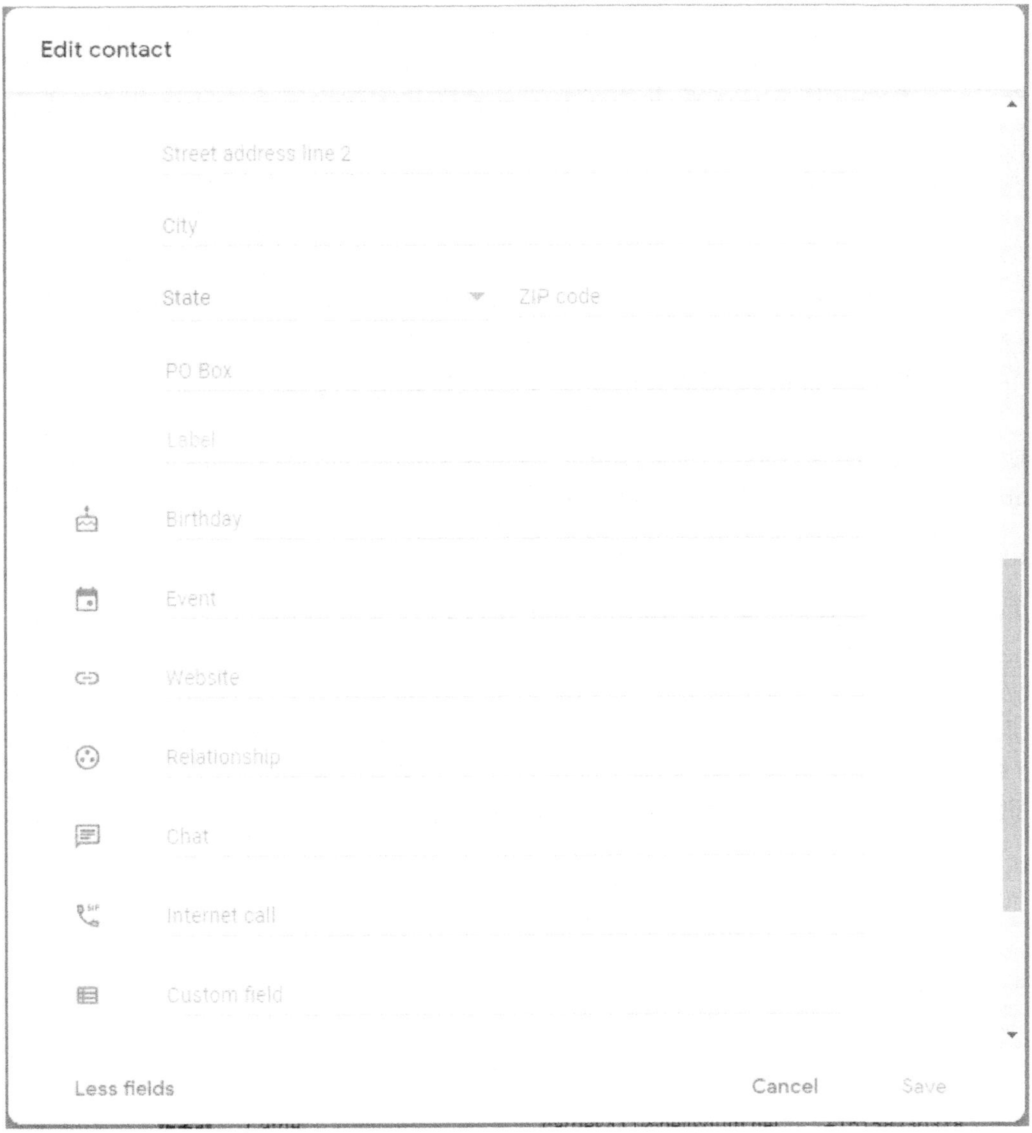

Chapter 11 – Contacts

Figure 11.4

Clicking on the contact's picture will allow you to change it to one from your Google Photos, or you can also upload one from your computer.

Clicking on the three vertical dots will bring up additional options that you can use to edit your contact:

- **Print** – This will let you print out all of the contact's information from your printer.

Chapter 11 – Contacts

- **Export** – If you need to export your contact to send to someone else so they can add it to their own contacts, then you can do that here. You can export it as a Google CSV, Outlook CSV, or vCard for iOS contacts (Apple).

- **Hide from contacts** – Here you can hide any contacts that you don't want to show up in your contacts list without actually deleting them. If you want them to show up again, then go to *Other contacts* (discussed later), find them in that list, and add them back by choosing *Add to contacts*.

- **Delete** – This option will remove a contact from your list permanently.

The *Duplicates* section of your contacts will show you any contacts that you have duplicated so you can merge all the information from the duplicates into one complete contact and then delete the extra ones.

If you have made some changes to your contacts and realized that you shouldn't have, then you are in luck, because there is an easy way to roll back those changes and get things back to the way they were. If you click on *Undo changes* on the side of your contact list, you will be able to roll back all of the changes you made over a specific time period. Just be sure that this is what you want to do, because it will also revert back the changes that you wanted to keep.

Chapter 11 – Contacts

Figure 11.5

Creating a Contact

Creating a new contact is a fairly simple process and only takes a few steps to complete. And if you create a new contact and need to add additional information later, you now know how to do so.

To make a new contact, click on the *Create contact* button and start filling in the fields that you want to use. Keep in mind that you don't need to use all of them just because they are there. Plus, you can click on *More fields* to show the extra fields I showed you in figure 11.4.

When adding the information you might notice that there are + signs next to some of the fields. Those are used to add additional fields of the same type. For example, if you want to have both a work and cellular number for a contact, you can click on the + next to their phone number to add a second phone number field (figure 11.6).

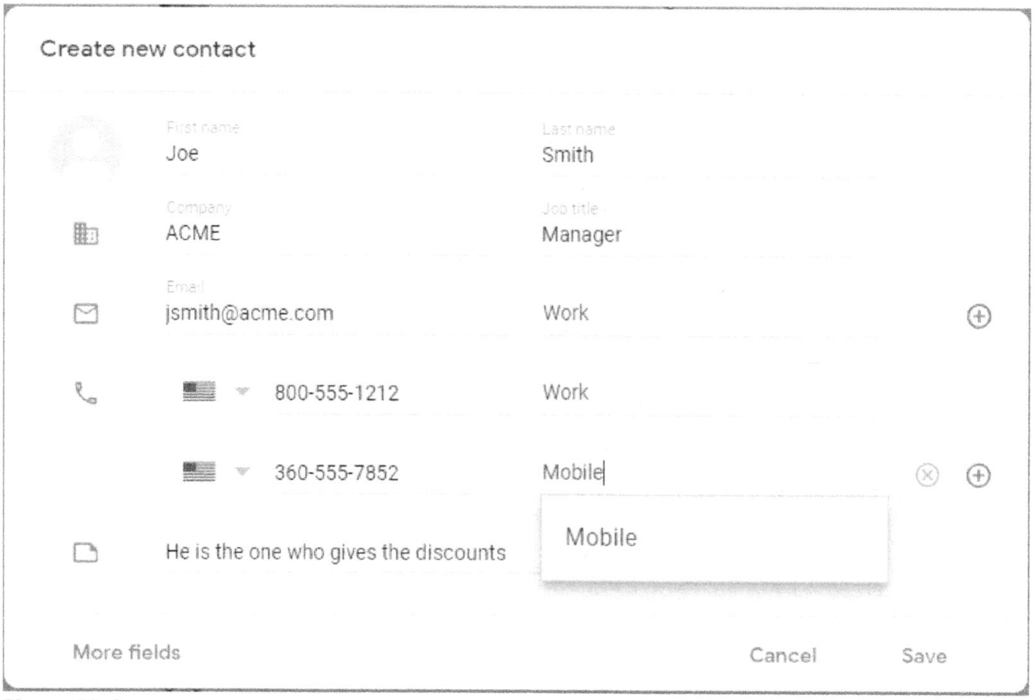

Chapter 11 – Contacts

```
Create new contact

                First name                          Last name
                Joe                                 Smith

                Company                             Job title
       🏢       ACME                                Manager

                Email
       ✉        jsmith@acme.com                     Work                    ⊕

       📞            ▼  800-555-1212                Work

                     ▼  360-555-7852                Mobile          ⊗       ⊕

                                                    ┌──────────────┐
                                                    │ Mobile       │
       📄       He is the one who gives the discounts└──────────────┘


       More fields                                       Cancel       Save
```

Figure 11.6

When you are finished entering in all of your information, click on Save. You will be shown your new contact, and then be allowed to edit it right away if needed. Then you will be able to search for that contact using any of the information you entered (figure 11.8).

```
       ⓙ       Joe Smith                          ☆   ✏   ⋮   ✕


       Contact details

       🏢       Manager, ACME

       ✉       jsmith@acme.com · Work

       📞      800-555-1212 · Work

               360-555-7852 · Mobile

       📄      He is the one who gives the discounts
```

Figure 11.7

462

Chapter 11 – Contacts

Figure 11.8

 FYI, the star icon next to the edit pencil will let you mark a contact as a favorite, and they will show up at the top of your contact list under *Starred Contacts*.

Labels

Labels are used to categorize contacts to make them easier to find (just like they are used in Gmail to make your messages easier to find and organize). By default, you will not have any labels in your contacts, but they are very easy to create and then assign to people.

If you look to the left hand side of your contacts, you will see the labels section with an option to create a label. All you need to do is click on *Create label* and give it a name (figure 11.9 and 11.10). Then click on Save when you are finished.

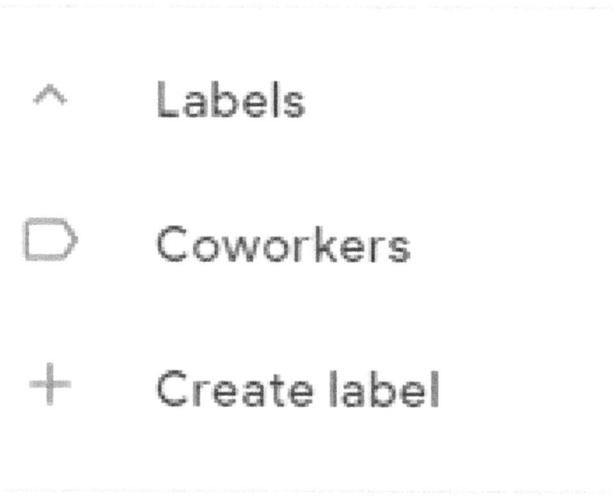

Chapter 11 – Contacts

∧ **Labels**

▱ Coworkers

+ Create label

Figure 11.9

```
Create label

Coworkers
_____


                                Cancel    Save
```

Figure 11.10

To assign that label to a contact, all you need to do is open that contact, click on the three vertical dots, and put a checkmark next to the label name. If you have more than one label created, they will all show up here, allowing you to choose one or more labels to assign to that contact.

Chapter 11 – Contacts

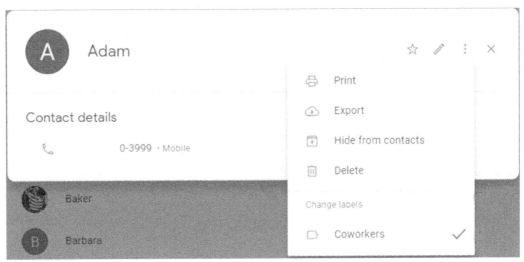

Figure 11.11

Now when you go back to your labels list on the left hand side of your contacts, you will see your new label listed there with the number of contacts assigned to that label next to it. Then when you click on the label name, it will show you only contacts with that label assigned.

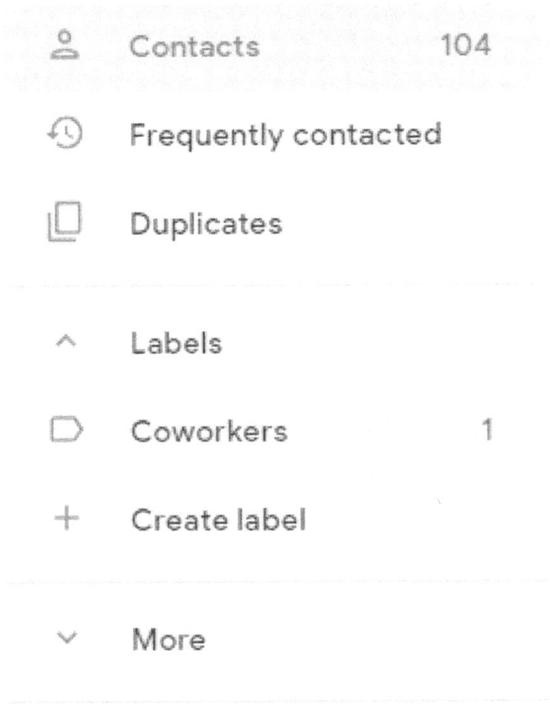

    Contacts   104

    Frequently contacted

    Duplicates

    Labels

    Coworkers   1

    Create label

    More

Figure 11.12

Chapter 11 – Contacts

Keep in mind that it will not move contacts from your main list to your label category, but rather only display them there *in addition* to them being on your main list.

Importing and Exporting Contacts
Google Contacts has the ability to import contacts from other sources as well as export your Google Contacts so they can be imported elsewhere, and the process is fairly easy to do. You will find the *Import* and *Export* choices under the More section on the left hand side of your contacts.

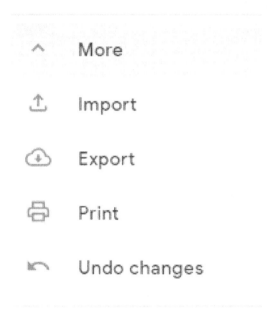

Figure 11.13

Importing Contacts
To import contacts into Google Contacts, they need to be in either a CSV or vCard format. For my example, I have some contacts in a CSV file (Contact List.CSV) that I will import into my Google Contacts.

Chapter 11 – Contacts

Once I click on *Import,* I will be prompted to select the file I want to import.

Figure 11.14

Once the import is complete, it will show you all of the contacts that have been imported and ask you if you would like to search for duplicates.

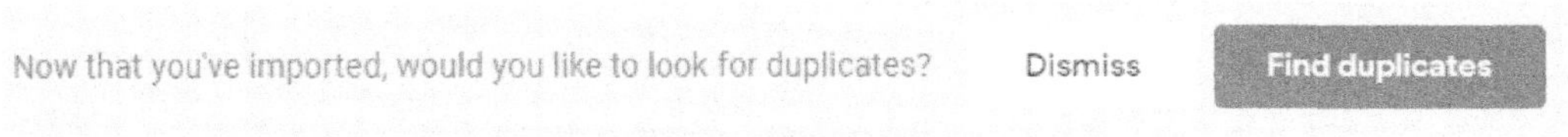

Now that you've imported, would you like to look for duplicates?   Dismiss   **Find duplicates**

Figure 11.15

If it does find duplicates, then you will have the option to merge the information for both versions into one contact so you don't have two of the same contacts with different information.

Exporting Contacts
The process for exporting contacts is just as easy as importing contacts, and all you need to do is click on *Export* and decide if you want to export all of your contacts, or only specific ones. Then you will have a few options as to what format you can export them to.

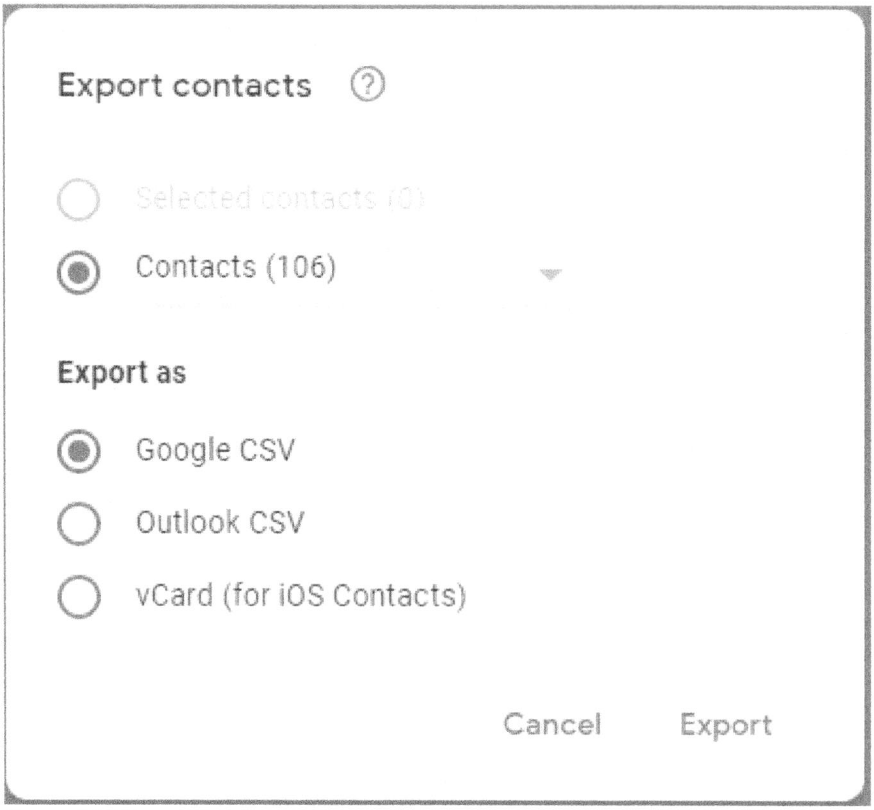

Chapter 11 – Contacts

> **Export contacts** ?
>
> ○ Selected contacts (0)
> ● Contacts (106) ▼
>
> **Export as**
>
> ● Google CSV
> ○ Outlook CSV
> ○ vCard (for iOS Contacts)
>
> Cancel   Export

Figure 11.16

Once you make those choices, click on *Export,* and you will be prompted to choose a name for your exported file and also where you want to save it to. Just make sure to save it somewhere that you can easily find it, like your desktop (etc.). Then you will be able to take this file and import your contacts into other places like another Google account or your Microsoft Outlook email client.

Printing Contacts
Printing out your contacts works in a similar fashion as printing out anything else in your Google Apps. It just comes down to what exactly you want to print out, and how you want it to look when printed.

If you were to click on *Print* on the left side of your contacts, you would be prompted to choose what contacts you want to print (like shown in figure 11.17). You can print out all of your contacts, or choose from categories such as *Starred contacts* or any label groups you've created. (Keep in mind that your options will most likely be different than mine based on your configuration.)

Chapter 11 – Contacts

Figure 11.17

You might have noticed that you can't choose *Selected contacts*. This is because you need to select the contacts you want to print BEFORE clicking on *Print* to be able to print out specific contacts. If I were to select three contacts from my list and *then* click on *Print*, I would see a different print dialog box (like shown in figure 11.18).

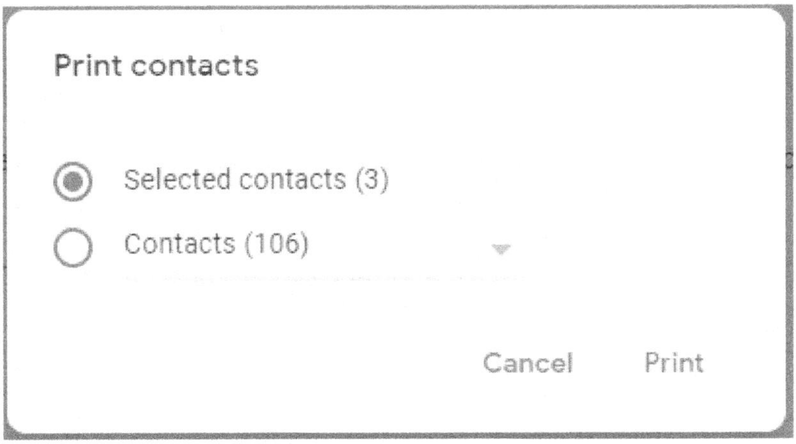

Figure 11.18

Then when I clicked on *Print* it would bring up the Print settings that you have seen many times before, and you can change your printer options from there if needed.

Chapter 11 – Contacts

Notice how it will print all three contacts on one page, so if you want to have a separate page for each, you will need to print them one at a time.

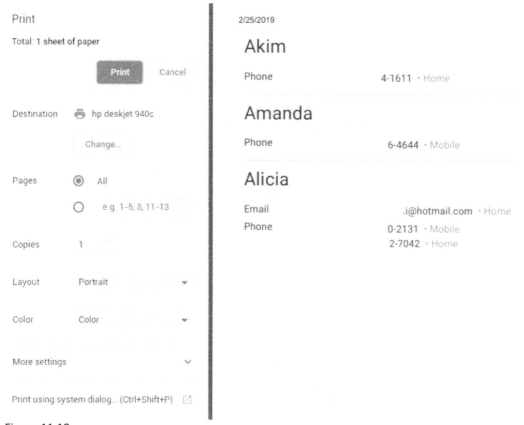

Figure 11.19

Other Contacts
Google Contacts does a pretty good job of keeping the contacts you use the most separate from other contacts that you might need in the future, but don't necessarily want to see mixed in with your main contacts.

This is where *Other contacts* comes into play, and they can be found on the left hand side of your contact list near the bottom (figure 11.20).

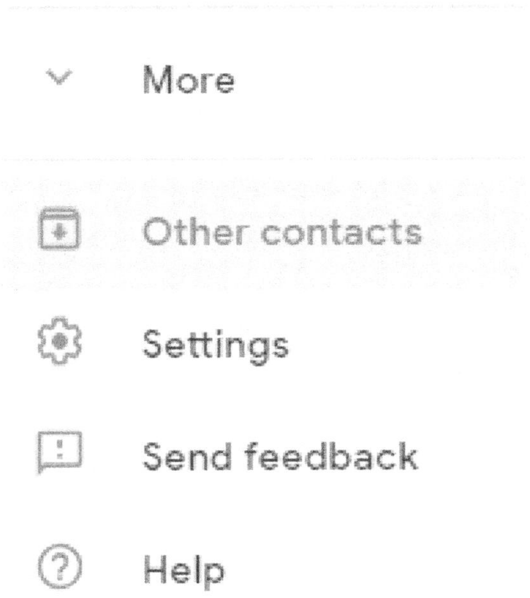

Chapter 11 – Contacts

   ⌄   More

   ▣   Other contacts

   ⚙   Settings

   🗨   Send feedback

   ⓶   Help

Figure 11.20

The *Other contacts* section is where Google places contacts that it pulls from things like email conversations and Google + associations. (By the way, Google+ is no longer around, since it never went anywhere to begin with. It was Google's attempt to make their own Facebook-type social media site.)

When you click on *Other contacts,* you will most likely see a bunch of contacts that you don't recognize from things such as one time emails that you had sent or received like customer support or product inquiries. You may also see duplicate contacts that you also have in your main contacts.

You can manage these other contacts the same way you manage your main contacts. There are options to edit and delete them, as well as an option to add them to your main contacts if you would rather have them there (figure 11.21).

Figure 11.21

I usually just leave them alone unless there are some that I want to have in my main contacts. You never know when you might need to use one of them,

Chapter 11 – Contacts

so it's good to have them around, yet out of the way so they don't make a mess of your main contact list.

What's Next

Now that you have read through this book and taken your Google Apps skills to the next level, you might be wondering what you should do next. Well, that depends on where you want to go. Are you happy with what you have learned, or do you want to further your knowledge on Google Apps, or maybe even get into the more advanced Google G Suite?

If you *do* want to expand your knowledge (or even get into G Suite), then you can look for some more advanced books or ones that cover a specific technology that interests you. Focus on one subject at a time, then apply what you have learned to the next subject. You can even sign up for a free G Suite trial to see if it's something you want to pursue.

There are many great video resources as well, such as Pluralsight or CBT Nuggets, which offer online subscriptions to training videos of every type imaginable. YouTube is also a great source for training videos if you know what to search for.

If you are content in being a standalone power user that knows more than your friends, then just keep on reading up on the technologies you want to learn, and you will soon become your friends and families go-to computer person (which may or may not be something you want!).

Thanks for reading *Google Docs Made Easy*. If you liked this title, please leave a review. Reviews help authors build exposure. Plus, I love hearing from my readers! You can also check out the other books in the Made Easy series for additional computer-related information and training.

What's Next

You should also check out my website at www.onlinecomputertips.com, as well as follow it on Facebook at https://www.facebook.com/OnlineComputerTips/ to find more information on all kinds of computer topics.

About the Author

James Bernstein has been working with various companies in the IT field since 2000, managing technologies such as SAN and NAS storage, VMware, backups, Windows Servers, Active Directory, DNS, DHCP, Networking, Microsoft Office, Exchange, and more.

He has obtained certifications from Microsoft, VMware, CompTIA, ShoreTel, and SNIA, and continues to strive to learn new technologies to further his knowledge on a variety of subjects.

He is also the founder of the website onlinecomputertips.com, which offers its readers valuable information on topics such as Windows, networking, hardware, software, and troubleshooting. James writes much of the content himself, and adds new content on a regular basis. The site was started in 2005 and is still going strong today.

Made in the USA
Monee, IL
24 June 2020